# ON THE WAY TO JESUS

## A JOURNEY THROUGH THE BIBLE

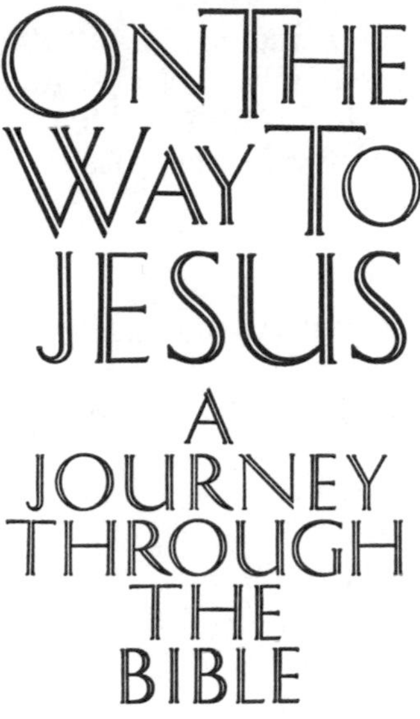


ALBERT H. BAYLIS

MULTNOMAH • PRESS
Portland, Oregon 97266

Scripture quotations in chapters 1–5, unless otherwise identified, are from the New American Standard Bible (NASB), © The Lockman Foundation 1960, 1962, 1963, 1968, 1971, 1972, 1973, 1975, 1977. Used by permission.

Most other Scripture quotations not otherwise identified are from the Holy Bible: New International Version (NIV), copyright 1973, 1978, 1984 by the International Bible Society. Used by permission of Zondervan Bible Publishers.

Cover design by Al Mendenhall
Interior design by Judy Quinn

Photograph by Kris Coppieters, Antwerp, Belgium

ON THE WAY TO JESUS

Portland, Oregon 97266

Printed in the United States of America



**Library of Congress Cataloging-in-Publication Data**

Baylis, Albert H.
On the way to Jesus

Includes bibliographical references and index.
1. Bible. O.T.—History of Biblical events.
1. Title.
BS1197.B37 1986 220.6'7 85-32088
ISBN 0-88070-105-6 (pbk.)

87 88 89 90 91 92 – 10 9 8 7 6 5 4 3 2

This book is dedicated to

THEOTA

God's special gift to me
for nineteen years,
now in the presence of our Lord Jesus
&
to the children
who continue to call her blessed
ELENA, AL, AND MARK

# CONTENTS

PART

3

## STRUGGLE FOR CONSISTENCY



PART

4

## RESTORATION AND HOPE

# FOREWORD

I took the manuscript of this book with me to lunch, so I could review it and write the foreword. Before long I found myself underlining several especially insightful sections. Soon I had forgotten why I was reading it—I was simply being spiritually fed.

Spending time with this fascinating material over lunch took me back to my first year of teaching at Multnomah School of the Bible, where my friendship with Al Baylis blossomed.

In my mind I was there again with the Multnomah faculty, eating soup and salad but digesting spiritual truths. Those were among the choicest education experiences of my life, when as a freshman faculty member I pumped my more experienced colleagues with questions. How refreshing it was to sit under such godly servants and bask in their wisdom.

That's the kind of wisdom Al fills this book with. Here's a man who knows the Word of God inside out and puts it together for us in a personal, practical way. I could almost picture him as a seasoned rabbi surrounded by a huddle of eager listeners. He doesn't simply teach the Old Testament; it's as if he personally reminisces through it.

How rare it is to read a Bible survey that goes beyond sterile skeletal outlines to wrestle with the meat of the Word. Al Baylis provides a veritable banquet. His writing is fluid and conversational, yet as meaningful and thought-provoking as the most profound theological study. His book is both fresh and wise, stimulating and seasoned.

Up to the light he holds the valuable jewel of the Old Testament, seeing in it the multi-facets of God's truth. And he rekindles the realization that God's Word is one word; that the Old Testament shouts ahead to the New.

Al has also solved a major problem for me: what to give as Christmas gifts to the one hundred Walk Thru the Bible seminar instructors in twelve countries around the world.

You won't have to discipline yourself to get through this book. And frankly, that's unusual for a Bible survey! You know you're reading a book that will change your life when you find yourself underlining, circling, and starring more material than you leave unmarked.

Thanks, Al. I took your book to lunch—and it made an impact on my life!

Bruce H. Wilkinson
President
Walk Thru the Bible Ministries

# PREFACE

"Why do you want to write a book?"

A student of mine caught me up short with that question as we returned from Christmas break. As usual, I had spent the entire vacation writing. Why *did* I want to write a book?

And why *this* book?

I have heard many a preacher say, "Christians know all they need to know about the truth. It's living it that is the problem." Yet year after year I discover that the students churches are sending to Bible college (their best young people) do not know that much.

Certainly living the truth we already know is a challenge. But it's hard to be challenged by truth we don't know! Too many of us are living on a subsistence diet of Scripture—and wonder why our strength is small. How do we receive motivation to live through difficulties, to face struggles, to avoid temptation, if it is not by the Word of God?

Yet when it comes to the heart of the Bible, most people are lost. Oh sure, they know and enjoy some individual stories like David and Goliath, Joshua and the battle of Jericho, Noah and the flood; but few have put them together to understand what the Bible is all about . . . *and where it is going.*

On the other hand, I believe most Christians would like to know their Bible better. They would like to be motivated by its message. Yet when they are taught the Bible, they often find themselves bogged down with facts and dates and names and places. They conclude that understanding the Bible must be a dull and tedious task.

And, then there is Jesus.

How does the front half of the Bible relate to Jesus and the New Testament? Except for a few specific predictions about Jesus—like Isaiah 53 and Isaiah 9—most Christians aren't really sure.

So now you know what I've been doing with my vacations!

I've been taking a trip through the heart of the Bible, thrilling to the dynamic of the Bible itself, and plotting a road map for those who have not seen the best sights before. It's a journey *On the Way to Jesus*—and I hope it brings the Bible alive for you.

A Scripture reading guide has been provided with each chapter as an aid for opening up the Bible on a daily basis. Thought questions, helpful for either group discussion or personal interaction, follow each chapter. But whether you are going to use the book for study or just for casual reading, *enjoy*. I've done my best to sweep away any dry cobwebs and produce a book which, like the Bible itself, is dynamic and challenging.

My vacations are spent. Your trip is just beginning. I wish you Godspeed.

Special thanks are due to a number of people for making this book possible. I am grateful to Larry Libby for his enthusiasm for this volume from the very beginning. The support of Rod Morris and the editorial work of Steve Halliday are also gratefully acknowledged.

My most faithful supporter and editor, however, was my wife, Theota. Her reward continues in this volume.

The interaction of John R. Kohlenberger III with major issues in the book was very helpful to me. John Johnson responded to the chapter on wisdom.

My daughter, Elena, saved Dad much time by helping with the word processing.

Albert Baylis
Portland, Oregon
September 1985

# PART 1.

# BASICS FOR UNDERSTANDING LIFE

'GENESIS 1 IS ONE OF THE MOST REMARKABLE PUT-DOWNS EVER ADMINISTERED. WITHOUT EVEN MENTIONING THEM, THIS PASSAGE UNDERCUTS THE FALSE GODS. THE WORDING LEAVES NO DOUBT THAT IT INTENDS TO SNUB THEM.'

---

CHAPTER

# 1.

# THE GOD OF CREATION

## A FRESH LOOK AT GENESIS 1

Like many a modern parent faced with raising children in a confusing world of drugs, disasters, and mind-bending ideas, Moses must have had his concerns. Certainly God did. The book of Exodus tells us about the beginnings of the nation of Israel under the leadership of Moses, the man of God. It records their last-minute rescue through the sea and their campout in the desert of Sinai. But that is just the beginning. These former slaves must now enter into a land inhabited by people who would make Hell's Angels seem like Sunday school teachers.

As the patriarch lay down to sleep at night, he must have worried about this people he was leading. They had every mark of early adolescence about them and yet they needed a stability few adults ever achieve. Sure, they had witnessed God's power to plague and decimate the Egyptians. They had passed through the sea without muddying their feet. But had they really become the people of Yahweh* in heart and mind?

How do you prepare a people to avoid the degrading tentacles of a deteriorated culture? How do you lay a foundation for a worthwhile life? What alloy do you use to strengthen their discernment to motivate them toward a better way?

**Yahweh* is God's personal name. Translated in many English versions as "LORD" (all capitals), it occasionally is rendered "Jehovah." Its significance will be discussed in chapter six.

The answer is torah.

*Torah* simply means *instruction*. "The Torah" came to be the name for the first five books of the Bible, Genesis through Deuteronomy. As we open the Bible we encounter that instruction—teaching given to prepare the Israelite people for their encounter with gross paganism.

But oh, what teaching! No dull classroom recitation here. These are *stories*. And understanding the history in them is not the boring calisthenics of learning names, dates and places, but involvement with dynamic and crucial events giving us insight into life itself.

## THE WORLD OF GENESIS ONE

So, let's join Israel in the desert.

Pack up your tent. Leave your modernized campers behind. Come as you are—and bring an appetite for manna!

As Israelites, we owe our allegiance to Yahweh God in a world where many gods are worshiped. Their names are strange to our modern ears: Baal, Molech, Ashtoreth, Anath, and El. They have not survived the millennia, though they were drawing rave reviews in Palestine at the time.

Stories about these gods form the belief-system of the world around us. These gods are like most men—and worse! They play and drink, and drink too much. They fight, deceive, and engage in licentious behavior. Just to give you the idea, let's take a quick X-rated look at El, the father of the gods.

El is a brutal, bloody tyrant. He not only dethrones his own father (not a new temptation for king's sons), but also castrates him. He slays his own favorite son, and cuts off his daughter's head. He also has a reputation for seduction of women.[1]

But perhaps El is the exception. Certainly the *goddesses* must possess fine and gentle spirits! Well . . . no. Consider the goddess Anath, called the "queen of heaven" and "mistress of all the gods."[2] She too is sensuous and violent. Here is a description (not recommended for children) of gentle Anath at work:

> Anath hews in pieces and rejoices,
> her liver extends with laughter,

her heart is filled with joy;
for in Anath's hand is success;
for she plunges her knees in the blood of
the swift ones,
her thighs in the gore of the fast ones.[3]

While the gods fight one another, Anath enjoys the carnage. If her father, the god El, does not grant Anath her request for a palace for Baal, then she assures us,

I shall trample him down like a lamb to
the ground;
I shall bring down his hoary head with
blood to the grave,
the gray hair of his old age with gore.[4]

No doubt this tale did a lot to encourage honoring one's father and mother in Canaanite culture!

Intrigue and murder, deceit and incest are what you get from these gods.[5] Israel's Ten Commandments are broken without hesitation by these supposed divinities. These gods were not sterling examples. Could belief in them produce sterling civilizations?

## THE NEED FOR THE TRUE CREATION STORY

These thoughts bring us face to face with a sobering fact. *People become like the gods they worship.*Their gods are their models. It would be disastrous if Israel thought Yahweh her God was like other gods. In fact, God warns his people that if they become as depraved as the people of Canaan, he will eject them too from Palestine (Leviticus 18:24-30). The Bible, then, begins with the most essential element of torah—the real story about the true God—so the people of God may live a free and wholesome life.

But if we're trying to learn about God, why tell the story of *creation*? Doesn't that center on learning about the world? About origins? Geology?

Not really. The Bible begins at the beginning not because Moses is a history buff obsessed with chronological order, but because understanding God's creation of the world gives us a clear picture of what God is like.

Have you ever noticed that apart from spending time with someone in a number of situations, it is difficult to really know him? He could be described accurately to you over the telephone (tall, generous, honest, enjoys tennis), but do you really have a clear picture? The best description would come by telling a number of stories about him. What did he do in a variety of situations? When confronted with a tough decision? When he was with his children? Now you understand and know him better. The same is true for God. The Bible communicates what he is like by many, many events. By studying these carefully, we begin to understand and know God. And remember: People become like the God they worship.

If we are going to learn about God through his activity, creation is the best place to start. It was and is[6] the critical event for a person's view of life. Knowing how God initiated my world helps me understand my own relationship to God more clearly. Then and now, the relationship (or nonrelationship) of God to the world controls our total view of life.

**Creator Most Worthy**

As Moses sat in his tent and thought of the challenges ahead for the people he led, as he worried about their encounter with violent and sensuous paganism, his mind may have reviewed the creation stories of his neighbors—such as the famous Babylonian creation story *Enûma Elish.*[7] In this story one of the three original parents of the gods, Ti'amet, is identified as the ocean. Marduk, a younger god who becomes the chief Babylonian deity, kills her.

> He split her open like a mussel into two
> parts;
> half of her he set in place and formed the sky
> therewith as a roof.
> He fixed the crossbar and posted guards;
> he commanded them not to let her
> waters escape.[8]

Half of her corpse was used to form the sky, the other to make the earth[9] (a possible beginning to the expression

"Mother Earth"?). The story continues:

Putting her head into position
he thereon formed the mountains.
Opening the deep which was in flood,
he caused to flow from her eyes
the Euphrates and Tigris.[10]

Even the most superficial reading of Genesis 1 catches the far purer and more profound character of the biblical story. Could this people—could any people—prefer the violence of the gods over the majesty and purity of Yahweh?

As Moses penned these words he must have fallen to his tent floor in adoration. The God of the Bible is more worthy than these gods. He is Most Worthy.

## OVERVIEW OF THE CREATION STORY

The worthiness of God saturates the very structure of Genesis 1. As we look here, the first thing to notice is the tremendous beauty and order. Let me briefly summarize the layout.

It all begins with a topic sentence worthy of the most cloistered English teacher:

In the beginning God created the heavens and the earth.

Nothing could be clearer than this. God created it all. "Heavens and earth" includes the universe as man knows it—the land we live on, the sky and solar system we see.

The details of that creation follow. Verse 2 describes the terrible chaos present as God starts his creative work.[11] The planet—if we can call it that—was "formless and void." It was without shape or order, and it was empty. Further, "darkness was over the surface of the deep [waters]." A dark watery chaos prevails. Finally, "The Spirit of God was moving over the surface of the waters." These three descriptions summarize the earth's desperate condition. The earth lacked productive energy. No life. No light. The only hope was the presence of the Spirit of God himself.[12]

The creative days which follow demonstrate that Israel's God is able to make a creation out of a desolate chaos, but more, he can do it in a beautiful pattern of harmony and wisdom.

Note the order of events:

| DAYS 1-3 | | DAYS 4-6 | |
|---|---|---|---|
| Day 1: | Creation of light & limitation of darkness (1:4-5) | Day 4: | Lights created: sun, moon & stars (1:14-19) |
| Day 2: | Creation of heavens & separation of the waters (1:6-9) | Day 5: | Birds and Sea creatures created (1:20-23) |
| Day 3: | Creation of dry land by limiting sea, & creation of vegetation (1:10-13) | Day 6: | Domesticated animals, insects, & wild animals created Man created in image of God (1:24-31) |

**DAY 7**

God rests from His creative work (2:1-3)

The Master Designer is at work. An examination of the chart shows that Days 4-6 parallel Days 1-3. Days 1-3 provide the basic divisions necessary to a living environment. Darkness must be dispelled and limited to part of the day if there is to be life on the planet. The watery chaos must be penetrated and separated, with much of it removed to the heavens so the remaining sea can be limited to part of the globe. With this, dry land appears and vegetation can be brought into existence.

Day 4, however, returns to the subject of light. Particular lights now are created to bear the already created light, marking out time on earth—days, seasons, and years. Day 5 answers to Day 2 by providing inhabitants for sea and sky. Day 6 provides land creatures to inhabit the provisioned earth of Day 3.

By the end of Day 3, the earth is no longer "formless." By the end of Day 6 it is no longer "void" or empty. Day 7 is an unparalleled day—a day to commemorate the completion of creation.

When biblical critics see this beautiful arrangement, they often jump to an unwarranted conclusion. To them the parallels prove that the account was invented. The facts were forced into this neat arrangement, they say. But this suggestion ignores the very point of the account. The creation story is all about ordering. That the creation is orderly—even artistically arranged—is not surprising. Has anyone ever read about the symmetry of a snowflake or a rose or the designs on many reptiles, and concluded that the writer must be inventing the order and beauty he describes? Israel's God is a God of order and beauty. More, he is a God of wisdom. To know the order of the universe and to have arranged that order is part of the wisdom of God (see Job 38—39, Psalm 104:24).[13]

But we have not exhausted this sublime account when we note its parallel structure. There is another thread woven through the passage.

It is *going* somewhere.

The lights are created to mark out days, seasons, and years. But for whom? On the sixth day, the Creator's activity comes to a sudden timeout. A divine discussion is held. God's creative work is climaxed by the creation of a being distinct from all others, a creature made in the image of God and therefore able to rule as his vice-regent over the lower creation (1:26-28).[14] Man—male and female—is the peak of God's creation. All that went before was designed with man as the climax.

Genesis 1:1 said it simply: "In the beginning God created the heavens and the earth." Genesis 1:2—2:3 said it profoundly: Out of disorder and chaos, God creates order and beauty and makes a habitation fit for a king—his royal creation, man.

### Torah in Genesis 1

Many valuable concepts, vital to the Israelite entering the promised land, are taught in Genesis 1. It is not too much to say that Israel's success or failure will depend upon her understanding about God and his relationship to man and the material universe as taught in this chapter. Here are a few of these vital truths.

*Concept #1: God is in charge.* He is in complete control of the universe. He is not a part of it. Nor does it control him. It came into existence at his command.[15] The earth is not a dead, defeated god. There is no god of the sea.[16]

For the pagan, the world was a fearsome place. The large sea-creatures were feared as semigods. "Baal's adversaries were gods like himself, or demons to be propitiated."[17] But for Israel there is only one God. The productive earth, the seasons, and the light were all good gifts from the hand of God; provided in his original creation. These gifts are not dependent on cultic magic or the whim of gods, but are gracious provisions from the very first. This is why praise to the Creator is in order.

This is Moses' warning to the Israelites in Deuteronomy 8. They are ready to enter the land. They have seen God's direct, supernatural provision of food in the wilderness. But when they settle in the land and harvest abundant crops, they might say, "My power and the strength of my hand made me this wealth" (Deuteronomy 8:17). Such a viewpoint is unacceptable heresy. They are to recognize God's hand in his provision for them—even through these ordinary channels. Centuries later, the apostle Paul would point out that failure to recognize the Creator and give him thanks was the critical first step toward the futility and darkness of idolatry (Romans 1:18-23).

The fallen culture around Israel believed that nature was non-regular, that it depended on the interaction of the gods and on man's attempts to influence them. Our culture today has largely accepted the idea of regularity, but ironically it is a regularity caused by *chance.* So men today face the same danger as the Israelite: to fail to honor God by recognizing the creation as a gracious, regular provision for which thanksgiving is appropriate.

*Concept #2: The surrounding gods are nonentities.* Genesis 1 is one of the most remarkable put-downs ever administered. Without even mentioning them, this passage undercuts the false gods. Of course, the events of this chapter go back beyond the time when these false religions arose. But the wording of the passage leaves no doubt that it intends to snub them. Words and phrases are chosen which intentionally belittle claims existing at Moses' time. The idea that the sea is the kingdom of another god, as we have seen, is rejected.[18] It is just water. The earth is merely land which can be seen when the sea is removed from it.

But what of the stars, the sun, and the moon?

The stars also are created—nothing more. The sun and the moon are downgraded to being "two great lights," a "greater light" and a "lesser light." Even the names "sun" and "moon" are avoided.[19] These are not gods with personal names, but mere functionaries. Though belief in the power of the sun and stars pervades history (Deuteronomy 4:19, 2 Kings 23:11, Isaiah 47:13), "in these few simple sentences the lie is given to a superstition as old as Babylon and as modern as a newspaper horoscope."[20]

No, the sun and moon and stars, far from controlling man, are to function for man's benefit. They provide a measuring device for time, to mark off seasons. How ironic and shameful that what God created for man's benefit and service has "ruled" man. The folly of the human mind is such that it subjects man to lesser things to avoid subjection to the true Creator God.

*Concept #3: God has a special interest in man*: "In the Mesopotamian creation account man's creation is almost incidental. He is there to serve the whimsical pleasures of the gods, giving them food and satisfying their personal needs."[21] But in the Genesis record man is the apex of God's creative work. Earlier acts of creation anticipate man's needs. The step-by-step march of the narrative is broken by a divine conference before the final step is taken: "Let us make man in our image and after our likeness." Man is not special by accident. He bears a similarity to God which distinguishes him from all earlier creation. This similarity enables humanity to function as rulers of the earth under God's design.

Since mankind is in the image of God and is at the pinnacle of God's creative work, men should recognize that it is entirely wrong to worship and serve images of the lower creation. It is a perversion of God's original calling for man to degrade himself by setting material things and lower creatures in a higher position than himself.

The sophistication of twentieth-century Western man rarely bows before images of wood and stone, but quite often before creations of plastic, steel, and brick. Things of his own design control him (see Isaiah 44:14-18). He toils not as God's vice-regent, but as a slave to *things.*

## ON THE WAY: FULFILLMENT OF GENESIS ONE

Creation does not stop in Genesis 1. Like many other concepts we'll discover as we make our way through the heart of the Bible, it continues to develop as we journey on the way to Jesus—the author and completer of history.

The teaching about the God of Israel as the true Creator God is a critical point in Israel's faith (see Psalm 33:6-11 and Isaiah 42:5-9). This belief forms the groundwork for the first four commands of the decalogue (Exodus 20:1-8). Only the true Creator God deserves my worship and commitment—and he deserves it *exclusively.* Because of the profound wisdom evident in the creation, man must bow in humble recognition of a sovereign and all-wise Creator, even when personal events and experiences go beyond man's ability to understand (Job 38—39; Isaiah 40:12-17).

### Toward a New Creation

But the notion of creation does not stop there. It goes on to a final and glorious completion in a new creation.

We have seen how God limited the chaotic elements of verse 2 and so made them a part of an ordered creation. The chaotic waters became the sea, which in turn became the habitat for the various forms of sea life. The total darkness becomes limited to nighttime and is further dispelled by the lesser light of the moon. Darkness and the sea, however, still hold for man a reminder of life as chaos—life apart from God (see Psalm 107:10-14, Psalm 139:7-12, Isaiah 60:1-3).

But that is not the final story.

This creation, marred by sin as recorded in Genesis 3, must yield to a new creation. It is not, however, simply a return to conditions of the original creation. It is an advance . . . a creation which does away with even the suggestion of original chaos. Compare the differences between the original creation and the new creation as prophesied in the book of Revelation.

| Original Chaos | Creation | New Creation |
|---|---|---|
| Darkness | Darkness limited to nighttime | No night (Revelation 22:5) |
| Darkness | Light & Darkness controlled by sun and moon | No Sun & Moon (Revelation 21:23) |
| Covered by Waters | Waters limited to Sea | No Sea (Revelation 21:1) |

This new creation is possible only because of the work of Jesus Christ, who as the light of the world vanquishes both moral and physical darkness. He who said, "I am the light of the world; he who follows Me shall not walk in the darkness, but shall have the light of life" (John 8:12) is also the one who will illumine the final habitation of believing men.

> And the city has no need of the sun or of the moon to shine upon it, for the glory of God has illumined it, and its lamp is the Lamb. (Revelation 21:23)

## The Journey to Man's Rulership

The special place of man, so central in the Creator's plan in Genesis 1, is celebrated elsewhere in Scripture. The most notable case is Psalm 8. Harking back to this creation account, King David marvels at the splendor and majesty of Yahweh in the creation. He sees the God of Creation as still able to show his strength through those regarded as weak (verse 2). But mostly the king praises God for the position he has given to man. Man is endowed with "glory and majesty"—a summary of the image of God. Man has been given rulership over God's creative work (verses 6-8).

Psalm 8 celebrates man's position, but does not explore the problem of sin and man's subsequent failure to justly exercise that rulership. Later the New Testament quotes the psalm a number of times, in each case tying the truth about man's rule to the work of Jesus. The writer of Hebrews is bold to note (in 2:5-10) that though the psalmist says God has subjected all things under man's feet, "we do not yet see all things subjected to him (man)."

There is a problem.

God as Creator subjected all things to man. That was the original commission. But in practice, complete subjection has never taken place.

The answer?

"But we do see Him who has been made for a little while lower than the angels, namely, Jesus." Jesus became man in order to bring to pass God's plan for man—a plan that could never come to pass under fallen humans who carry out God's righteous rule inconsistently and irregularly.

Jesus is the perfect man who becomes the perfect author of men's salvation through his death on the cross. Because of this he alone is able to bring man to the place of honor and glory that God intended for him (Hebrews 2:9-

10). Even so, we do not yet see this full subjection. Jesus has been given authority over everything, and in that sense God already has put "all things in subjection under His feet" (Ephesians 1:22, quoting Psalm 8:6). But we still live in a fallen world where injustice and man's inhumanity to man too often prevail. We await Christ's return when "he must reign until he has put all his enemies under his feet" (1 Corinthians 15:25 NIV).

Under the rule of Jesus Christ, the perfect man, God will bring all things into the order and design he originally intended. Jesus himself will present this harmonious kingdom back to the Father. Then everyone will recognize that there is no God besides Yahweh, the God of Israel.

God will be all in all (15:28).

Creation will be complete.

# FOR PERSONAL INTERACTION & DISCUSSION

SUGGESTED SCRIPTURE READINGS:

Genesis 1:1—2:3
Revelation 21:1-4 and 22:1-5
Hebrews 2:5-9
Job 38:4-21
Psalm 8

1. What problems were solved for the Israelites by understanding God's creation of the world?
2. Check out each of the following mythical beliefs. Is it mostly "ancient" or "modern"?

    astrology
    materialism
    crude polytheism
    idolatry
    sun worship
    belief in the irregularity of nature
    culturally approved perversion and violence
    "chance" as the cause of life

3. Why is thanksgiving an important response to God as Creator? What is the result of failing to be thankful?
4. What importance is given in Genesis to the creation of man? Why is being created in the image of God significant? What is man's place in the creation? What does this mean as far as man's responsibility today?
5. Why is everything not in subjection to man at the present time? What has been accomplished by Jesus to advance God's program for man?
6. Why do you think light and darkness have become synonymous with truth and error? In what sense is Jesus the light (John 1:1-18)?

'LISTEN TO THE FIRST
RECORDED WORDS IN ALL
HUMAN HISTORY—NOT
THE PRIMEVAL GRUNT OF
NARROW-BROWED
NEANDERTHAL
. . . BUT *POETRY.'*

CHAPTER

# 2.

# MAN AND HIS RELATIONSHIPS

## THE ADDED CONTRIBUTION OF GENESIS 2

Blood will I form and cause bone to be;
Then I will set up *lullû*, "Man" shall be
his name!
Yes, I will create *lullû*: Man!
Upon him shall the services of the gods be
imposed
that they may be at rest.

"Who am I?" is a modern question. But the need for man to know his place in the world is as old as creation.

According to the Babylonian creation legend above, Marduk creates man to make life easier for the gods.[1] The God of the Bible, however, does not need food and drink. Rather than being a taker, God is a *giver.* As Paul puts it, God is not served by human hands, "as though He needed anything, since He Himself gives to all life and breath and all things" (Acts 17:25).

Genesis 1 featured a sovereign Creator who shaped the material world for man. Genesis 2 provides a second dimension to the picture of life as God intended it. As before, *telling the story* communicates most effectively man's place and significance.

## THE STORY OF MAN

Like Genesis 1, our story opens with a summary title (2:4) followed by the prevailing situation (2:5-6)—which God's action will change.

TITLE: "This is the account of the heavens and the earth when they were created. . . ."

SITUATION: "Now no shrub of the field was yet in the earth, and no plant of the field had yet sprouted, for the LORD God had not sent rain upon the earth; and there was no man to cultivate the ground."

The problem is clear. Certain things have not occurred because man's creation is still future.[2] Our story, then, begins prior to the sixth day. It is written not to fill in details left out of the majestic chapter 1, but to give us information to help us understand man's place in the world.

### Relationship to God

If you want to know about relationships you need details.

I can give you facts about my three children—their birthdays, height, weight, and other physical characteristics. But you still know nothing of my relationship to them. This you would learn better by hearing how I try to encourage them, discipline them, or put them to bed at night. Chapter 2 gives us this kind of detail about man's creation and God's relationship to him.

Man, like the animals, is created from the ground (2:7, 2:19) and is a physical being. In Genesis 1 this was indicated by man's creation on the same day as the animals. Physically, man is an animal . . . some more than others! But man is more than an animal. Man was created in the image of God. In Genesis 2 the special nature of man is marked out by the personal way God gives to man the breath of life. By this direct transfusion man becomes a "living being."[3]

Though man is not deity, he has a special tie to

God—the tie of personal relationship initiated by God himself.

## God's Provision for Man

God demonstrates his care for man when he provides him with a "paradise" (2:8-17). Adam's home is a bountiful, parklike garden. This new inhabitant of earth will not have to scrap and scratch for food.

But this is no Walden Pond. No placid creek with pond here, but a massive and mighty river, suitable for wide-scale irrigation. It is superior to the rivers later civilizations relied on—and is actually their source. Northwesterners should think bigger than the Columbia. Midwesterners, the Mississippi. Egyptians, the Nile.

In this magnificent setting man could exercise his creativity and rule by cultivating, pruning, and otherwise caring for the garden. There is no rush to subdue the whole earth. No one's in a hurry. Yahweh has provided a productive beachhead from which to start. As the human race grows, the model garden can be creatively extended.

Additionally, in his great kindness Yahweh designates all the trees in the garden as sources for food. Man need not ask divine permission. He does not have to pray about it. This is man's realm by God's sovereign design. Of course, there is a minor restriction (2:17), but it is the *abundance of provision* that is stressed here. "The prohibition (v. 17) is completely embedded in the description of God's fatherly care for man."[4] Even the prohibition of this one fruit must be for man's good. But it is mentioned along with the penalty to prepare us for the events of the next chapter.

## The Creative Counterpart

The climax of God's care is the gift of a counterpart. The creation of man, including both male and female, was the high point in Genesis 1. Likewise, in Genesis 2 the provision of the woman is the final and most special of God's gifts. Only in this context do the words "not good" appear in describing God's creation—"It is not good for the man to be alone" (2:18). This announcement does not contradict the "very good" of 1:31. Creation is "very good" *after* the creation of both male and female (1:27). But man without woman forms an incomplete humanity which is "not good."

So crucial is the creation of the woman that it is preceded by a heavenly discussion (2:18). Only the creation of humanity merited such a discussion in chapter 1. The woman is the most significant of God's provisions for Adam.

Now comes a parade! This procession of the animals created by God[5] occurs for a couple of reasons. Adam needs to initiate his rule by naming them. In the ancient world the right to name indicates rule.[6] As God's agent, Adam begins to organize the creation.

Yet there also is a more basic reason, made clear in the final review of this zoo-in-motion: "But for Adam there was not found a helper suitable for him" (2:20). Of course there wasn't; God was not surprised. Remember verse 18? But now *Adam knew his need.*

And so God creates the woman. His "fanciful" method displays his wisdom. By using a part of the man to create the woman, there can be no doubt that the woman is on the same level as Adam. To deny her is to deny himself. Commitment to each other and dependence on each other must be total.

Adam recognizes the significance of God's action, but even more celebrates the unique value of the gift. Listen to the first recorded words in all human history—not the primeval grunt of narrow-browed Neanderthal . . . but *poetry*:

> This is now bone of my bones
> And flesh of my flesh;
> She shall be called Woman,
> Because she was taken out of Man (2:23).

Poetry in recognition of woman.

## The Answer

"Who am I?"

The Babylonian myth would answer, "You are a product of the gods to make their life easier."

The Bible would say, "You are a personal creation of Yahweh, who cares for you and has created certain relationships for your own good as you rule his gift, the earth." This knowledge of God's order and created relationships is considered obsolete today. As a result, our age suffers the anxiety of enjoying no secure place or relationships in the world.

## UNDERSTANDING RELATIONSHIPS[7]

### Relationship to God

It is not enough to know that God is the sovereign Creator.

The Israelite must realize that Yahweh *cares*.

Knowing God as Creator calms our fears and eliminates our superstitions. But to know that God initiates and desires personal fellowship with us motivates us to love and response. God's personal commitment to man began by sharing his divine breath and providing a productive environment. But most striking to both the Israelite and to us is God's immediate presence in the garden. There was direct fellowship with God from the very first (compare 3:8-9). If Eden were England, teatime would have been anticipated with great delight!

Moreover, God is called *Yahweh* in Genesis 2. Genesis 1 used the term *Elohim*, the general name for the Supreme Being—"God" in English. Genesis 2 adds Yahweh to Elohim. Yahweh is the personal name for God and stresses his relationship and commitment to his people.[8] Its presence here supports the central theme: Yahweh, the God of Israel, created man personally and desires only good for man.

Of course, this original fellowship was ruined by man's sin (our next chapter). But this does not make

Genesis 2 irrelevant for later readers. The same Yahweh revealed here is the Yahweh who delivered the Israelite readers from Egypt. His care and concern have not changed—though circumstances have. He still wants to be with his people. This same Yahweh wants to give Israel a bountiful land "flowing with milk and honey". To enjoy this land—and God's fellowship as well—Israel, like Adam and Eve, must obey.

### God's Order of Life

Our story makes clear that God is sovereign over man, and that animals are in turn subject to man's oversight (2:19-20). The relationship of the man to the woman is a bit more complicated—and has been ever since!

Everything in this chapter points to the woman as the climax of the story. God's method of creating her from Adam, the failure to find a suitable partner among the animals, and Adam's poetic enthusiasm all introduce the woman as being on a level of creation equal to the man. This is the primary focus and must not be moved to the edge of the picture.

But is there anything in this instruction which suggests the relationship between the man and the woman? The apostle Paul finds it significant that the man was created first, then the woman (1 Corinthians 11:8-9, 1 Timothy 2:13). But, say Paul's critics, if being created last indicates the highest creature in Genesis 1, then being created last would mean the woman was higher than the man in Genesis 2.[9] True enough; but only if you forget the theme of Genesis 2. All the items following man's creation in Genesis 2 relate to God's gracious provisions for Adam. Of these, the woman is the highest—so high as to be on the man's level. But that does not eliminate the apostle's point. The woman was created after the man and *for* the man.

Neither does the word *helper* by itself suggest that woman is man's inferior—nor even that she is under his leadership. The word is used of God as man's helper

(Hosea 13:9, Psalm 115:9-11), and certainly God is not under man's leadership. Even when *helper* is used for other human aid, usually for military allies, it does not imply inferiority.[10] But here again, the context must not be neglected. Consider what it would mean if God were "brought into existence" to be a helper to man in any of those passages in which he is called man's helper. Ah, what a far different thought!

In Genesis 2, *helper* specifies the woman's major role. So the word itself suggests no inferiority; it is the man who is incomplete. Yet it is still true that the woman is created "for the man" to aid him in achieving God's mandate for humanity. "The woman is not described as the man's servant, his valet, his little errand girl whom he needs for this or that, but as the help equal and adequate to him and without whom he cannot be a man."[11] Thus, no inferiority of being or function is implied. Nonetheless, she is in fact created to function in relation to the man to achieve God's purpose for mankind.

The man then exercises leadership by naming the woman. Just as he classified the animals, so now he designates her "Woman." The name he chooses shows that he recognizes she is on his own level.[12] As this account continues into the next chapter, there are at least two more indicators that God designed woman as man's equal, functioning as an equal ally under his leadership. These indicators will be discussed then.

A major concern of the Old Testament is that people understand and follow God's order. It is expressed in the phrase from Proverbs: "The fear of the LORD is the beginning of wisdom." Genesis 1—3 instructs in God's wisdom. It presents his intended order. This wisdom is relevant for today, and by its light we need to examine our own practices relative to both equality of male and female, and to roles. Many roles advocated for woman may violate her equality by implying an inferior servitude rather than her real status as man's ally or counterpart. Also, roles that we think imply leadership may not be so certain. Some husbands, for instance, insist on keeping household finances and paying the bills. Is this necessarily the husband's role? Or may he delegate that responsibility to his wife? She just might be better at math!

Also, the man must remember that being the leader does not mean he is the most intelligent or the more gifted. Many men get all tangled up in the telephone booth trying to uncover their costume with the "S" on it. A good leader is one who recognizes the value and capabilities of those who are equal to him in standing—and often superior to him in certain abilities.

## The Model for Marriage

This initial male and female design, we are told, is God's plan for marriage (2:24). Though every man's wife is not formed from one of his ribs, God's design is that men seek a counterpart in life.[13] When a man and woman come together in this way, they—like the first man and woman—become one in God's order.

This prescription for marriage was surprising for the ancient world. A man is to *leave* his father and mother and cleave to his wife. The instruction is clear. The new unity is to be foremost. The son's former loyalty to his parents—though strong in the culture of that time—is not to interfere with his devotion and commitment to his wife. God has initiated a unity that is stronger than obligation to father and mother! In the patriarchal world no stronger affirmation could be made about this relationship.[14]

To "leave" parents and "cleave" to a wife become the clear hallmarks of the marriage union. By them it is publicly recognized that the son has started his own family and has left his parents' household.

Though sexual union is a significant part of this "cleaving," sexual union by itself does not qualify as marriage. Even betrothal is stronger than sexual union as a marriage claim (Deuteronomy 22:23-27). Sexual union apart from public leaving is fornication (1 Corinthians 7:1-2). The back seat of a car is not an acceptable place to initiate marriage. The mother's tent, after public arrangements, is (Genesis 24:67). Fornication and adultery are perversions of the "one flesh" pattern of marriage, for they attempt a "one flesh" physical experience without the commitment of marital unity. And so Paul condemns becoming "one flesh" with a prostitute (1 Corinthians 6:15-16). Joining with a prostitute does not make a marriage. Rather, such a union is fornication, and is to be avoided as a tragic sin against God's ideal for the body (1 Corinthians 6:18).[15]

## Vocation

Popular ideas of Eden's garden often include the picture of no responsibilities—as if Adam and Eve spent all their days on the beach. If Eden is no Walden, neither is it Sun City, Arizona.

We have seen that God gave man certain tasks. In 1:28 he is to subdue the earth. Even within the garden God prepared, the man is to till, prune, and generally care for the garden. Adam, created in God's image and like God himself, engages in meaningful, creative activity. He is not made to graze all day without a creative thought, plan, or responsibility. Man, even in "paradise," has tasks and goals—and the freedom to carry them out creatively.

Keeping the wolf from the door, however, was not man's concern. There was an abundance of food and a magnificently large river. Famine was not on the horizon. Man's work became a burden due to a tragedy of his own making. But even after sin's entrance, work can be positive. Man still bears responsibility for subduing the earth. As the Old Testament wisdom books (Proverbs, Ecclesiastes, and Job) clearly teach, "Man is meant for an orderly role in an orderly cosmos. His rightful duty is to discern that order and find his responsible share in it. Scientific endeavors, therefore, in the fields of biology, chemistry, geology, mathematics, forestry, and others, should be looked upon as honorable as they seek to discern the order of the universe."[16]

# ON THE WAY: FULFILLMENT OF RELATIONSHIPS

## Restoration of Relationship

Why tell the Israelite of a time when man lived in a much finer setting, when mankind had direct contact and fellowship with God? Sacrifice was not offered in the garden. No temple was there as a place to approach God. No priesthood had been appointed. God himself visited Adam and Eve in the garden. The contrast with the daily experience of the normal Israelite is remarkable.

One reason this wonderfully open past relationship to God is recorded is to allow every man to understand why God does not communicate openly and directly today. Surely all serious people have wondered why God seems so difficult to talk to—and even more, to hear from! The Scriptures confirm that God hides himself from man. God's direct revelation to Moses was considered exceptional (Numbers 12:6-8). Other prophets received their messages in dreams and visions (Numbers 12:6), and the rest of the people received God's message through these prophets. Moses is said to have spoken "face to face" with God, and yet the same passage makes clear that he did not directly view God's face (Exodus 33:11-23). In Eden, God communicated directly with man because man was perfect from God's creative hand. But, as we shall see, that perfection is no longer the case.

Though our story begins to explain why God's presence is hidden, there is another reason for it. It also points with hope to the future. The story of man's *formerly* open communication with God helps us understand the relationship God desires with man *now*. And so the story builds the foundation for what God will do in the future. In progressive stages God is bringing to pass his plan in history for restoring man to direct fellowship with himself. With Christ, a new level beyond the revelation to Moses was reached (John 1:17-18). The instruction which came through Moses was direct, but the truth revealed by the one who is God among us outshines Moses in glory. After the coming of the Holy Spirit at Pentecost, every believer experiences a new level of fellowship with God (2 Corinthians 3:18). Believers enjoy a restored relationship through Jesus Christ (Ephesians 2:11-18).

But there is still *more to come.*

One day we shall know *fully* just as we are fully known by God (1 Corinthians 13:12). Then we shall be like our Savior because "we shall see Him just as He is" (1 John 3:2). Then will come to pass the future blessing Jesus promised: "Blessed are the pure in heart, for they shall see God" (Matthew 5:8).

**The New Creation**

The New Testament emphasizes God's plan to restore man by announcing a new creation that we can experience *already* (2 Corinthians 5:17). As believers we participate already in the new order of living—*eternal life.* As citizens of the kingdom (Colossians 1:13) we have a whole new set of relationships and a totally new identity—"the old things passed away; behold, new things have come" (2 Corinthians 5:17). Old identities are severed; a new relationship to God is what counts (Ephesians 2:10-13).

But the full implementation of this new creation is still future. As the apostle John describes his vision of the future in Revelation 21:1—22:5, the theme of a restored world is announced. We saw earlier that this coming new world has no hint of the original chaos in Genesis 1:2. Now compare the new order with the scene in the garden of Eden, and note the similarities:

- No need for a temple.
- God is directly present.
- There is a river.
- The tree of life is there.

Yet the new creation is not a return to the gracious provisions of the garden. It is an *advance.* Note the differences from the garden:

- The presence of God and Christ is continuous.
- The throne of God is there. His perfect order and rule is guaranteed.
- Eternal life is secured.

What was lost in Eden is more than regained. For those redeemed by Christ, a new humanity has begun!

**The New Humanity**

For a new creation there must be a new humanity. God began the old creation with one man. Adam was it. He was humanity. Eve was created as his complement, and together they were man (Genesis 5:2). In starting a new creation, God begins it with the man Christ Jesus.

Paul compares these two men in 1 Corinthians 15:45-49. He calls Adam the "first man" and he calls Christ the "second man" and the "last Adam." How many men does that leave between Adam and Christ? How many men does it allow after Christ? For Paul there were *only two real men*. Only these men are heads of humanity. Adam was humanity as God created it. But by his sin he placed all of his humanity out of fellowship with God (Romans 5:12-19). The new human race begins with Christ. All who are his by God's grace and through faith in him become part of this new humanity. Under Adam we suffered the results of sin. Under Christ we enjoy the accomplishments the Son of God has brought. We are counted righteous before God. We have life and have entered into Christ's righteous reign (Romans 5:16-19, 8:1-10).

Severed from our citizenship in the old creation, we still live in it and still experience in these physical frames the results of the failure of our original "Old Man." We often struggle with temptation and groan with the rest of a creation out of gear (Romans 8:22-23). But there is eager anticipation of our final redemption out of this creation (8:29) and the changeover when we shall wear the likeness of the New and Last Man (1 Corinthians 15:49, Romans 8:29).

Behold, the tabernacle of God is among men,
and He shall dwell among them,
and they shall be His people,
and God Himself shall be among them,
and He shall wipe away every tear from
their eyes;
and there shall no longer be any death;
there shall no longer be any mourning,
or crying, or pain;
the first things have passed away
(Revelation 21:3-4).

# FOR PERSONAL INTERACTION & DISCUSSION

SUGGESTED SCRIPTURE READINGS:

Genesis 2:4-25
Romans 5:12-21 and 8:12-39

1. With what you know from these three sources—(1) ancient pagan beliefs, (2) modern secular beliefs, and (3) the Bible's teachings—compare what each one says about mankind's purpose and our relationship with God (or the gods).
2. What can we learn in Genesis 1 and 2 about God's concern for man? What difference do you think this should make in your life?
3. Describe as fully as you can what the garden of Eden provided for man and woman. What do these things tell you about the role and purpose of mankind?
4. What kind of bearing does Genesis 2 have on the most important relationships of your life? Are any relationships which are crucial to human survival not addressed in Genesis 2?
5. What events in Genesis 2 show the full equality of the female with the male?
6. Look over this list of behavior patterns from various cultures. Which ones do you think violate biblical teaching on equality? Which are adequately supported by biblical teaching? Which are merely cultural practices that are neither condemned nor supported by the Bible?
    - When both husband and wife travel by car, the husband drives.
    - Only the wife wears a wedding ring.
    - A man allows a woman to enter a door before him, as he holds open the door.
    - The wife rather than the husband is primary caretaker for their children.

- When walking together on a sidewalk, the man keeps himself between the street and the woman.
- When walking together with a heavy load, the woman rather than the man carries it.
- When walking together with a heavy load, the man rather than the woman carries it.
- The wife is responsible for housecleaning and meal preparation for her husband and children.
- When walking together, the woman walks a short distance behind the man.
- The husband must be his family's "breadwinner."
- The husband makes all financial decisions for his family.
- The family will move to follow the husband's/wife's occupation.

7. Why is sexual union not an adequate definition for marriage? What disruptive effects come from violating the marriage pattern of Genesis 2?
8. Genesis 2 indicates God's direct presence with man in man's original state. What is the importance of this? Does God's presence with us have the same importance today? If so, how do we experience God's presence?
9. What is the New Humanity and the New Creation? Why is Jesus, as the second and last Man, necessary for God's plan of restoring mankind? How is he important to your own relationship to God?

'GOD HAD SAID IT WAS ALL "VERY GOOD." BUT IT IS *NOT* ALL GOOD. IN FACT, A LOT OF IT DOESN'T MAKE SENSE.'

---

CHAPTER

# 3.

# THE MESS WE'RE IN

## THE REALITY OF SIN IN GENESIS 3

Travel in ancient times was no Boy Scout expedition.

In an account of his traveling the coast of Palestine and Phoenicia during the time of the judges, Wen-Amon, an official of Egypt, spells out some of the difficulties he encountered: He is robbed. His ship is tied up in harbors. He is caught in a storm and is forced to land and face attack by local townspeople.[1]

Perhaps an even less peaceful scene prevailed inland. The Bible pictures the danger.

> In the days of Shamgar the son of Anath,
> In the days of Jael, the highways were deserted,
> And travelers went by roundabout ways
> (Judges 5:6).

The Israelites of Moses' time had their problems too, not only from outsiders but also from their own ranks. There was rebellion against Moses (Numbers 16). There was complaining about God's choice of diet (Numbers 11). There was idolatry (Exodus 32:4, Amos 5:25-26). The caseload of disputes between Israelites required Moses to get help by appointing judges (Exodus 18). This world is no Eden.

What happened? How did the world get into the mess it's in?

Genesis 1 and 2 by themselves do not explain man's experience in the world. It is not until the tragic events of Genesis 3 that we understand. God had said it was all "very good." But it is *not* all good. In fact, a lot of it doesn't make sense.

> There is futility which is done on the earth, that is, there are righteous men to whom it happens according to the deeds of the wicked. On the other hand, there are evil men to whom it happens according to the deeds of the righteous. I say that this too is futility (Ecclesiastes 8:14).

How is it that there is oppression on the earth God created? How is it that a girl was brutally murdered on a local college campus and a family was murdered in their own home? And does it makes sense that all these victims were believers in Jesus Christ?

The most important thing for a man to know is the God who is the sovereign, personal Creator of this world. Next comes man's understanding of his own function in God's scheme for life. But we will be hopelessly confused and defeated if we do not also understand that *things are not as they once were.* A great change has come which has cast a shadow of imperfection and impossibility on what went before. Without knowing of this great change, we would be frustrated and conclude that the Bible's picture of God cannot be reconciled with life as we know it.

After Genesis 3, man finds himself in the frustrating position of the little boy whose bedtime prayers included the following request: "Lord, please help me save my money for a baseball bat . . . and don't let the ice cream man come down this street." This third chapter of Genesis, then, tells us how we got into the mess we are in. And—more important—by reading Genesis 3 we also understand God's view of this mess.

## THE STORY OF MAN'S FALL

### Background

Genesis 2 provides part of the background for the story of the Fall. There the prohibition against eating from the tree of the knowledge of good and evil was introduced as the only restriction in the midst of overwhelming and abundant provision by God.

What kind of a tree was it? Certainly *not* an apple tree. Its name is provided: "a Knowledge-of-Good-and-Evil tree."

But what was its significance? Why was it there?

First, we should remind ourselves that it was not a sinister tree. All of God's creation was pronounced "good" by the divine author himself. The name "Good-and-Evil" does not brand the tree as partially evil, but mentions two extremes in order to include everything in between.

We do the same thing in English. We say someone "searched high and low," meaning they searched everywhere. In Genesis 1:1, "heavens and earth" includes the whole solar system. In Psalm 139:2, David says God knows him when he sits down and rises up. The meaning is, "God knows me no matter what I'm doing." The knowledge of good and evil involves knowing the whole moral spectrum, just as the tree of life related to living forever. This tree, then, has to do with moral knowledge.[2]

Again we are forced to conclude that though it is not good to experience both good and evil, yet moral knowledge is good. And Genesis confirms our conclusion, for God himself says, "Behold, the man has become like one of Us, knowing good and evil" (Genesis 3:22). Significantly, the New Testament adds that the spiritual person is marked by this very quality: "But solid food is for the mature, who because of practice have their senses trained to discern good and evil" (Hebrews 5:14). Infants lack this discernment (Deuteronomy 1:39), and King Solomon prays for it as part of the wisdom he desires (1 Kings 3:9).

We can only conclude that God had intended to use the tree of the knowledge of good and evil to bring the man and the woman to a higher level of moral perception. Would God, after Adam and Eve built a history of obeying the command to abstain from this tree, have commanded them to partake? Or would abstaining from the tree in itself have been the key ingredient to learning moral discernment?

We cannot say. Either is possible. We can know only that God's creation of the tree was for a positive purpose. The serpent, introduced in 3:1, gives us a second problem in understanding the background of the temptation. The text informs us that the serpent was "more crafty than any beast of the field which the LORD God had made." This immediately alerts the Israelite reader that a real serpent is in view—not a serpent as found in many of the myths.[3] This serpent is a creation of God.

But this leaves us unprepared for the remainder of the narrative. As much as any Israelite of Moses' time, we are surprised to read of a talking serpent. Not only does this serpent talk, but it is able to reason—to a degree that is convincing to a human! How does this fit with the earlier distinction between the animal and human level of creation? How does this fit with the search among the animals for a helper and the absolute failure to find a candidate? Beyond all this, the serpent knows about the prohibition. And it is impossible to deny that its aim is to cause the woman to disobey God.

No answers to the dilemma are provided for us. We are forbidden by the passage to make the scene mythical. We seem to be forbidden by the nature of the conversation to conclude that the serpent is one of God's good creatures and nothing more.[4]

The above two limits make the interpretation of the New Testament the only satisfactory one. The New Testament writers understood the tempter of Genesis 3 to be Satan (see John 8:44, Revelation 12:9, Romans 16:20). It is clear from the Genesis narrative that a sinister mind is at work in the serpent. The Israelites were aware of the use of the serpent as a god.[5] They also recognized that false gods were demonic (Deuteronomy 32:17, cf. 1 Corinthians 10:20). Our account of the entrance of sin into human experience assumes an already fallen intelligence—devilishly so![6]

**Overview of the Temptation**

The serpent approaches the woman, who already knows about the forbidden tree, though the command not to eat of it was given prior to her creation (2:16-17). Adam, no doubt, was responsible for communicating this to her.

Why did the tempter approach the woman rather than the man? Because of some weakness of nature particular to the woman? There is no reason to assume so. He may have chosen Eve because her information was secondhand, giving him more room to increase doubt when he raises the question, "Has God said . . . ?" Satan has always found this a successful approach, calling into question what has been passed down from prophet, eyewitness, and apostle.

The serpent doesn't stop at questioning the God-given prohibition. He wants the woman to *focus* on the restriction: "Has God really said that you can't eat from any [every] tree of the garden?"

The woman is quick to the defensive, but her reply shows the serpent succeeded in directing her to focus on the single divine prohibition. Eve's reply differs in at least three ways from the original command.[7]

| *Original Command* | *Eve's Reply* |
| --- | --- |
| From any (every) tree of the garden you may eat freely. | From the fruit of the trees of the garden we may eat. |
| Tree of life is in the middle of the garden. | Tree of knowledge of good and evil is in the middle. |
| From the tree of the knowledge of good and evil you shall not eat. | God has said, 'You shall not eat from it or touch it.' |

The first difference seems almost insignificant. Perhaps it is. If there is any difference, it involves a shift of emphasis. The original command emphasizes the generosity of God's provision of every tree in the garden. Matched against that the restriction is so slight as to be insignificant. In Eve's reply, however, the bountiful provision is reduced to simple *permission*—so that the restriction becomes the focus. Her answer is truthful, but lacks the enthusiasm she might have expressed for God's goodness.[8]

The second difference from the account in chapter 2 involves the garden's geography. In 2:9 the tree of life is identified as being in the middle of the garden. Eve identifies the *forbidden* tree with the phrase, "the tree in the middle of the garden." Now, Eve's geography may not be entirely bad. The forbidden tree is closely associated with the tree of life in 2:9, and both may be toward the center of the garden. But even if both are in the center, Eve's identification of the forbidden tree by this single description overlooks entirely the tree of life and its positive appeal. Her language again shows that the serpent has been successful at focusing on the restriction.[9]

The third difference from God's command is Eve's addition to the original restriction against eating. She says that not only are they not to eat of the tree, they are not to *touch* it. Again the restriction looms larger in Eve's eyes than it really is.

The serpent's reply becomes more bold (3:4-5). Now that the woman is focusing on the restriction itself, he contradicts God's warning about the penalty. He does so in the most direct way possible. Where God had said, "You shall surely die," Satan says, "You shall surely not die."[10] He must relieve Eve of the idea that she will suffer the announced penalty. He says in effect, "You won't really reap what you sow."

To make his own contradiction of God's word seem more reasonable, Satan invents a false motive for God. "God," he says, "has really invented a nonexistent penalty to keep you in your place. He is afraid you will rise to his level. If you knew as much as God knows, you would become a threat to him."

Eve's response is fatal.

She divorces her God-given reason from God's word and relies instead on her limited experience. The tree looks like a good tree. And it was, wasn't it? Eve eats and gives to Adam who also eats, and so she invents disobedience. Here is one case where necessity was not the mother of invention.

## The Immediate Results of Sin

Here come the clothes!

We were told following the woman's creation that Adam and Eve were naked and not ashamed (2:25). Now they immediately recognize their nakedness *as a source of shame* and attempt to clothe themselves. This is remarkable when one considers that they were the only humans around. A Jewish commentator summarizes the original view of nakedness before the Fall: "They looked upon the sexual organs in the same way as we regard the mouth, the face and hands."[11] This has not been true since. Adam and Eve quickly set about to remedy their sense of shame with temporary garments. This partial remedy was continued by God with more substantial clothing (3:21), and has remained a social necessity. Throughout the Scripture the concept of nakedness and shame are connected (cf. Ezekiel 23:29, Revelation 3:17-18). It was not so from the beginning.

A second experience previously unknown was a sense of fear arising from guilt. The human pair hide themselves from God—as best they can. God comes and graciously directs a discussion in a way that gives man opportunity to recognize and fully confess his sin.[12] Adam admits to fear (3:10). This fear, arising out of his sense of shame, separates him from an open, transparent relationship with God. So he hides. "Fear and shame are henceforth the incurable stigmata of the Fall in man."[13]

If these first two experiences sound as modern as a page in the local psychiatrist's notebook, the third reaction of man does nothing to lessen the impression. The man attempts to avoid taking the responsibility for his failure. He shifts blame to the woman and ultimately to God himself: "The woman you put here with me—she gave me some fruit from the tree, and I ate it" (3:12 NIV). The woman points to the serpent who deceived her (3:13).

Eve's answer discloses a reversal of the divine order: Male and female were to have dominion over the beasts (1:26). God does not accept Adam's excuse either (3:17). Again, the divine order has been reversed. Adam was to be subject to God, not to his counterpart.

At this point it is possible to suggest a more significant reason why Satan used a serpent to tempt the woman. The theme of the divine order for Creation and the satanic desire to incite rebellion against God's rule make this format for the temptation especially potent. Satan not only causes them to sin in direct disobedience and rebellion against the divine command, but the sin also directly flouts the divine order. Humanity's charge to rule over the beasts is violated, as is the man's responsibility for leadership. Eve listens to a beast and Adam follows her lead.[14]

According to 3:22, what the serpent said came true. They became like God. They knew good and evil. Their eyes were opened (3:7). But all this occurred in the most perverse way, rather than in the way God intended. They knew good and evil by adding sinful experience to the good they had already experienced. But one thing the serpent said was not at all true: In spite of what Satan claimed, death surely *did* come to the first human couple on the day they ate. Adam had been created from the ground with the capacity to die; he was mortal, though as long as he remained faithful to God death could not touch him. But as soon as he sinned, death came.

Adam, like Paul in Romans 7:11, could say, "Sin . . . put me to death" (NIV)—though both men were still breathing. Death was first seen in man's guilt and fear before God. It would ultimately send man's body back to the dust (Genesis 3:19).

## UNDERSTANDING TEMPTATION

Paul told the believers at Corinth, "We are not unaware of his [Satan's] schemes" (2 Corinthians 2:11 NIV). Elsewhere he refers again to "the devil's schemes" (Ephesians 6:11), schemes that should be clear to all believers. They are plainly revealed in Scripture. The temptation of Eve gives flesh and blood reality to the effectiveness of several of these strategies:

*Scheme #1—Satan attempts to have us view God's standards as unreasonable restrictions.*

It is important to recognize that the command not to eat of the tree of moral knowledge involved no hardship for Adam and Eve. They were not hungry without its fruit. There was no nutritional lack in their diet. They could not even achieve boredom of menu simply by avoiding this one tree.

Our focus should not be on limitations we do not understand, but on the evidence that God has been gracious to us. These should convince us that any limitations are for our good. The divine remedy for this temptation is clear:

> Rejoice always;
> pray without ceasing;
> in everything give thanks; for this is
> God's will for you in Christ Jesus
> (1 Thessalonians 5:16-18).

Read Philippians 4:4-7 as well. Thanksgiving is the antidote! It is impossible to be thankful and subject to the devices of Satan at the same time. Restrictions and circumstances we do not understand can then be accepted by faith as coming from the good hand of God.

That the restriction was incidental and involved no sacrifice brings out a further observation concerning this Satanic scheme. The more *insignificant* and *unimportant* the restriction, the more useful it becomes for

Satan-inspired rebellion. A decade plus as both parent and teacher has provided repeated confirmation. Point out to a complaining child or student that the restriction they are denouncing is hardly worth the effort because it is of so little consequence, and they will invariably reply: "That's what makes me so upset!"[15]

*Scheme #2—Satan questions whether God has spoken (3:1).*

This is a regular Satanic approach. Because God speaks primarily through selected individuals—prophets—and even then primarily in dreams and visions, it is possible to doubt that the message of the prophet is really a message from God.

To further complicate the picture, Satan often produces counterfeit or false prophets. So it is impossible for believers to accept just anyone's word that he is a prophet. The Bible prescribes strict, objective tests to deal with this situation (see Deuteronomy 18:14-22). It is right to question whether God has spoken through a particular individual. God's word will stand up to the tests which God himself has instructed his people to use. In this way they will avoid being duped by false claims.

But the prophets and apostles of the Bible have already been clearly vindicated as spokesmen of God. To reject their instruction in favor of an appealing personal experience is to fall into this snare of the devil.

*Scheme #3—Satan attempts to convince men they will not reap what they sow.*

"God will not penalize," Satan repeats with defeating regularity. "God wouldn't do that . . . He's just trying to hold you in line . . . He just doesn't want you to have any fun." Many religious teachers adopt this demonic device when they proclaim that God would never send anyone to eternal punishment.

Just as many cigarette smokers believe they will be the exception to the normal health problems caused by smoking, men and women seem ready to believe that somehow they will be exempted from the results of sin outlined in the Bible. We like to think that "just this one sin" will have no effect on our future, our family, or even our fellowship with God. Adam and Eve's sin affected the whole race!

*Scheme #4—Satan encourages dissatisfaction with our God-appointed role.*

Ambition is a noble characteristic if its antonym is laziness. There is, however, a destructive type of ambition based on a dissatisfaction with what God has given me to do and be.

This dissatisfaction says, "I would like to be up front and noticed" when God has given the gift of helps. (How we *desperately* need more people with the gift of helps.) This dissatisfaction causes a young mother to wish she were free from her role to pursue an independent career. A husband looks elsewhere than to the wife of his youth for some experience of pleasure—no matter how superficial and fleeting. A wife believes her home would be much better off if she were the leader.

Ambition is wonderful when directed toward faithfulness to God in the circumstances and role God has placed you in—whether temporary or permanent. It is self-defeating and destructive when it seeks to break out of God's pattern for life.

*Scheme #5—Satan wants us to use human reason to judge God's word.*

When Eve was ready to judge the situation by her own limited understanding—apart from God's instruction—the battle was all but over. The tree *looked* like a good tree, both nutritionally and aesthetically. Of course it was! And didn't it hold out the promise of wisdom, as its name suggested? From her perspective, and with the facts at hand, it was reasonable—*if she neglected God's instruction*—to think that eating would be beneficial.

Satan would like us to demand that God's revelation be acceptable to our limited understanding before we follow it. Naturally, men using this method find much wrong with God's word. Why? Because we are using an imperfect yardstick—our own ignorance plus our own imperfection.

## ON THE WAY: THE COMPLETION OF TEMPTATION

### Satan's Failure as a Tempter

The beginning of the end for Satan's deception of mankind occurs in the life of Jesus of Nazareth. The first creation and first humanity were victimized by the original liar and murderer, the devil (John 8:44). God's plan for restoring humanity involves, as we have seen, the Last Adam and Second Man, Jesus Christ.

It is not surprising therefore to discover that Jesus also faces satanic temptation in a one-on-one encounter. The Bible records only two temptations in which actual conversation takes place between the devil and men. One is with the first humans. The other is with the Second Man. This is not coincidental. Neither is it coincidental that this second temptation follows the voice from heaven which declares Jesus to be the chosen Son with whom the Father is well pleased (Matthew 3:17, Luke 3:22). Luke even inserts the genealogy of Jesus at this point—tracing his line right back to . . . Adam![16]

Jesus, unlike Adam and Eve, is actually hungry; but he refuses to violate God's will for him by making life easy through the misuse of supernatural power. He is willing to submit himself to the divine order and plan. There is no rebellion against an assigned role here!

Satan also tempts Jesus to seek rule and position independent of God's sovereign control (Luke 4:5-7). The devil has always tempted men to think of themselves as captains of their own fate and souls. Those he has deceived always boast, "I will be like God," whether they are a king of Babylon (cf. Isaiah 14:14), the director of a bank, or a hardworking grease-monkey. Jesus rejects this temptation and repeats the commandment of God. Though rule will eventually be his in the Father's appointed time, he will not seek it by disobeying God's direct command.

Finally, not unlike the temptation of Eve, Satan affirms that God will take care of Jesus and not allow him to suffer physical harm (Luke 4:9-11). But Jesus refuses to test God's word as if it could not be accepted as given.

Jesus maintained his complete subjection to God's role for him throughout his earthly life, even though that role involved not only temptation but also suffering (Philippians 2:5-11). This qualified him to be the author of salvation for all who follow him (Hebrews 2:10, 5:8-10).

**Satan Judged at the Cross**

Following Jesus' announcement that the time for his crucifixion had come (John 12:23-28), Jesus and his disciples ate the Passover meal together (John 13—17). Jesus tries to encourage the disciples, who are anxious about any future that would not include him (14:1-5). He tells them they will not be without miraculous help (14:12-17). He himself will hear and answer their prayers. The Holy Spirit will be sent to replace him as their Helper. In fact, *it is to their advantage* that Jesus return to the Father, because the Holy Spirit as the Helper will guarantee their effectiveness through convicting the world of sin, righteousness, and judgment (John 16:8-11). And the Spirit will reveal to them all the truth about coming events which they were not yet able to understand (John 16:12-13).

What encouraging guarantees!

In a world of limited warranties, "lemon" laws, and "come-ons," Jesus' promises to his disciples were so fully kept that the world was turned upside down. But hidden in the discussion of the Spirit's convicting work is a significant notation: "*The ruler of this world has been judged*" (John 16:11). Because the usurper of the rule of this world met his judgment in Jesus' crucifixion, the disciples would be able to proclaim a message of freedom from the fear of death. Jesus died to "render powerless him who had the power of death, that is, the devil" (Hebrews 2:14, cf. Colossians 1:13).

**Victory Proclaimed**

With Satan judged at the cross, it's all over except the shooting.

Lest there be any doubt, Jesus was raised to proclaim victory over death and to ascend to the right hand of the Father. By this, his authority over every other power is guaranteed (Ephesians 1:18-21). Those powers against which the Christian struggles in spiritual battle (Ephesians 6:12) may be withstood in the might of the conquering Messiah. The armor of Ephesians 6 includes armor that Isaiah predicted would be worn by the King at his coming (Isaiah 11:5, 52:7, 59:17). *Yet the believer may wear it now!* And we need to wear it, for the battle rages all around us. Paul, hearing of the obedience and holiness of the Roman Christians, can encourage them with the fact that "the God of peace will soon crush Satan under your feet" (Romans 16:20).

Think of it! Fellowships of believers, when obedient, may expect to carry out the work of Jesus the Messiah, extend his kingdom, and implement his victory over Satan *even now*.

**Victory Consummated**

Though Christians may begin to implement Christ's victory now, they must still recognize that real bullets are flying. To know you're on the winning side and that you personally have been enabled to succeed in spiritual battles with the enemy should be more than encouraging. But the ammunition is still live, and a person can be wounded if he fails to follow his instructions. And even if he does follow orders, his battlefield conditions are not Eden! Listen to the apostle as he chides the Corinthians about their ease while he is undergoing hardship. It is as if they are already reigning with Christ:

> You are already filled, you have already become rich, you have become kings without us; and I would indeed that you had become kings so that we also might reign with you. For, I think, God has exhibited us apostles last of all, as men condemned to death; because we have become a spectacle to the world, both to angels and to men. We are fools for Christ's sake, but you are prudent in Christ; we are weak, but you are strong; you are distinguished, but we are without honor. To this present hour we are both hungry and thirsty, and are poorly clothed, and are roughly treated, and are homeless; and we toil, working with our own hands; when we are reviled, we bless; when we are persecuted, we endure; when we are slandered, we try to conciliate; we have become as the scum of the world, the dregs of all things, even until now" (1 Corinthians 4:8-13).

This is not the time to reign as kings! That day is coming.

Today we must live as aliens and pilgrims in a world that still tempts us to sinful desires (1 Peter 2:11).

Today we walk in subjection and humility before God and his word, that he may exalt us "at the proper time" (1 Peter 5:5-6).

# FOR PERSONAL INTERACTION & DISCUSSION

SUGGESTED SCRIPTURE READINGS:

Genesis 3
Luke 4:1-13
Ephesians 6:10-20
Philippians 4:4-8
1 Peter 5:5-11

1. How should understanding the story of man's sin make a difference in the way we view life?
2. In what ways can people learn good and evil today? Which ways are positive and which negative?
3. What evidence do you see that satanic temptation is involved in the serpent's conversation with Eve in Genesis 3? Which of these New Testament verses—John 8:44, Romans 16:20, Revelation 12:7-17, and Revelation 20:7-10—give hope for ultimate victory over Satan?
4. In what ways are "fear and shame . . . the incurable stigmata of the Fall in man"? In what ways do fear and shame keep us from being truly free as human beings?
5. Why is our mental focus so important in avoiding sin? What remedies are available to keep us from falling into a poor mental attitude that makes us more prone to sin?
6. In what ways does Satan try to dupe people today into missing the true word of God?
7. Why are Satan's schemes for temptation so appealing? Are some people more susceptible to these than others are?
8. In facing temptation, how does Jesus' mental focus contrast with Eve's?
9. In Luke 4:1-12, what is the importance of each step in Jesus' progressive victory over sin? How can you practice each of these steps in your own life?

10. Since Satan, though now judged, is still very much active, how should that affect our involvement with material possessions? How should it affect our outlook toward those who oppose the Christian message? How should it affect our political and cultural involvement with the world around us?

'SO THE ALBUM OF THE FIRST FAMILY CLOSES. ONE SON IS BANISHED. THE OTHER'S BLOOD HAS WET THE DUST TO WHICH ALL MEN WILL RETURN.'

CHAPTER

# 4.

# THE EFFECTS OF SIN

LOSS OF ORDER & BALANCE, GENESIS 3—11

"Humpty Dumpty was pushed."

So reads the subway graffiti. And perhaps he was. We'll never know.

There's no question, though, about the extra nudge in the fall described in the Bible. Mankind fell, and the fall was certainly aided. And like the Hump, man has been unable to get it all together since.

There's another rhyme. It's about Little Jack Horner. You remember modest Jack—the boy sitting in a corner for who-knows-what offense with his very own Christmas pie. Inserting his thumb yields one plum, and our hero draws an entirely illogical conclusion: "What a good boy am I."

How like society these two are!

Ever since the Fall man has been attempting to conduct business as usual, convinced that he can get it all together. Some optimistically proclaim that life is on an upward trek. If only it were so! But the results of sin won't go away. Pretending is the most dangerous approach. Sin may be relabeled as an "alternate lifestyle" or "termination of pregnancy," but its results will not go away. Fallen man fails to recognize the deterioration of his own civilization.

Genesis 3:14—11:9 outlines in broad strokes the swift deterioration of society following sin's invasion into man's homeland. The problems man will face are first announced by God as judgment for disobedience. Then the failures of two civilizations testify to the persistence of the temptation to rebel against the divine order.

## PREDICTIONS OF THE STRUGGLE

### Struggle with the Serpent

The interrogation by God (3:11-13) led from the man to the woman to the serpent, confirming again the order of responsibility from the divine viewpoint. God does not question the serpent as to why he tempted the woman—an omission which points again to an *already fallen* intelligence. The curse or judgment of God is announced in reverse direction.

First, the serpent is addressed. The penalty fits both the beast of the field and the demonic personality behind the scene. This curse does not involve a change in the serpent's digestive system so that dust becomes nutritionally beneficial. The dust is not its regular diet, but an unpleasant effect of the previous line: "On your belly shall you go." As a beast of the field the serpent was classed as having the highest mental capacity among the wild animals—much as dolphins and great apes are popularly viewed today. As a wild animal he is demoted to a place of dishonor: He is to crawl in the dust (cf. Micah 7:17).[1] Because he helped to undermine the divine order, his place in the wild animal hierarchy has been changed.

More critical is the point that the struggle which began at the temptation between the serpent and the woman would continue into the future. To limit the struggle to snakebites is to cancel out the significance of the initial interchange between the serpent and the woman. Just as the original encounter involved a demonic intelligence, so the curse of the serpent involves Satan. Satan himself will meet his demise through the action of a woman's offspring. But, as with many curses, the words are cryptic and can be fully understood only upon the fulfillment of the curse. Here the significance of the woman's seed and of God's ultimate plan to overcome the effects of the Fall is just beginning.

**Struggle with Multiplying**

As with the previous struggle, this struggle introduces no new function on the part of the woman. Childbearing was part of God's original intention (1:28). The Fall has increased the pain of an event which was to be totally beautiful.

Those who, like myself, have participated with their wives in classes designed to help control the labor process and who have invaded the labor room and the delivery room, can testify that it is still beautiful—but there *is* pain. The husband can be there to encourage, but he cannot share any of that pain. Modern medicine can (and should) relieve it as much as possible, but some of it seems necessary to the process itself. As with all human functions, the Fall has made the task more difficult. The pain of childbearing is not the last pain the woman will experience because of the children she brings into this world.

**Struggle in Marriage**

In addition to the struggle with multiplying, the woman will face tension in the very relationship which was the hallmark of her creation—her marriage to her husband: "Yet your desire shall be for your husband, and he shall rule over you" (3:16). This verse, like all personally threatening verses in Scripture, has been interpreted in many ways. Some have understood the verse to mean that the woman has a physical and emotional tie to her husband that makes it *easy* for him to exercise his leadership and rule in the family. But that view fails to see that the context concerns *judgment*. None of the rest of God's statements are blessings for the one being addressed.

Another view holds that these words teach a desire for harmony and rest in the husband, but that his response is harsh rule. This fits the context of a curse better, but the word for rule does not by itself suggest harshness. It is used for both God's rule and man's rule.

A third approach fits the context of a curse and the use of the words elsewhere. This view says that the woman will desire to dominate her husband, yet he is to rule over her. This view is supported by a look at the parallel wording in the very next chapter involving God's discussion with Cain. In 4:7 God informs Cain that sin's "desire is for you, but you must master it." Sin wanted to overcome and dominate Cain, but he had the responsibility to rule over it.[2]

Likewise in 3:16, the woman desires to dominate her husband (as sin did Cain), but it is the husband's moral responsibility to maintain leadership. This involves no new arrangement, as we have seen, but rather a difficulty brought on by the Fall. What was formally a highly compatible arrangement will become beset by the difficulties of fallenness on both sides. Here the wife specifically is cursed with the desire for control.

Men, however, also need to recognize that while it is their moral responsibility to be the leader in the home, their leadership has not always followed the model of rule revealed in the love of Yahweh for Israel—and that of Christ for the Church. So in Ephesians 5, Paul reminds the woman to be in subjection and exhorts the husband to love his wife. Each emphasis meets the particular temptation attached to their divinely assigned roles.[3]

We are not saying of course that every wife is bent on undermining her husband. We are saying that the Fall introduced this particular weakness. Just as there is discord between man and ground, discord has entered also the most intimate and fulfilling of relationships. Yet the message of Genesis 2 concerning God's best gift to man at the creation is still true: "He who finds a wife finds a good thing, and obtains favor from the LORD" (Proverbs 18:22).

### Struggle in Subduing the Earth

The curse for the male reduces the joy of creative lordship over the earth by adding a struggle with the ground. Woman's intermittent pain is paralleled by this constant pain for the man. Again, the contrast with the pre-Fall situation is not complete. Satisfaction with work accomplished is a gift of God (Ecclesiastes 3:13), yet it is modified with the knowledge that the earth will win this struggle and man will return to the dust (cf. Ecclesiastes 5:11-20).

## SIN'S PROGRESS

The next events in Genesis graphically catalog the Fall's impact upon the race. These stories focus on judgment. Within the first family comes the judgment on Cain (chapter 4). Then there is judgment on the whole ancient civilization by the Flood (6—8). Following this is judgment within Noah's family (9:20-27). Finally, the post-Flood civilization is judged by confusion of languages (11:1-9). All these judgments highlight the scope of failure which dogs the human family as a result of the Fall.

### A Family Album

Not only was the husband-wife relationship affected by the Fall (Genesis 3:16), but so was the relationship between brothers (Genesis 4). Here we see all those vile monsters that have been our daily companions as fallen men: envy, hypocrisy, malice, and guile. The list comes from 1 Peter 2:1. Remarkable how it agrees with our story, isn't it?

Why was Cain's sacrifice not acceptable to God? Some have believed it was due to its lack of blood. But Scripture allows other sacrifices besides animal sacrifice, so this may not be the reason. Others have suggested that we have here the original distinction between external religion and true devotion.[4] In other words, Abel came with the right motivation, while Cain came grudgingly. This may be supported by the observation that Abel brought the firstborn of the flock, not simply any animal. Cain's offering is merely described as from the fruit of the ground.

But notice the point of the passage. Yahweh warns Cain that he must act properly toward God. If he does not he is responsible for his sin (Genesis 4:7).[5] Cain's failure to control his anger leads to murder, and *God's sovereignty proves undiminished by man's fall.* He acts as judge against injustice on earth.

And so the album of the First Family closes.

One son is banished. The other's blood has wet the dust to which all men will return. Though man is able to advance in the arts and technology after the Fall (4:21-22), Abel's blood will not be the last emblem of fraternal strife (4:23).

**A Civilization Falls**

The Bible next records the progress of the first civilization from Adam to Noah. It is a story marked by a dismal conclusion. In contrast to the Babylonian flood story, which has the gods destroying mankind because they were making too much noise, the Bible cites the moral failure of man. "The wickedness of man was great on the earth, and . . . every intent of the thoughts of his heart was only evil continually" (6:5). Man's inner life has gone the wretched limit. Society reaps the tragic results: *"The earth is filled with violence"* (6:13).

Once again the sovereign God judges the moral failure of man, and this time destroys the ancient world by flood. Civilization must start anew through a single family whose head "walked with God."[6] But what happens as soon as that family gets off the boat and resettles? The family patriarch gets drunk and one of his sons acts shamefully toward him in his drunken and naked state.[7] Depravity is not eliminated by the Flood—only judged.

The subsequent curse upon Canaan, the son of Ham, is not a curse on the Negroid race, but on the Canaanites—the very people Israel would expel from the land for their wickedness. The curse is not on Ham himself. If it were pronounced on Ham it would be experienced by *all* of his sons. God graciously limits the curse to only a portion of Ham's descendants. Canaan is no doubt chosen because of a propensity toward the same weakness as his father. The curse is fully vindicated when the Canaanites actually practice again the indecencies which brought on the curse.[8]

### The New Civilization—Genesis 8-11

Let's check the score. Following the fall of Adam and Eve, Cain kills Abel. *Failure in the family.* Score: 1 to 0. Eventually that whole civilization fails (2 to 0). Noah's family settles in again and before you know it, 3 to 0. But what of the civilization which arises from that family? The answer: 4 to zip. The Bible has portrayed in each of these civilizations first the evidence of sin in the initial family and then the rebellion of each society.

No better example could be found of this universal deterioration than the rebellion of Babylon. Here arises a plot against God's instruction. These men are *not* trying to create the ancient world's forerunner to Skylab—the passage doesn't condemn space exploration. Neither are they trying to reach God's throne. The rebellion here is pure and simple. It is a rebellion against God's instruction which came immediately after the Flood: "Populate the earth abundantly and multiply in it" (Genesis 9:1,7; cf. 1:28).

The men found the plain where Babylon was built and decided to build a city with a tall tower that could be seen for miles around in order that they might not be spread out over the earth. Yahweh takes a decided interest in this building program, though it is insignificant compared to him. He has to "come down" to see this oh-so-tall edifice—generally considered a Babylonian ziggurat or temple-tower.[9]

But he does seem worried, doesn't he? After all, he says that "nothing which they purpose to do will be impossible for them" (11:6). The passage, however, is not speaking of technology, but *morality*. Yahweh concludes: "If I let them get away with this, they will stop at nothing." And so he initiates a judgment to counter their rebellion. The introduction of languages makes this rebellious unity of mankind a practical impossibility. Yahweh scatters them throughout the earth.

### Conclusion

But what of all this failure?

Why recount these ancient events for the benefit of the Israelites who so newly have become a people under God? Their ancestry, of course, has been traced through Shem to Noah and back through Noah and Enoch to Seth. It has not been a perfect ancestry, but it has been preserved by God's grace and has been the object of his special selection. The promised seed continues. But the theme of moral rebellion has been even more center-stage. Moral rebellion is the reason the Canaanite nations are being dispossessed (Leviticus 18:24-25). Israel's own success in the land is dependent upon her recognition of the need for submission to God's sovereign rule (Leviticus 18:26-30).

Not all descendants of Noah are blessed by God. The moral sin of the Canaanites is anticipated in the sin of Ham and predicted in the curse on Canaan. Just so, the selection process would continue. Not all the sons of Abraham would secure God's blessing. And so, within Israel it could be assumed that God would judge and discard those who insist on the route of rebellion.

The first eleven chapters of Genesis stand as a monument to Israel's solemn privilege as God's current standard-bearers in the midst of general rebellion—but also as a monument of warning that the human tendency is to rebel and allow society to deteriorate. If this happens, God will judge.

## ON THE WAY: FULFILLMENT OF THE HUMAN FAMILY

Like a well-fought tennis game in which the competitors fire the ball from one side of the court to the other, the themes of judgment and grace alternate throughout the Bible. In both themes God is seen to be the sovereign Lord of the universe.

But God's ultimate purpose is not limited to displaying his sovereignty in a world that continues to burst open at the seams. *Reversal* of this process is God's ultimate plan. Judgment must culminate. Grace must conquer.

## Reversal of Babel

The judgment of different languages which came at Babel forced man to move out to populate and exercise dominion over the earth as God had commanded. But it also introduced a barrier to the unity of the human race. As long as man is in a state of rebellion against God, unity would be dangerous. God would use national desires and interests to control the rise of evil in various populations (cf. Acts 17:26-27).

In the Old Testament, speaking in tongues is always a judgment. It is at Babel. It is in Isaiah 28:11 where the language which God promises to speak to Israel is the language of the Assyrian invader. Because they have rejected the clear message of the prophet, God's next message to them will be captivity. Such speaking in tongues was promised in Deuteronomy 28:49 as God's judgment on Israel for rebellion against his covenant with her. A century after Isaiah, Jeremiah would predict a similar judgment of tongues and exile for Judah (Jeremiah 5:15).[10] Paul censures the Corinthians for using tongues in an Old Testament manner (1 Corinthians 14:20-25). Used in a way that people cannot understand, tongues should only be used for judgment. Yet under the gospel, the Corinthians are attempting to be an instrument of grace to their unbelieving neighbors. Only words that are understood can bring grace.

This is the context of Acts 2—the day of Pentecost, a day on which a distinct signpost was given. Christ's death fifty days earlier brought judgment to climax. The critical battle was won. The victory was sure. The tide of defeat had been stemmed and now God was bringing his program to completion. All humanity would come to unity under Christ. The first signal of this ultimate unity and the clear indication that we have entered the last phase of God's program was the overcoming of the language barrier by the coming of the Holy Spirit.

In Revelation 7:9-10, what was signaled at Pentecost comes to harmonious completion before the throne of God and before the Lord Jesus as a great multitude from "every nation and all tribes and peoples and tongues" cry out in unison: "Salvation to our God who sits on the throne, and to the Lamb."

**Unity in Christ**

The creed of religious liberalism more than a generation ago was captured in the slogan: "The Fatherhood of God and the brotherhood of man." Undoubtedly they were right. All men owe their existence to the sovereign Creator. And all men are related. As the apostle put it, "And He made from one, every nation of mankind to live on all the face of the earth" (Acts 17:26).

But the physical brotherhood of man has not produced a spiritual unity of peace, harmony, and love. Cain and Abel were brothers, but just as surely as this initial brotherhood cracked under the weight of envy, jealousy, and strife, so sin continues to fracture the hope of universal brotherly harmony.

To achieve a true unity of peace and love, mankind needs help from the outside. That help arrived when the sovereign Creator became the sovereign Redeemer. In a demonstration of both judgment and grace, the author of life died (Acts 3:15).

But what did he achieve in his death?

He achieved that very unity which has eluded man. No greater spiritual division of mankind existed in the first century than between Jew and Gentile. Yet the Gentile who had no covenant with God receives the news: "But now in Christ Jesus you who formerly were far off have been brought near by the blood of Christ. For He Himself is our peace, who made both groups into one . . . thus establishing peace" (Ephesians 2:13-15).

*What Good News!* By faith in Christ alone, men are able to enter God's redeemed family (Ephesians 2:8-9).

The unity established by Christ's death must not be violated in our relationships with one another. Those who are Christ's are to preserve this unity by dropping the ways of the old life and implementing the new life received through Christ. It is significant that Paul mentions the characteristics of humility, gentleness, patience, forbearance, and love in connection with preserving this unity (Ephesians 4:1-3).

I was teaching a Bible class in which a department manager for a major retail chain participated. When we studied these characteristics in Ephesians 4, he immediately responded: "This is just the opposite of our training in business." Yes, that's right. Men are often concerned to protect themselves, to fulfill themselves, to be themselves—even at the expense of others, whether they be our mates, children, or fellow workers. God's concern is for unity . . . for building each other up until we *all* attain to the unity of the faith and total maturity (Ephesians 4:12-13).

You see, Paul's concern is for the whole body to reach maturity in Christ *together*. It is part of our man-made Christianity to think we can achieve maturity as isolated individuals. This is not God's plan! Some things we should do in our inner room by ourselves (Matthew 6:5-6), and others we should do secretly to avoid parading righteousness (Matthew 6:3,17-18). But the things which preserve unity and build toward a fuller experience of unity require commitment to one another. No closet holiness here!

Yet what church has unity and peace as a part of its doctrinal statement? Are these not considered the most dispensable items when a disagreement develops in a church body? These *are* significant doctrines! The unity Christ provided for in his death must be put into practice by believers so that unity may increase in our relationships with one another. This is the route of maturity.

If there is shallowness of life among believers today, might not this be the reason? Jesus said it plainly: "By this all men will know that you are My disciples, if you have love for one another" (John 13:35).

## FOR PERSONAL INTERACTION & DISCUSSION

SUGGESTED SCRIPTURE READINGS:

Genesis 3:14-24, 4:1-12, 6:5-22, 9:18-27, and 11:1-9
Ephesians 4:1-16

1. How does living in a fallen world affect human relationships? Does Genesis 4—11 help us understand our current world situation? What examples come to mind?
2. Why do peace and harmony on earth always seem out of reach, despite the fact that so many people seem to genuinely desire such peace? What are the causes for war, divorce, estrangement, and bitterness?
3. How can a Christian have a positive attitude in the light of all that is wrong in the world? What should be our attitude when the difficulties introduced in this chapter come uninvited into our lives? Does a "positive thinking" mentality gloss over the real problems of a fallen world? Are the ideals of peace and unity unrealistic in light of man's sinful tendencies?
4. How does Christ's first coming, his death, and the coming of the Spirit on the day of Pentecost signal a reversal of the disharmonies of the Fall? How much of this reversal can be experienced now? How can it be experienced?
5. How does the scene in Revelation 7:9-12 picture the ultimate harmony God desires? What is the testimony of this group? Why is this testimony significant for mankind?
6. Why can't a Christian attain maturity in isolation? Look at the teaching in Ephesians 4 about the relationship of believer to believer. What are the key ingredients for growth? What attitudes and actions are taught? What actions and attitudes destroy peaceful relationships?

PART

2.

# GOD'S PLAN FOR REVERSAL

'BEING GOD'S CANDIDATE
FOR BLESSING IS NOT A
TRIP TO DISNEYLAND.
BECAUSE GOD IS GOING TO
BLESS ABRAHAM, HE'S
GOING TO MAKE HIM INTO
A MAN OF FAITH.'

---

CHAPTER

# 5.

# A NEW BEGINNING

## THE COVENANT WITH THE PATRIARCHS

Do you remember when zoom lenses first came out?

I can remember sitting down to home movies made with a zoom lens. Before that, all we had for entertainment was the projector's reverse switch. Now we were entranced by the wide-angle shot which gradually—after practice—narrowed the field of vision until what was previously a small detail now took up the entire screen.

In much the same way the camera of Genesis narrows our field of vision to a single individual. Suddenly the screen is filled with the craggy Semitic face of one man.

In Genesis 1—11 we were faced with cosmic issues: the sovereign Creator, the divine order for life, the destructive and debilitating effects of sin, God as sovereign moral ruler, and man as God's designated regent—yet unable to rule himself. Genesis 12 builds on these themes, but focuses our vision on the cosmic importance of one person's life. Genesis 1—11 crunched more than 2,000 years of human history—and perhaps much more—into less than twenty percent of the book. Genesis 12—50 deals with only four generations.

God has focused on one family before. He began with Adam and Eve, but the account quickly moves on through generations to the Flood. He began all over again with Noah and his family. But again, from a few critical incidents in their lives the camera scans to the failure of civilization.

With Abraham we are beginning again.[1]

Abraham—initially "Abram"—is God's chosen instrument for starting his program of reversal. The development of God's program of redemption begins to take shape in the story of Abraham. God intends all the world to be in proper relationship with himself. This universal redemption, however, will come about by selecting not everyone, but a few—initially one.

While previously we were given a broad, panoramic understanding of life as it is, now we focus on God's special work which makes *history* into *his story* . . . the Story of Reversal.

## THE PROMISE TO ABRAHAM, ISAAC, AND JACOB

God's selection is announced to Abraham in the form of a promise:

> And I will make you a great nation,
> And I will bless you,
> And make your name great;
> And so you shall be a blessing;
> And I will bless those who bless you,
> And the one who curses you I will curse.
> And in you all the families of the earth
>   shall be blessed (Genesis 12:2-3).

This promise forms the backbone to the rest of Genesis. It is repeated with each succeeding generation. Isaac receives it in Genesis 26 (twice). Jacob receives it in Genesis 28 and Genesis 35. Only one string is attached to the promise. It is stated in Genesis 12:1: "Now the LORD said to Abram, 'Go forth from your country, and from your relatives and from your father's house, to the land which I will show you.'" Abraham took up the offer God had made and came to the land of Canaan (Genesis 12:4).[2] Abraham has made his decision, and though he has much to learn about the life of faith, the promise is his. God is only too willing to reassure Abraham about this, even when the old patriarch struggles with problems and doubts.

The promise to Abraham is reaffirmed by God on at least five occasions. It includes the following elements:

- The promise of a great nation through Abraham (12:2, 18:18)
- The promise of a great name (12:2)
- The promise of innumerable offspring (13:15-16)
- The promise of the land of Canaan (12:7, 13:14-17, 15:18-21, 17:8)
- The promise of universal blessing through Abraham (12:3, 18:18, 22:18)
- The promise to be the sovereign Protector of Abraham and his descendants (15:1, 17:8)

This last element holds good even when Abraham himself causes the problem by not wholly trusting God's protection (12:10-17, 20:1-7). God confirms this promise to Abraham by going through a covenant or contract procedure used in the culture of the time (Genesis 15:12-21). Animals were split apart and those making the contract would pass between the pieces. God, in symbolic form—"a smoking oven and a flaming torch"—passed between the divided animals by himself. By this God bound himself irrevocably to his promise.[3] Abraham was the passive recipient of an unconditional covenant. Or as the biblical writer puts it, "On that day the LORD made a covenant with Abram, saying, 'To your descendants I have given this land, from the river of Egypt as far as the great river, the river Euphrates'" (Genesis 15:18).

## THE FAITH OF ABRAHAM

But let's face it . . . Abraham walked around in that land for twenty-four years with nothing but promises.

Well, promises plus verbal assurances whenever he was depressed enough to ask. Abraham gets a lot of ceremonies but no offspring. What is God up to? Why is he taking so long?

It appears God wants to do more with Abraham than drop promises on him. Abraham had received an irrevocable promise from God. But being God's candidate for blessing is not a trip to Disneyland. Because God is going to bless Abraham, he's going to make him into a man of faith. Because God is going to make Abraham a blessing, God will take whatever time is necessary. And God has never let time bother him.

### Blessing or Difficulties?

Abraham arrives in the land. No doubt he expects only good times now. Yet he encounters famine. He heads for that perennial haven from crop failure, Egypt, with its dependable Nile. This unforeseen development leaves Abraham insecure. He finds it difficult to appropriate God's promise of protection: "I will bless those who bless you, and the one who curses you I will curse" (Genesis 12:3). He is afraid for his own life and allows Sarah (still known as Sarai) to be taken into the harem of Pharaoh. He even accepts wealth in his new role as brother-in-law to Pharaoh.

But in spite of Abraham's lack of faith, God still acts as his Protector. "The LORD inflicted serious diseases on Pharaoh and his household because of Abram's wife Sarai" (Genesis 12:17 NIV).

Abraham is a Typhoid Mary to Pharaoh. He is hustled out of the country by military escort—gently, no doubt. Abraham is being stretched. And foreign kings may well hope he learns to trust more. They will be blessed or cursed based on their treatment of him.[4]

### Two Steps Forward—Genesis 13

The next snapshot of Abraham catches an entirely different picture. Abraham is magnanimous toward his nephew Lot—allowing him to choose the best pasturage in this land that had been promised to Abraham. To this giant step of faith, God responds in kind. Abraham had given Lot his choice: "If [you go] to the left, then I will go to the right; or if to the right, then I will go to the left" (13:9).

Yahweh now says to Abraham, "Now lift up your eyes . . . northward and southward and eastward and westward; for all the land which you see, I will give it to you and to your descendants forever. . . . Arise, walk about the land through its length and breadth; for I will give it to you" (13:14-17). Abraham *couldn't give the land away*. In this walk through the land—another ritual of his culture—he symbolically lays legal claim to it (cf. Joshua 1:3-4). This high point of faith is followed by the building of another altar of worship (Genesis 13:18; cf. 12:7-8).

The next challenge to Abraham's faith is brought on by nephew Lot's association with Sodom (Genesis 14). As the result of an ancient military conflict, Lot and his household are carried away. In a lightning military strike which brings to mind the later activity of the judges—remember Gideon with his three hundred men in Judges 7?—Abraham rescues Lot as well as the goods and people of the Sodom coalition. Here Abraham's faith nearly orbits. He recognizes God as his Protector, Savior, and Provider. After tithing the confiscated booty, he refuses to take anything from the king of Sodom lest the king be able to say, "I have made Abram rich."[5] Abraham has confirmed his commitment to Yahweh as his Provider, the one who is *God Most High*, Possessor of heaven and earth (14:22).

**God's Response—Genesis 15**

The Lord again appears to Abraham in a vision (Genesis 15) in response to Abraham's act of faith above. He affirms Abraham's stand and encourages him in it:[6]

> Do not fear, Abram,
> I am a shield to you;
> Your reward shall be very great (15:1).

Abraham is undoubtedly encouraged by this, but quite naturally he wonders when God will get started on fulfilling the promise. How will there be a great nation, a multitude of offspring who will inherit this land, if Abraham is childless? When will he receive a son? According to the custom of his time, as it now stood a servant named Eliezer would inherit everything.[7] For his part the servant would be responsible for giving Abraham and Sarah a proper burial—a fine prospect for the promise!

God repeats only the promise itself—that Abraham's descendants would be as uncountable as the stars (15:5). And *that satisfies Abraham.* God's clearly stated word was enough for Abraham. Here the biblical writer makes it plain that God was pleased. This is the writer's only comment in the whole of the text about God's view of things: "Abram believed the LORD, and he credited it to him as righteousness" (15:6 NIV).

God's clear word about descendants and the mention of the land (15:7) prompts another question from Abraham. True to human experience, the resolution of one troubling item prompts the raising of another that has been stirring beneath the surface. *As long as my doubts are getting addressed without censure,* Abraham must have thought, *what about the land?* Again God deals with Abraham in a way that encourages his faith and certifies God's promise in the strongest terms. He gives him that irrevocable covenant in a form that could not be misunderstood by Abraham. Nor could its clear intention be later doubted ("Did God really say, 'You will possess this land'?"). In addition, God adds details about the land and nationhood so Abraham need not be anxious (15:13-16).[8]

### One Step Backward—Genesis 16

But even if God's word is clear, human frailty has a way of finding alternate routes apart from the path of faith. Sarah comes up with such a route. It was quite acceptable in the culture of the time, but was not what God intended by his promise. She suggests that her servant be her substitute to overcome her barrenness. As the ancient Nuzi tablets indicate, this was a legal procedure by which the child of Hagar would be born as Sarah's. Sarah then could "obtain children through her" (16:2).[9]

Though humanly acceptable, this approach brings its own problems when Hagar tries to use the pregnancy as a means of elevating her own status (a Proverbs 30:23 situation).[10] As in the situation with Pharaoh, even this failure comes under the protective hand of God. Even this substitute son is Abraham's descendant and receives God's protection and a promise of future greatness (16:9-12 and 21:13-21).

**Beginning of Fulfillment—Genesis 17**

Thirteen years elapse after the attempt at do-it-yourself fulfillment. Abraham now is ninety-nine and Sarah only ten years younger (17:1,17).[11] After these apparently silent years, God comes to Abraham as God Almighty—the one who is not limited by human agendas. He has come to signal the beginning of fulfillment!

He does this by announcing three changes:

Abram's name is changed to Abraham. This signals that God intends to bring to pass his covenant with Abraham, but not through Ishmael. Abraham could see himself as "Abram" ("exalted father") through Ishmael; but God strains his faith by renaming him Abraham ("father of many"). Ishmael would be blessed, but the nation possessing the land of Canaan will come not through Ishmael, but through Isaac (17:7-8,21).

A second alteration is the introduction of the outward sign of circumcision. It was common in the ancient Near East to have a sign to indicate a covenant's existence. The sign of the covenant with Noah was the rainbow (Genesis 9:12-16). The sign of the Mosaic Covenant would be the sabbath day (Exodus 20:8-11, 31:12-17). For Abraham and his descendants, circumcision is the sign of God's covenant with him. To refuse this sign and to fail to practice it as a family would be to reject that covenant. When Moses later postpones the circumcision of his son, God's judgment is aroused even though God had called him to lead the Exodus (Exodus 4:24-26).

A third change indicating that God was about to begin fulfilling the promises in his own supernatural way is the renaming of Sarai as Sarah ("princess"), and the announcement that she will be blessed by becoming the mother of nations and kings. Abraham's reaction is a mixture of reverence (he fell face down) and bemused astonishment (he laughed).

If only God Almighty could be *realistic* and recognize Ishmael as the way of fulfillment! Twenty-three years earlier there was some hope . . . but now barren Sarah is eighty-nine! God, however, is unmoved by human "realism." He will bless Ishmael,[12] but the covenant will come through Isaac.

**Sodom Revisited—Genesis 18-19**

The first episode of Lot and Sodom marked the high point of Abraham's faith during the initial period in the land. A second episode with Sodom again marks Abraham's development as a man who is a prince with God. The judgment on Sodom reminds us of God's continuing sovereignty as judge of all the earth (as in Genesis 4—11). Abraham's descendants ultimately would receive the land when God again brings judgment on the nations of Canaan (Genesis 15:16). But for now, Sodom and all the surrounding cities have reached the point of injustice necessary for Yahweh's formal investigation. As in the tower of Babel incident, Yahweh says, "I will go down now, and see" (Genesis 18:21, 11:5).

Much like the story of Noah, this setting of judgment becomes the scene for God's choice and blessing. Yahweh, present in appearance as a man, announces the approaching conception of Isaac. Sarah laughs, but Yahweh—in line with his previous announcement as God Almighty (chapter 17)—rebukes them. "Is anything too difficult for the LORD?" (Genesis 18:14).

Another mark of Abraham's standing with God is Yahweh's own choice of Abraham as the father-designate of a nation chosen to model his justice (18:17-19). "Shall I hide from Abraham what I am about to do, since Abraham will surely become a great and mighty nation, and in him all the nations of the earth will be blessed?" The status God himself has given to Abraham gives Abraham a legal standing in the land—a standing significant enough that Yahweh should honor him by informing him of his plans and allowing him to plead the cause of as few as ten innocents in Sodom.[13]

So Sodom is destroyed, but God's grace in providing a saving plan is present as well. At the Flood, Noah was God's route of salvation for the future. After the waters accomplished their judgment, "God remembered Noah" (Genesis 8:1). After the burning sulfur has exacted the divine penalty on the cities of the plain, "God remembered Abraham" (Genesis 19:29)—*and delivered only four people.*

**Failure Revisited—Genesis 20**

The prince-designate of Palestine does it *again.* Abraham once more becomes his own worst enemy by placing the promise in jeopardy. In Genesis 12 he allowed Sarai to enter Pharaoh's harem. In Genesis 20 he allows Sarah to enter Abimelech's harem. Sarah, renamed "Princess" because the promise will come through her womb, is threatened with violation by a Canaanite king immediately after Abraham is told that she will give birth to Isaac within a year.

But if Abraham is his own worst enemy, he has God Almighty for a friend. God keeps Abimelech from violating her and allows him to repent of his sin of ignorance. God requires him to make intercession *through Abraham.* How different this is from the episode with Pharaoh. There God allowed an indignant Pharaoh to hustle Abraham away. Here, Abraham is no doubt as embarrassed, but God forces Abimelech to honor him anyway.[14]

Sarah will become a nation's mother through the promise in spite of Abraham's weakness. So sure is God's promise that Abraham cannot give her away. And now that God has begun to implement his promise, kings will recognize the status of Abraham even in his weakness.

### The Son of Promise

Laughter has come to the house of Abraham, because Isaac (which means "He laughs" or "May He [God] smile"), son of promise, is born. Abraham laughed at the absurdity (17:17), Sarah laughed at the impossibility (18:12). Now she laughs with rejoicing and others will laugh with her (21:6).

But a difficult decision has also come to Abraham. Following Isaac's weaning, the prospect of a rivalry and divided inheritance arises. Abraham is concerned for his son Ishmael, but is directed by God to follow Sarah's wish to send him away. God assures Abraham that Ishmael will also achieve nationhood because of Abraham, but the promised line must come through Isaac.

### Climax of Testing

The story could have ended with the birth of Isaac. The issue of descendants and God's method of fulfilling the promise is resolved. But the story stretches to an even higher climax. There can be no doubt now that Abraham is blessed of God—as even the local king now recognizes: "God is with you in all that you do" (Genesis 21:22). The nations seek out Abraham for a friendship treaty in order to assure their own future blessing. But just as the story settles down for a smooth landing, the promise is in jeopardy again—*this time by God himself.*

The final issue to be branded into the mind and soul of Abraham and our Israelite readers is the necessity of faith.

Is *Yahweh* the God of Abraham? Or is *the promise* the god of Abraham? To paraphrase Satan's accusation against Job: "Does Abraham serve God for nothing? You have blessed him with flocks and herds and provided him a son through his barren wife. You protect him against kings even when he is less than honest. Just ask him to give up his son, and he will curse you to the face." Abraham has had the faith to live with the promise in view. Does he have the faith to put the promise on the altar? He is asked to cancel out the only concrete fulfillment he has experienced.

Words are sparse on the way to the altar as the story becomes painfully slow and detailed (Genesis 22). Caring to the end, Abraham carries the dangerous items himself. The boy, as all boys, is observant and inquisitive: "Where is the lamb?" The heartbroken father's explanation answers a question too painful to face: "God will provide the sacrifice." It seemed he had—in the son who was to be the heir. More prophetic than he knew, Abraham spoke only what he had experienced of God. *God provides.* He always does. Sometimes he waits until the raised knife has removed all question of divided motive.

The Father of Israel has shown future descendants that commitment to God ("I know that you fear God," Genesis 22:12) is the whole duty of man. This leads to a new affirmation of the covenant of promise heightened by Yahweh's taking an oath in his own Name (22:15-18).

Two final duties remain for the patriarch. First, to bury Sarah (Genesis 23)—thereby gaining the only property in Canaan he ever owned. He looked not for property he could buy at discount rates, but for the fulfillment of the promise. Other kings had their cities, but Abraham looked forward to the city that would come from God.[15]

His second duty was to find a wife for Isaac. God is faithful in this as well. Abraham's servant carries back to the eastern relatives the story of Yahweh's blessing on Abraham and receives Yahweh's aid in finding Isaac's bride, Rebekah.

## The Blessing Goes On

The remainder of Genesis confirms that the covenant God made with Abraham continues on to his descendants, Isaac and Jacob. These men also become the fathers of the nation of Israel. The Abrahamic Covenant with its many features (blessing, descendants, nationhood, the land of Canaan) is repeated to Isaac and Jacob (Genesis 26:2-5 and 26:24 for Isaac; Genesis 28:10-15 and 35:11-13 for Jacob).

In fact, Isaac's experiences of Genesis 26 are a microcosm of the events we have seen in Abraham's life. He experiences famine—but is told not to go to Egypt. He encounters a Canaanite king, Abimelech, and tries to pass off Rebekah as his sister. (This is not the same king Abraham encountered; "Abimelech" is a hereditary title like "Pharaoh.") But God blesses him to the extent that the Canaanite king recognizes his need for a covenant with Isaac.

God's choice of Jacob as heir of the promise is announced at the birth of the twins—from a previously barren wife. The story of Jacob becoming heir takes up the balance of Isaac's life (Genesis 27 through 35). Acting like divine bookends, two repetitions of the covenant enclose the diary of the heir-apparent in a strange land.[16] The first includes a promise of protection for the time he is out of the land of promise (Genesis 28:15). Though Jacob's actions and plots are far from defensible, the recognition that God is blessing him is required by all involved (Genesis 30:27, 31:24-29).

The critical midpoint of this story finds Jacob wrestling with God and being renamed (Genesis 32). Like the proverbial used car salesman, this man has "worked the angles" all his life. He encountered and ultimately prevailed over one of his own kind in Laban. But he cannot go back. In front of him is Esau, a victim of earlier plotting. He can only pray to the God of the covenant, acknowledge God's grace, and lean on his promise (32:9-12). What other security is there? Jacob wanted more than anything else to be blessed of God (32:24-29). He struggles all the way into what God wanted to give him—and prevails.

The story of Jacob as patriarch in the land (Genesis 37—50) is largely the story of Joseph and Judah. Joseph's own summary of his experience capsulizes the major theme: "God sent me before you to preserve for you a remnant in the earth, and to keep you alive by a great deliverance. Now, therefore, it was not you who sent me here, but God" (Genesis 45:7-8). Jacob heads out of the land in a different direction than he traveled in his youth.

As he nears the borders of Canaan, God reconfirms the covenant with him and again promises to bring Israel back into the land (46:1-4). What God had explained to Abraham (Genesis 15:13-16)—that they would be strangers in a foreign land from which they would return to take possession of Canaan—is under way.

The blessing goes on. It cannot stop. God has sworn by himself to Abraham.

## ON THE WAY: FULFILLMENT OF THE ABRAHAMIC COVENANT

### The Foundation for God's Developing Plan

The Abrahamic Covenant is the spring from which the rest of God's plan of redemption flows. In the Old Testament it is the foundation for the rest of the covenants.

The Law, or *Mosaic Covenant,* marks the beginning of the nation that was promised to Abraham, Isaac, and Jacob. And the entrance into the land under Joshua is the beginning of God's fulfilling the promise of land (cf. Joshua 1:6).

The kings promised as part of Abraham's descendants include first Saul, but later David and his line. God's promise to David in 2 Samuel 7:8-16, the *Davidic Covenant,* promises his descendants will have perpetual rulership over the land and nation promised to Abraham.[17]

Even when Israel becomes a nation in exile because of her unfaithfulness to God, God promises restoration. Note those elements of Jeremiah 30:18-22 which correspond to the elements of the Abrahamic Covenant.

| *Abrahamic Covenant* | *Jeremiah 30:18-22* |
| --- | --- |
| BLESSING AND LAND | "I will restore the fortunes of the tents of Jacob and have compassion on his dwelling places; and the city shall be rebuilt on its ruin, and the palace will stand on its rightful place." |

| | |
|---|---|
| DESCENDANTS | "I will multiply them, and they shall not be diminished." |
| GREAT NAME | "I will also honor them, and they shall not be insignificant." |
| NATION | "Their children also shall be as formerly, and their congregation shall be established before Me." |
| PROTECTOR | "I will punish all their oppressors." |
| GOD | "And you shall be My people, And I will be your God." |

This notion of restoration of the nation introduces the *New Covenant*, a future covenant to be given to the nation as an improvement over the Mosaic Covenant which the nation consistently violated (Jeremiah 31:31-37). This New Covenant will include *inner enablement* for living in God's ways—a covenant which will be written on the heart. God will not only provide the instruction, but the change of heart necessary to follow his teaching.

The progression of God's plan through the Old Testament is traceable by following these covenants—all based on the Abrahamic Covenant. See the chart below.

| | |
|---|---|
| **Abrahamic Covenant** | **Mosaic Covenant** - *Nation Formed.* |
| | **Davidic Covenant** - *Line of Kings over Nation.* |
| | **New Covenant** - *Enablement for Blessing.* |

**God is Faithful**

Our survey of God's work with Abraham shows that God sovereignly gave the covenant to him—in the clearest terms language and culture allowed—as an *unconditional covenant.* From entering the land onward, Abraham's obedience or disobedience did not change God's decision to work through Abraham. Of course, Abraham's great acts of faith bring from God a reiteration of the promise and statements of approval and acceptance (Genesis 15:6, 22:15-18). But statements of God's intention to fulfill the promise are just as clear after Abraham's *failure* to act in faith (Genesis 17:17-22). And after Abraham's death it is God's dealings with Abraham—and not Isaac's activity—that are given as the basis for confirming the promise to Isaac (Genesis 26:3-5, 26:24).[18]

The prophets also proclaim God's faithful determination—even while Israel stands under God's judgment for near-continuous disobedience:

> Thus says the LORD,
> Who gives the sun for light by day,
> And the fixed order of the moon and the
> stars for light by night,
> Who stirs up the sea so that its waves roar;
> The LORD of hosts is His name:
> "If this fixed order departs
> From before Me," declares the LORD,
> "Then the offspring of Israel also shall cease
> From being a nation before Me forever"
> (Jeremiah 31:35-36).

Clear enough? If not, turn to Malachi 3 where some have returned to the land from the Babylonian captivity. They have not been obedient. But what does God promise? To send his messenger to bring chastening so Israel's worship might be pleasing to the Lord once again. And he finishes with these words: "For I, the LORD, do not change; therefore you, O sons of Jacob, are not consumed" (3:6).

Yahweh does not change. He cannot bless unrighteousness, but he also cannot—he will not—change his promise with Abraham, Isaac, and Jacob.

And this is the point which confuses many readers of the Old Testament. God promised Abraham a nation, land, and blessing upon himself and the world. He will fulfill his promise, but not when the nation is disobedient.

Perhaps an illustration will help. I could promise to buy my daughter a new car. I could make that promise in unconditional and irrevocable terms. We could even split a few animals on the front yard and I could walk between them. Or, as a more recent substitute, I could sign my name in blood. The bargain is clear. She will get the car.

But when? I may find that the tender age of sixteen, when she first receives her license, is not the time to fulfill my contract with her. Having a new car then may do her more harm than good. I may decide to give her the car at age seventeen because she seems to exhibit a special maturity for her age. But within six months, I find she is having problems fulfilling other responsibilities because she is spending so much time with the car. I exile the car to the garage indefinitely—putting it on hold until I believe she is ready. Have I violated my contract? No, I have not.

In terms of the Abrahamic Covenant, this means God is committed to fulfilling his promise to Abraham, but he is not obligated to do it all at once, or to bless every generation no matter how rebellious they are. God's promise to Abraham does guarantee the *conclusion* of the matter. *It will come to pass.* It does not guarantee the nation unrestricted blessing at all times.

## Jesus, The Son of Abraham

The New Testament immediately introduces Jesus as "the son of David, the son of Abraham" (Matthew 1:1). Tracing the line of Jesus back to Abraham is important because God had already indicated it was through Abraham that blessing for all the nations would come. God was bound to his own oath. "Because God wanted to make the unchanging nature of his purpose very clear to the heirs of what was promised, he confirmed it with an oath" (Hebrews 6:17 NIV).

Several announcements mark the significance of Jesus' birth. Among them is the *magnificat* of Mary (Luke 1:46-55). She finishes with these words:

> He has given help to Israel His servant,
> In remembrance of His mercy,
> As He spoke to our fathers,
> To Abraham and his offspring forever.

The promise is not dead, but very much alive in the child within her womb! Is anything impossible for God? The child who will fulfill the promise is not the son of a barren woman, but the son of a woman who has not had sexual intercourse at all. *What a way to mark out the special nature of this Son of Abraham!*

Zechariah, the father of John the Baptist, prophesied concerning Jesus:

> Praise be to the Lord, the God of Israel, because he has come and has redeemed his people. He has raised up a horn of salvation for us in the house of his servant David (as he said through his holy prophets of long ago), salvation from our enemies and from the hand of all who hate us—to show mercy to our fathers and to remember his holy covenant, the oath he swore to our father Abraham (Luke 1:68-73 NIV).

Israel expects restoration to full nationhood, and Zechariah by the Holy Spirit predicts it will come through Jesus. Such restoration is confirmed by the apostle Paul who emphatically denies that God has cast away his people, the physical descendants of Abraham (Romans 11:2). He points out that there has always been a faithful minority, a "remnant," who truly knew God in Israel.[19]

This is true in the present age as well. There is a remnant of faithful Israelites who are now participating in the Church (11:5), Paul himself being a prime example (11:1). Paul sees the blind state of most of Israel at the present time as "a partial hardening" that "has happened to Israel until the fullness of the Gentiles has come in; and thus all Israel will be saved" (11:25-26). He then quotes the Old Testament promises: "The Deliverer will come from Zion, He will remove ungodliness from Jacob. And this is my covenant with them, when I take away their sins."

Ross Parker and Hughie Charles in 1939 wrote the song "There'll Always Be an England." It encouraged hope at a time when England needed her spirits lifted. It's a fine national sentiment, especially for those with English blood in their veins. But only one people really have such an assurance. There'll always be children of Israel—not because Israel is faithful, but because God has given his word to Abraham.[20]

### Jesus, the Seed of Abraham

The seed, the descendants of Abraham, would also be the mediators of blessing to all the nations of the earth (Genesis 22:18, 12:3). This also comes to pass through Jesus. Jesus is *the seed*—the descendant of Abraham *par excellence*. Just as at a later time the Israelite king would represent the whole nation, so Jesus is God's chosen representative for the nation.

The good news of Jesus Christ—that God would justify the Gentiles by faith—was proclaimed to Abraham, Paul says, in the promise: "All the nations shall be blessed in you" (Galatians 3:8). Jesus, in fact, came under God's judgment on the cross "in order that in Christ Jesus the blessing of Abraham might come to the Gentiles, so that we might receive the promise of the Spirit through faith" (Galatians 3:14). But the full extent of this Gentile blessing is revealed only in the New Testament. The Old Testament foresees ultimate Gentile redemption but does not foresee the nature of the Church—a body in which there is no distinction between Jew and Gentile. Both are fellow members in the Body of Christ, the Church (Ephesians 3:6).

Paul reminds his Gentile readers of their relationship to God before they came to believe in Christ (Ephesians 2). No more desperate condition could be described than that of Ephesians 2:12—"You were at that time separate from Christ, excluded from the commonwealth of Israel, and strangers to the covenants of promise, having no hope and without God in the world." But God has done something new. He has made a "new man" (2:15), the Church, which includes both Jew and Gentile.

The Gentile experiences not only the blessing through Abraham's Seed as originally promised, but more: Since God has placed all who believe, whether Jew or Gentile, as equal members in Christ, the Gentile finds himself a part of Christ, the Seed of Abraham. This is the essence of Paul's proclamation of the gospel—that "the Gentiles are heirs together with Israel, members together of one body, and sharers together in the promise in Christ Jesus" (Ephesians 3:6 NIV). "If you belong to Christ, then you are Abraham's seed, and heirs according to the promise" (Galatians 3:29 NIV).

You can't do better than that. What was previously a very narrow spot on the screen—one man—has now opened up to a glorious, wide-angle vista.

For Israel it's because of God's faithfulness to his promise.

For Gentiles like myself, it's called *GRACE.*

# FOR PERSONAL INTERACTION & DISCUSSION

SUGGESTED SCRIPTURE READINGS:

Genesis 12:1-7, 18:1-15, and 22:1-19
Ephesians 2:8—3:6

1. Abraham was God's choice to bring blessing to the world. Did Abraham have an easy life? What advantages did he experience? What difficulties and frustrations? What about Isaac and Jacob?
2. What factors in God's working with Abraham do you see as similar to God's working today in believers? What factors are unique to Abraham's special calling? What makes Abraham a man of faith?
3. What do Abraham's failings and God's response to them tell us about God? What do they tell us about Abraham? Is Abraham more "human" than the rest of us? Or less?
4. How does a thoroughly human Abraham become accepted as righteous before God? How does a person do this today?
5. Imagine yourself living in the next tent over from Jacob. What is it like to be his neighbor? How can such a schemer have fellowship with God? What was Jacob's attitude toward God's promise?
6. What makes the Abrahamic Covenant so important to understanding the Bible? How does the miraculous survival of the Jewish people relate to this covenant?
7. What is the "good news" for Gentiles? Why was Jesus' work necessary to achieve this good news?

'HOW MANY PLAGUES WOULD IT TAKE BEFORE YOU RECONSIDER WHETHER THIS WAS SUCH A GOOD BARGAIN? CUT YOUR LOSSES, PHARAOH, AND LET THEM GO! DON'T BE A FOOL.'

C H A P T E R

# 6.

# A REDEEMED PEOPLE

## CALLING OUT A PEOPLE FOR GOD

Thanks to the efforts of Cecil B. De Mille in his screen spectacular *The Ten Commandments*, much of the English-speaking world has no difficulty picturing the drama of the Exodus. We can relive the emotions of a mass of all-too-common people with their doubts, complaints, and hopes, who at last scurry between two walls of water in an escape to freedom. Though we know the plot, we feel the tension as the Egyptian chariot force hesitates momentarily before literally taking the plunge.

But the Exodus is more than a mass movement of tons of water. More, in fact, than the beginning of freedom for an oppressed people. The Exodus is truly a creation—a creation of that nation which would be distinctively God's people. The Exodus for Israel is not the "luck of the draw," nor is Moses the George Washington of a new democracy.

Step by step, the book of Exodus records for us the process of God redeeming this enslaved people. Like most of God's operations, it seems exceedingly slow—especially for those who cry out to God for help. *Why does he take so long? When will God answer?* These are questions Abraham asked . . . questions asked again by the descendants of Abraham . . . and questions still asked today.

The book of Exodus has answers to these questions. For it recounts not simply a spectacular miracle or even a score of them, but a revelation of Yahweh, the true God. The goal of God's activity here is to have his people learn to *know Yahweh.*

## THE REDEMPTION FROM EGYPT

### Egypt, the Artificial Womb—Exodus 1

God does his creating in the most unlikely wombs. A great nation was promised out of Sarah's barrenness. The descendants of her womb become a people through the surprising hospitality of Egypt. Oh, it started out well enough with Joseph being sent ahead by God. In fact, Egypt continued to be a positive birthing station: "The Israelites were fruitful and multiplied greatly and became exceedingly numerous, so that the land was filled with them" (Exodus 1:7). It is no accident that these words repeat God's blessing given originally to Adam (Genesis 1:28) to Noah (Genesis 9:7) and to Jacob (Genesis 35:11).

The text is telling us that *the Creator God is the God of this people.* The people of Abraham experience blessing originally intended for all mankind because they have come into relationship with God through his covenant with Abraham, Isaac, and Jacob.

But the artificial womb turns hostile. New leadership first tries harsh labor, then infanticide. Finally, being born a male Hebrew becomes a capital offense. Yet none of these steps can stem the blessing of God (Exodus 1:12,20).

Out of this last, most oppressive step, God raises up a deliverer. Oppression was Egypt's fatal mistake. It placed Egypt in a hostile relationship with Yahweh because of his covenant with Abraham: "I will bless those who bless you, and whoever curses you I will curse" (Genesis 12:3). By perverting its role as host, Egypt fell from the place of being blessed to the place of being cursed.

Pharaoh[1] has taken on an awesome Opponent who delights in proving his strength out of weakness. From the desperation and pain of a powerless Hebrew mother, God raises up a deliverer. Moses rides in a frail mini-ark to safety,[2] and God rears his leader with Pharaoh's groceries.

But if Israel's hopes were riding on having an inside man at the Kremlin, these hopes are dashed as Moses must flee to the wilderness. Here again there is irony in God's providence. The very taunt thrown up to Moses by his own fellow Hebrew becomes the reason Moses must go to the desert. "Who made you ruler and judge over us?" (2:14) stands as a concise summary of Moses' need and as a clear pointer to the focus of the Exodus—*Who* indeed?[3]

But to the Hebrews in bondage, the signs of God's concern must have seemed minimal. Ignorant of God at work behind the scenes, they could only cry out in their misery. Let us not forget that this was *real groaning*—and without knowing the purpose for it.[4] How much of life is like this—where the reasons for our pains will become clear in God's purposes generations later?

God has not forgotten, however. "God heard their groaning and he remembered his covenant with Abraham, with Isaac and with Jacob. So God looked on the Israelites and was concerned [knew] about them" (Exodus 2:24-25).

God heard . . . God remembered . . . God looked . . . and God knew. All terms of involvement. For God to remember is not to imply prior absent-mindedness. God's "remembering" is a way of saying he is about to act. God *remembered* Noah and acted by causing the flood waters to recede (Genesis 8:1). God promised to *remember* his covenant with Noah to never again destroy the earth with a flood (Genesis 9:15-16). God *remembered* Abraham and his concern for his nephew and so delivered Lot from Sodom. God *remembered* Rachel and her request for a son by causing her to conceive (Genesis 30:22). God is now ready to act on the basis of his covenant with

Abraham, Isaac, and Jacob. This guarantee of God's impending intervention switches the scene back to the preparation of Moses.

**Yahweh Encounters Moses—Exodus 3-4**

To date, God has been in the background. But now God begins an outright program of revealing himself to this people nurtured in the womb of idolatrous Egypt. His revelation to the deliverer comes first.

From the middle of a burning bush, God identifies himself as "the God of your father, the God of Abraham, the God of Isaac, and the God of Jacob." This is not empty repetition or even name-dropping. It announces God's intention to keep his covenant. He will rescue Israel[5] and bring her into the land promised to Abraham. Moses will be his prophetic spokesman to lead Israel out of Egypt.[6]

Moses' questions and problems provide the background for the critical themes of this book. Moses' first problem is his own inadequacy for the task. He has no current standing in Egypt. The answer is that God will be adequate: "I will be with you" (Exodus 3:12). This leads to Moses' second problem: Who is the God of Abraham? What is his Name? If Moses is to represent Yahweh in polygamous Egypt, He would need more than the title *God* in a country that had multitudes of gods under various names. These two questions introduce the first major theme: *the name Yahweh.*

Up to this point in Exodus the name *Yahweh* has not been used. The title *Elohim* (translated "God") has indicated the Creator's interest in Israel to bless them. But the rest of the book is the story of Israel's and Pharaoh's increasing understanding of God as Yahweh.[7] The statement, "I am Yahweh," makes its imprint on each unfolding episode which follows.

But why does this name make a difference?

What's in a name, anyway? In most of our naming, the answer is "Not much." Sometimes, as in our family, the first son will be named after his dad. For our second son we chose the name *Mark.* No, not because it is a "biblical" name. We just liked it! Many biblical names also have little ultimate significance. Some, like "Moses," match the situation at birth. Others reflect a renaming, as in Jacob's case, to reflect a change of status.[8] But the name of God? Surely God's self-chosen name must be significant.

It is, therefore, not merely the name, but the meaning of the name that is being emphasized here. And what is God's name? It appears in the Hebrew Bible as יְהוָה, which transliterated into English would read YHWH. In most English Bibles this name is not given, but is represented by the word LORD, printed with all capitals. Some Bibles use the name Jehovah, but this is not really accurate. Because of its tie with the verb "I AM" (Exodus 3:14-15), most Hebrew scholars are convinced the name ought to be pronounced "Yahweh."[9]

But again we must ask, What does it mean? The explanation to Moses is, "I am who I am. This is what you are to say to the Israelites, 'I AM has sent me to you.'" God also said to Moses, "Say to the Israelites, 'Yahweh, the God of your fathers—the God of Abraham, the God of Isaac and the God of Jacob—has sent me to you.' This is my name forever, the name by which I am to be remembered from generation to generation" (Exodus 3:14-15).[10]

Tomes have been written on the meaning of this Name. But our best clue is the use of the same word for "I am" in this very discussion with Moses. For God has given as his first answer to Moses' objections the promise "I will be with you" (3:12). The word for "I will be" is the same word translated "I am" and it has the same significance.[11] God answered Moses' objection that he had no standing with Pharaoh by assuring him that his own Presence would be enough standing for both of them. God was assuring Moses: "I am present with you when you stand before Pharaoh. Go, for I am with you."

So in the name YHWH is wrapped up the notion that God is present to help. In other words, God is faithful. He is there to act on behalf of those who know him. "I am who I am" means: "I am there, wherever it may be . . . I am really there!"[12]

Furthermore, the name Yahweh is associated with the fulfillment of his promise. *As Yahweh* he has promised to bring Israel out of her misery in Egypt and bring her into the land of the Canaanites. The repeated "I am YHWH" in this book will continue to emphasize the one who has come into relationship by covenant with this people, and so is committed to faithfulness to them.

A second theme introduced by Moses' objections is *the theme of plagues and the response of the Pharaoh* (Exodus 3:18-20). Moses is commissioned to approach Pharaoh about Yahweh's right to demand worship from his people. Pharaoh, Yahweh predicts, will reject Yahweh's sovereignty, thus setting up the confrontation between Yahweh and Pharaoh over the rights to the sons of Israel.

Moses' concern that he might be rejected as a prophetic spokesman for God is answered when God turns the staff of Moses into a serpent as a sign of his commission. Don't miss the humor of it. The sign Moses so desperately wants chases him around. Two other signs also are provided (Exodus 4:1-9). With these three signs Moses' status as a spokesman for Yahweh will not be in doubt.

Following the answer to Moses' objection that he is not an adequate orator, another theme is introduced—*the theme of the firstborn.*

> When you return to Egypt, see that you perform before Pharaoh all the wonders I have given you the power to do. But I will harden his heart so that he will not let the people go. Then say to Pharaoh, "This is what YAHWEH says: 'Israel is my firstborn son, and I told you, "Let my son go, so he may worship me." But you refused to let him go; so I will kill your firstborn son'" (Exodus 4:21-23).

The firstborn son had the place of privilege and responsibility in the family. He was also granted an extra share of the inheritance. Israel as Yahweh's firstborn was to stand in the place of privilege. Israel was his designated leader among the family of nations. If Pharaoh was not willing to recognize this special relationship, the justice of correspondence ("eye for eye") would come into play. Pharaoh's firstborn would not be recognized by Yahweh.

But the next event involves Moses' firstborn (Exodus 4:24-26). This is not accidental, though its meaning is not totally clear. What is clear is that Moses comes under Yahweh's judgment. Why would Yahweh try to kill his chosen spokesman? The answer is tied to the fact that Moses' firstborn had not been circumcised. How can Moses represent Yahweh, the God of Abraham, Isaac, and Jacob, when he has not circumcised his own son? This would be like the president of Chrysler Corporation appearing in a television commercial for Chryslers, then driving a Toyota home. Circumcision is the sign of faith in what God promised to Abraham (Genesis 17:9-14). Zipporah, Moses' wife and perhaps part of the problem, circumcises Gershom to save Moses.[13]

Yahweh claims the right of his firstborn to serve him. And he claims the right to Moses and Moses' son. Yahweh's right to all of Israel will become an institution in the redemption of every firstborn son as a mark of the Exodus (Exodus 13:11-16).

### Who Is Yahweh?—Exodus 5-6

The people of Israel accept Moses as spokesman for Yahweh with a demonstration of the signs, but Pharaoh, as predicted, is adamant in his refusal to let the people obey Yahweh by going into the wilderness to sacrifice (Exodus 5:1-3).

Now, a festival in the wilderness certainly looks suspicious. Are they really going to have a Sunday school picnic and return to Egypt as good slaves? Isn't this idea of a religious retreat simply an attempt at escape?

Pharaoh thought so. Wouldn't you?

You might until you recognized that all Yahweh is trying to establish at this time is his right to receive worship as Israel's God. If Pharaoh will recognize this right, then

Pharaoh can come under the blessing of those who bless Abraham's descendants. But of course, Pharaoh has already violated Yahweh's people by putting them under the yoke of slavery and worse. Abraham's descendants will come to birth as a nation, even if God has to use Caesarean section or worse on Egypt. Much better for Egypt if she is cooperative with the divine program. The program will not suffer. Those who don't submit will. Some things never change!

But Pharaoh has had his chance, and he has now formally rejected Yahweh with the haughty answer: "Who is Yahweh, that I should obey him and let Israel go? I do not know Yahweh and I will not let Israel go."

Because Pharaoh reacts by increasing the workload, and the people of Israel respond by accusing Moses and Aaron of causing their ruin, Moses complains to God. God's response? A reaffirmation of his activity as Yahweh. In these eight verses the expression "I am Yahweh" is repeated for emphasis four times and is both the opening and closing statement. Because he is Yahweh, his promise will be fulfilled. He not only makes covenants, he establishes them by his active intervention.

### A Plague or Ten—Exodus 7-14

There are ten plagues and twelve miracles in this section. The ten plagues are preceded by a miracle of authentication and followed by a final miracle of judgment. Prior to all the plagues, Yahweh announces the certainty of Pharaoh's obstinacy:

> I will harden Pharaoh's heart that I may multiply My signs and My wonders in the land of Egypt. When Pharaoh will not listen to you, then I will lay My hand on Egypt, and bring out My hosts, My people the sons of Israel, from the land of Egypt by great judgments. And the Egyptians shall know that I am Yahweh, when I stretch out My hand on Egypt and bring out the sons of Israel from their midst (Exodus 7:3-5 NASB).

*The Plagues and Pharaoh.* But what about hardening Pharaoh's heart? Was it right for God to harden it? Did Pharaoh harden it first?

Much of the discussion on this issue misses the point of these events. Egypt has already violated her privilege as hosts to Yahweh's covenant people. She has enslaved them, murdered them, and now rejected any claim of Yahweh to their service for even a few days. Egypt is *already* due for judgment. Attempts to prove that Pharaoh hardened his heart first are futile.[14] Yahweh has hardened Pharaoh's heart so he would do something no sane ruler would ever contemplate: encourage Yahweh to multiply the evidence of his power at Egypt's expense.

As you read through these plagues, think of yourself as a businessman running Egypt. Surely you would like to hold on to such a work force as the Israelites. But how many plagues would it take before you reconsider whether this was such a good bargain? The land is decimated step by step. Cut your losses, Pharaoh, and let them go! Don't be a fool.

The magicians are no fools. By hook or crook they duplicate the first three miracles. But don't miss the irony here. They make *more blood* from water when water that isn't blood is nearly impossible to find. They produce *more frogs* when the land is crawling with the squishy things. When Yahweh is making blood out of water and producing frogs, almost anyone can do it! If these magicians were so great an answer to Moses and Aaron, why couldn't they reverse the plagues? And let's not forget the first miracle where they lost their serpents.

But, as I say, they are no fools. Following the third plague they advise Pharaoh: "This is the finger of God." But guess what? "Pharaoh's heart was hard and he would not listen, just as Yahweh had said" (Exodus 8:19).

Yahweh didn't want Pharaoh to do the reasonable thing once he saw he was out-plagued. If Pharaoh just used his judgment, cut his losses, and let the people go, the crucial place of the Exodus in Israel's history would not have been so clear. What is it that Yahweh says to Pharaoh before the seventh plague?

> By now I could have stretched out my hand and struck you and your people with a plague that would have wiped you off the earth. But I have raised you up for this very purpose, that I might show you my power and that my name might be proclaimed in all the earth (Exodus 9:15-16).

And again, what reason does Yahweh give to Moses for Israel not yet being free?

> Go to Pharaoh, for I have hardened his heart and the hearts of his officials so that I may perform these miraculous signs of mine among them that you may tell your children and grandchildren how I dealt harshly with the Egyptians and how I performed my signs among them, *and that you may know that I am Yahweh* (Exodus 10:1-2).[15]

And again, following the announcement of the culmination of plagues—the death of the firstborn:

> Pharaoh will refuse to listen to you—so that my wonders may be multiplied in Egypt (Exodus 11:9).

Pharaoh had said, "Who is Yahweh?" Before Yahweh is finished with Egypt, God declares concerning the crossing of the sea:

> I will harden the hearts of the Egyptians so that they will go in after them; And I will gain glory through Pharaoh and all his army, through his chariots and his horsemen. *The Egyptians will know that I am Yahweh* when I gain glory through Pharaoh, his chariots and his horsemen (Exodus 14:17-18).[15]

*Plagues and the Gods.* Not only does Yahweh want the full extent of wonders to be performed, but he wants to make clear who the true God is. These plagues vindicate Yahweh as the true God in a land of gods, a land ruled by a Pharaoh regarded as the incarnate son of the god Re. Pharoah is to learn that the earth is Yahweh's (Exodus 9:29). So Yahweh announces, "Against all the gods of Egypt I will execute judgments—I am Yahweh" (Exodus 12:12 NASB).

In fact, many of the individual plagues directly demonstrate Yahweh's power over the gods. The Nile River was considered sacred, yet it was turned to blood. Associated with the river were the gods Khnum, Hapi, and Osiris (for whom the Nile served as his bloodstream).[16] The goddess Heqt, the wife of Khnum, was represented as a frog. "The frog was one of a number of sacred animals that might not be intentionally killed, and even their voluntary slaughter was often punished with death."[17] And where was the sky goddess Nut, from whose domain came the hail? Isis and Seth, responsible in part for agricultural crops, seem to have been overwhelmed. A number of gods are identified with the sun, including the sun god Re. Certainly these gods failed in allowing a heavy darkness to blanket Egypt for three days.

**Yahweh and Israel—Exodus 12-17**

But if the plagues are to teach the Egyptians that Yahweh is God, the Israelites themselves are not so far ahead in their own understanding of Yahweh. Yes, they initially accept Moses (with signs in tow) as God's prophet. But even that attitude changes when Pharaoh does not immediately respond to Moses' demands. The Israelite foremen actually call a curse on Moses and Aaron for the increased workload: "May Yahweh look upon you and judge you!" (Exodus 5:21). Yahweh's people have little faith or endurance.

God's purpose in the plagues was not simply to force the Egyptians to let Israel go, nor even to punish them for their injustice to Israel, but to bring about a climactic deliverance to be remembered by Israel "that you may tell your children and grandchildren how I dealt harshly with the Egyptians and how I performed my signs among them, and that you may know that I am Yahweh" (Exodus 10:2).

To really know God as Yahweh was a goal not yet achieved among Israel. The events following the plagues are intended to increase their faith and leave a clear message for their children.

*Ceremonial Events.* Ceremonies can be either stale ritual or vital reminders. God commanded a number of ceremonies as part of Israel's annual calendar so the meaning of the Exodus would not be lost to future generations (Exodus 12:40—13:16).

The Passover meal would be Israel's annual reminder of the final plague when Israel's firstborn were passed over by the angel of death. Just as a lamb was consumed on that first Passover night when its blood marked the doorposts of Yahweh's people and protected their firstborn sons, so a lamb would be eaten yearly to commemorate the deliverance they experienced.

Passover was part of the larger Feast of Unleavened Bread. Going without yeast for a full week would remind the people of the quick flight from Egypt—too quick for baking normal bread. And the giving of each firstborn animal and son to God keeps alive the memory that God delivered his firstborn, Israel, from Egypt at the cost of Pharaoh and Egypt's firstborn.

*The Crossing of the Sea.* Finally comes the event we all associate most with the Exodus—crossing the Red Sea. Popular conception has it that the Israelites unwittingly got caught up against the sea. Not so, says the Bible. Yahweh instructed them to camp there to draw Pharaoh into his trap!

> Pharaoh will think, "The Israelites are wandering around the land in confusion, hemmed in by the desert." And I will harden Pharaoh's heart, and he will pursue them. But I will gain glory for myself through Pharaoh and all his army, and the Egyptians will know that I am Yahweh (14:3-4).

For the Egyptians this would be a final lesson. For Israel it would be a tremendous test.

As the encamped Israelites see Pharaoh's mighty army approach, they are terrified. They are forced to cry to Yahweh for help, but they attack Moses with their sharpest tongue-lashing: "Was it because there were no graves in Egypt that you brought us to the desert to die?" (Exodus 14:11).

The test: to wait and see Yahweh deliver. They need do nothing but learn this lesson: "Yahweh will fight for you" (Exodus 14:13-14).

Oh, the lesson they learned! The Song of Moses reflects their newfound reverence for this powerful God who had delivered them in the face of "impossible" odds.

> Yahweh is my strength and song,
> And He has become my salvation;
> This is my God, and I will praise Him;
> My father's God, and I will extol Him.
> Yahweh is a warrior; Yahweh is His name.
> Who is like Thee among the gods, O Yahweh?
> Who is like Thee, majestic in holiness,
> Awesome in praises, working wonders?
> Yahweh shall reign forever and ever
> (Exodus 15:2-3,11,18 NASB).

*On the Way to Sinai.* Now they have surely learned who Yahweh is. But Yahweh, who sees the heart, knows that a consistent response of faith is not achieved by one experience—*no matter how impressive.* The ingrained habit of squealing when squeezed is too near the surface in all of us. The inconsistency of this motley crew is obvious on the pages of this book. Our own is safely tucked away in the folds of minds practiced at focusing on our finer moments.

But let us document the trek nonetheless. The lessons here loom clear. Yahweh is faithful. Yahweh is patient. Yahweh responds in grace.

Yahweh tests them as he tests us—not to tempt to sin, but to cause increasing recognition of his ways.

At Marah it is bitter water.
At Elim they are short of food.
In the Desert of Sin it is no water at all.
Finally, they face war with Amalek.[18]

None of these experiences seem like easy street. And this group knows how to grumble! Yet they must learn that Yahweh is sufficient for their need. He was sufficient for repulsing Pharaoh's army and he is sufficient again for the attack by Amalek. In between, their faith must recognize that Yahweh provides. "Give us this day our daily bread." Yahweh puts up with their testing, an indication that he still considers that they do not fully know him.

Their peace, safety, and survival are threatened, but are never in doubt. The hardships they meet along the way are to teach them that Yahweh saves from each one. Praise comes to Yahweh as others see his power to save (Exodus 18:8-12).

*The Challenge at Sinai.* All this experience with Yahweh was designed with one goal in mind: that Israel might commit herself unreservedly to following Yahweh. How does God summarize Israel's journey? "You yourselves have seen what I did to Egypt, and how I carried you on eagles' wings and brought you to myself" (Exodus 19:4).

God has been carrying them the whole time!

But are they ready to obey?

Are they ready to trust Yahweh unreservedly as the One Who Is Present to carry out his covenant with Abraham, Isaac, and Jacob? If so, they can take their unique place among the nations: "Now if you obey me fully and keep my covenant, then out of all nations you will be my treasured possession. Although the whole earth is mine, you will be for me a kingdom of priests and a holy nation" (Exodus 19:5-6).

The people believe they are ready to take on that commitment which has eluded them so far. "The people all responded together, 'We will do everything Yahweh has said'" (19:8).

## UNDERSTANDING THE EXODUS

### Yahweh as the Sovereign God

The Exodus, as we have seen, involved a complex of events—more than just the miraculous crossing of the sea. It involved God hearing the prayers of distressed sons of Israel, raising up a deliverer, and judging Egypt and Pharaoh, and Israel celebrating the Passover and Unleavened Bread. But primarily it involved God demonstrating himself to be Yahweh—so all would know that Yahweh is the true God of the *whole earth* (Exodus 9:29). His sovereign control of events in order to bring about his purposes is everywhere evident.

At times God's purposes seem to ride on something as fragile as papyrus coated with pitch, and even the odd, selective pity of Pharaoh's own daughter. But if we think this is really the case we have missed the point. The sovereign Creator God is able to bring about his purposes as easily through insignificant persons and incidental events as he is through massive use of natural forces.

Yahweh was present with them even when they did not know it.[19] God's sovereign control of circumstances produced deliverance out of the most calculated oppression. The darkest hour was the hour closest to success. It is then that God *must remember* because he is Yahweh—the one who has promised and the one who will fulfill. It is he who finally causes all things to work together for good to those who are the called according to his purpose.

### Yahweh as Creator of Israel

Not only is Yahweh the sovereign Creator God, but he is the one who in the Exodus created the nation of Israel. This is especially indicated by the pronouncement, "I will take you as my own people, and I will be your God" (Exodus 6:7). Yahweh, through Isaiah, reminds the people of the Exodus in these terms:

> I am Yahweh, your Holy One,
> The Creator of Israel, your King
> (Isaiah 43:15 NASB).

The tie between Yahweh as Creator and Yahweh as Israel's God is so close that the sign of Israel's covenant with Yahweh is the keeping of the sabbath day:

> So the sons of Israel shall observe the sabbath, to celebrate the sabbath throughout their generations as a perpetual covenant. It is a sign between Me and the sons of Israel forever; for in six days Yahweh made heaven and earth, but on the seventh day He ceased from labor, and was refreshed (Exodus 31:16-17 NASB; cf. 20:10-11).

But for what purpose did Yahweh create Israel by redemption from Egypt? Israel's place in God's program is stated in 19:5-6.

> Now if you obey me fully and keep my covenant, then out of all nations you will be my treasured possession. Although the whole earth is mine, you will be for me a kingdom of priests and a holy nation.

Just as Yahweh created this nation from Abraham as he promised (Genesis 12:2), so they are to be the means of blessing to the world (12:3) by being intercessors for the world. Even Pharaoh recognizes something of this as he finally exhorts Israel to leave after the death of the firstborn. He adds: "And also bless me" (Exodus 12:32).

**Yahweh as Judge**

We do not appreciate too much the *lex taliones*—"an eye for an eye and a tooth for a tooth." But it is simply a formal way of stating that the punishment ought to fit the crime. In other words, it is a call for simple justice.

We saw in Genesis that God retains his sovereign right to judge even after man's fall into sin. Remember Cain? Remember the Flood and Babel? Remember Sodom and even Lot's wife? So here at the Exodus, God demonstrates his rule as judge by hardening Pharaoh and decimating the land of Egypt. These are not simply great miracles, they are great "judgments" (Exodus 7:4; also 6:6, 12:12). The hardening of Pharaoh is necessary to provide the opportunity for this judgment (Exodus 7:3), though God could have obliterated Egypt in one swipe (Exodus 9:15-16).

**Yahweh as Yahweh**

"Be yourself" is frequently good advice—though we hope it's not given to social misfits. Surely the major theme of this book, a theme that includes all the previous themes, is that Yahweh is being himself. He is Yahweh—and that is good news indeed!

He promised Abraham a great nation to whom he would give the land of the Canaanites. As Yahweh he is going to establish the covenant he made with Abraham by consolidating this people into a nation and by bringing them into the land. Childs puts it beautifully: "The name of Yahweh functions as a guarantee that the reality of God stands behind the promise and will execute its fulfillment."[20]

He is Yahweh because he is faithful, even though the people are slow to respond. Psalm 78 reminds us of this negative side to the Exodus:

> He did miracles in the sight of their fathers . . .
> He divided the sea and led them through . . .
> He guided them with the cloud by day . . .
> He split the rocks in the desert . . .
> He brought streams out of a rocky crag . . .
> But they continued to sin against him,
> rebelling in the desert against the Most High.
> They willfully put God to the test (12-18).

Psalm 105 praises Yahweh for being faithful to his covenant without mentioning the failure of the people:

> Egypt was glad when they left,
> because dread of Israel had fallen on them.
> He spread out a cloud as a covering,
> and a fire to give light at night.
> They asked, and he brought them quail
> and satisfied them with the bread of heaven.
> He opened the rock, and water gushed out;
> like a river it flowed in the desert.
> For he remembered his holy promise
> given to his servant Abraham (38-42).

What's in a name? All God's promises are in his Name because HE IS and HE IS PRESENT to bring them to pass. But God himself proclaimed his Name before the people. Listen to our God and know him:

> Yahweh, Yahweh, the compassionate and gracious God, slow to anger, abounding in love and faithfulness, maintaining love to thousands, and forgiving wickedness, rebellion and sin. Yet he does not leave the guilty unpunished (Exodus 34:6-7).

## ON THE WAY: THE COMPLETION OF THE EXODUS

The Exodus marked out God's choice of Israel to bring restoration to mankind. As such, it marks out the truth that God is acting in history to bring to pass his promise to Abraham—and through that promise, universal blessing to the world. It also provides a working model or pattern for God's future activity in completing that restoration.

### Passover and Firstfruits

Paul observes that Christ is our Passover (1 Corinthians 5:7). Crucified at Passover, Jesus was God's Passover Lamb. The shedding of his blood, accepted by faith, delivers men from the judgment of death. It was at the celebration of the annual Passover that Jesus announced his death and its significance for his followers: Taking the cup of wine, he proclaimed it symbolic of his blood to be shed for his followers. And using the unleavened bread of the feast, he proclaimed it symbolic of his body to be given in death (Luke 22:13-20).

Jesus thereby initiated a new and greater Passover out of the celebration of the original Passover. This New Passover would do more than bring deliverance from a local plague of death in Egypt. It would provide deliverance from the death that plagued all mankind since man broke his relationship to God.

## The New Exodus and Firstborn Son

Israel, as Yahweh's firstborn, would represent Yahweh to the world. Yet history showed her failure to live as a kingdom of priests. After various measures of lesser judgment failed to consistently revive the nation, Yahweh finally removed his people from the land he had promised. At the time of this exile to Babylon, Ezekiel the prophet writes about Yahweh, again drawing on the theme of the Exodus: "I am Yahweh."

Just as Moses announced that Pharaoh, Egypt, Israel, and the world would know who Yahweh is by the plagues on Egypt and the deliverance of the Hebrews, so Ezekiel announces that Israel and the nations will again "know that I am Yahweh." This recognition of Yahweh as the true God of Israel, however, would come through judgment and destruction of the land God gave to Israel. Not unlike Egypt, "their land will be stripped of everything in it" (Ezekiel 12:19-20). The false gods would again be overcome—but this time they are idols Israel herself has set up (Ezekiel 6:1-7). The people would die by plague, sword, or famine, though some would be spared and taken into captivity (Ezekiel 6:8-14).

But this is not the end of Ezekiel's proclamation of Yahweh. Yahweh is judging his people, but he is not deserting them. They still have a future. Just as he initially proved himself to be Yahweh, he will again bring them into the land promised to Abraham:

> This is what the Sovereign LORD says: "When I gather the people of Israel from the nations where they have been scattered, I will show myself holy among them in the sight of the nations. Then they will live in their own land, which I gave to my servant Jacob. They will live there in safety and will build houses and plant vineyards; they will live in safety when I inflict punishment on all their

> neighbors who maligned them. Then they will know that I am Yahweh their God" (Ezekiel 28:25-26).

This return to the land would involve a restoration to nationhood as God's covenant people (Ezekiel 34:25-31, 20:36-44). A new inner motivation to live under Yahweh's rule will be given by Yahweh. Cleansed and renewed, Yahweh will be able to bless his people (Ezekiel 36:24-38). Again, Yahweh will dwell with them (Ezekiel 37:24-28).

Yahweh restores them because of his Name (Ezekiel 20:44, 36:22-23). He is faithful to his promise. He cannot deny himself.

Isaiah also pictures a New Exodus and entrance into the land. Just as Yahweh created the nation by deliverance through the sea the first time, so now he will make a supernatural way through the wilderness (Isaiah 43:14-21). This New Exodus is marked out by the announcement, "In the desert prepare the way for Yahweh" (Isaiah 40:3), and by the expectation of the Servant of Yahweh—the New Israel who will achieve Israel's original mandate of universal blessing (Isaiah 42:1-9).

### Jesus, New Israel, and Firstborn

It is not surprising that the New Testament recognizes the appearance of Jesus as the one who will achieve God's plan for Israel. Matthew's Gospel raises the curtain on Jesus' role as Yahweh's Servant/Son who will achieve for Israel what she failed to achieve for herself. Matthew sees Jesus' return from Egypt as a fulfillment of Hosea 11:1: "Out of Egypt I called my son" (Matthew 2:15). In Hosea, this description refers to the Exodus by Israel. The verses which follow note Israel's consistent failure to follow God:

> When Israel was a child, I loved him,
> and out of Egypt I called my son.
> But the more I called Israel,
> the further they went from me.

They sacrificed to the Baals
 and they burned incense to images
 (Hosea 11:1-2).

Israel failed as God's firstborn son.

But now God had sent his Son and Servant, Jesus, to represent Israel and achieve for her and the world what she had never achieved on her own.

Matthew returns to this theme in identifying John the Baptist as announcing the New Exodus of Isaiah 40:3, and by the identification from heaven itself of Jesus: "This is my Son, whom I love; with him I am well pleased"—a quotation of Isaiah 42:1 (Matthew 3:1-3, 3:16-17). Almost immediately, as if to test the heavenly announcement, Jesus is led by the Spirit into the wilderness to be tempted. And what were the tests? Hunger, testing God, false worship.

Because Jesus answers the tempter with Old Testament Scripture, it is common to make the application that believers are to be ready to give answers from the Bible when they are tempted. This is certainly a good lesson, but it misses the real point of Jesus' answers. Christ's answers came not from scattered locations in God's word, but from Deuteronomy 6—8. And what is Deuteronomy 6—8? It is Moses' reminder to Israel's second generation about the sins of the first generation in the wilderness. They are to learn from these failures to live by obedience to the word of God without complaining or testing God or yielding to false worship.

Jesus, Matthew is telling us, achieved what Israel regularly failed to achieve because of disobedience. As Yahweh's Son and Servant he will not only bring Israel's restoration, but also light to the Gentiles.

# FOR PERSONAL INTERACTION & DISCUSSION

SUGGESTED SCRIPTURE READINGS:

Exodus 3, 6:1-9, and 12:1-13
Matthew 3:1—4:11

1. What is the significance of the announcement in Exodus 1:7 that the Israelites were fruitful and multiplying?
2. Why was the enslavement and persecution of the Israelites a fatal mistake for Egypt? How does this relate to the promise to Abraham in Genesis 12:3? What similar situations in modern history are examples of this?
3. How do you explain the suffering of the Israelites in Egypt? Why does God allow the killing of innocent babies—even among his own people? What evidence is there that God is still in charge during this period of suffering?
4. Does the phrase "God remembered" imply that God had forgotten? What happens when God remembers someone? What kind of a relationship does God's remembering imply?
5. Why is the name "Yahweh" central to understanding the book of Exodus? What does this name mean? How is this name related to God's presence? Why is it sometimes called God's covenantal name? Why is this name an encouragement to all believers?
6. What right of Yahweh is debated in Exodus 5? How does Pharaoh's rejection of this right bring the plagues on Egypt? Does Yahweh have this right today?
7. Why was it right for God to harden Pharaoh's heart? In what ways was this God's moral judgment on

Egypt? Can God harden the hearts of national leaders today?

8. What did God plan to teach Egypt through the plagues? How would the plagues accomplish this?
9. How do the magicians' actions and responses provide insight into God's greatness?
10. What three common worries are dealt with in Exodus 15:22—17:7? What does Israel learn about Yahweh in facing these concerns? How does God's view of these difficulties differ from the view of the people? What does this teach us about faith today?
11. How is Jesus' crucifixion related to the Passover? Compare Jesus' New Passover and its benefits to the original Passover. Why is the original Passover so central for Old Testament believers? How is the Passover which Christ achieved central to the New Testament message of good news?
12. How did Israel fail as God's firstborn? Why is the promise of a New Exodus important for Israel? Why is it important that Jesus achieve this New Exodus for Israel and succeed as God's firstborn?

'A LINKUP WITH YAHWEH IS A POWERFUL OPPORTUNITY, BUT ALSO A DANGEROUS ONE. JUDGMENT ALWAYS BEGINS AT THE HOUSE OF GOD. TO BE A SON IS ALWAYS TO INVITE CHASTENING.'

CHAPTER

# 7.

# A NEW NATION

## ONE NATION UNDER GOD

God's plan for reversal began with the covenant with Abraham—a single individual. It now has grown to include a people delivered out of Egyptian slavery. They have been transported by God's grace "on eagles' wings" to Mount Sinai. What is God's next step? The giving of the Law—otherwise known as the Mosaic Covenant.

When Christians think of the Law certain ideas surface. Check these to see if they fit your notion of the Law.

- The Law is a step backward from living by faith as Abraham did.
- The Law is opposed to God's grace.
- The Law is good only for showing us we're sinners.
- The Law introduces salvation by works.

The Law has received a bad press. It has always been a difficult subject for Christians, and there has been widespread disagreement on how to understand the Law and its place in God's program.

The Law in general has been treated like a white elephant gift from a relative. You can hardly throw it out, yet you do not want to put it in a prominent place.

Of course, many do not mind displaying the Ten Commandments suitably framed. But what about those other laws—clean and unclean, dietary restrictions, special festivals and new moons, "an eye for an eye." What to do with them? How can they be part of the Scripture Paul recommends as profitable for instruction in righteousness (2 Timothy 3:16-17)?

Only by understanding the place of the Law as given at Sinai can we hope to properly understand its place in the Scripture.

## WHAT WAS THE LAW?

### A Gracious Gift of Yahweh

The introduction to the Law begins with these words: "I am Yahweh your God" (Exodus 20:2). We have seen already how important this identification is in the book of Exodus. According to Exodus 6:6-8, there are three stages for God's gracious action as Yahweh. The first stage, deliverance from Egypt, is complete, and the third stage is yet to come: possession of the land promised to Abraham. At Sinai, stage two has arrived: "I will take you as my own people, and I will be your God."

The Law is not a bogus door prize. It is the opportunity of a lifetime. These people are about to become the people of God. They have been chosen to enter into a covenant with God in which Yahweh commits himself to them as his people and they recognize Yahweh as their God.

Let us make clear that they are not entering this relationship by works. What works have they done? Crossing the sea when God opened its waters? Complaining about lack of food and drink? Beating the Amalekites when God was their warrior? What have these people done to qualify themselves? The answer is clearly *Nothing*. "Israel certainly had demonstrated in her past actions no qualifications for this undeserved favor."[1] They have simply received God's gracious promise to Abraham and were graciously delivered from Egypt.

Now, as a people chosen of God, they are to become his nation. "Blessed is the nation whose God is Yahweh, the people he chose for his inheritance" (Psalm 33:12).

**A Constitution for a Nation**

Israel does not reject the opportunity to become God's nation (Exodus 24:3-8). They covenant with God to keep his Law. The Law becomes their constitution and national legislation.

Part of the Christian's confusion over the Law comes from expecting to find only "spiritual" things in the Bible. But the Bible here records God's purpose of starting a nation. Nations need laws.[2] And these laws must include statutes which cover criminal as well as civil cases.

A recent court case in Oregon involved a public school teacher who wore a religious turban to work. Oregon law covered this situation and the instructor's teaching certificate was removed when she refused to abide by the law. It is not only the Mosaic Law which covers seemingly incidental things such as dress. Our modern building codes and public health laws also have their counterparts in the Mosaic Law (Leviticus 13:12-17, 14:33-42; Deuteronomy 22:8).

But let us recognize a great difference between our laws and the Mosaic Law. Our laws are the efforts of men to legislate justice for the common good. The Mosaic Covenant was given by God and therefore is "holy, righteous and good" (Romans 7:12).

All legislation is legislated morality, but all legislation is not good. Is a progressive income tax right? Is it right to imprison a man who owes debts? Should victims of crimes be compensated? The difference between our laws and the Mosaic Law is that the Israelites need not debate these questions. God gave them a legal code which, if kept, would ensure his blessing on the nation (Exodus 15:26, 23:25-26).

What a privilege to have your national laws given by God! The psalmist rejoices over Israel's unique place:

He has revealed his word to Jacob,
his laws and decrees to Israel.
He has done this for no other nation;
they do not know his laws
(Psalm 147:19-20).

### A Covenant with Yahweh

The study of ancient Hittite treaties reveals a similar pattern to the arrangement in the Mosaic Covenant.[3] This has had significant impact on confirming the historical validity of the Law. It has also helped us gain further insight into the nature of the covenant.

Of course, the biblical material itself tells us this is a covenant (Exodus 24:7). But understanding covenant forms of the time helps us recognize the importance and significance of various features. For instance, the Hittite king-vassal covenants always started with *an identification of the king* who was extending the covenant. This was followed by the *gracious actions* and provisions which the king had given in the past, and which call for a response of gratitude and loyalty. The *requirements* that follow are those which the covenant names as the appropriate, grateful response.

This is the very pattern we find in Exodus 20. The king is named: "I am Yahweh your God" (20:2). The benefits the king already has provided, though they were undeserved, are named: ". . . who brought you out of Egypt, out of the land of slavery" (20:2). This gracious action is the basis for a response of loyalty (20:3-17). Just as the king of the Hittite treaties expected loyalty to him, so Yahweh, the one who delivered them from bondage and to whom they owed their very lives, expected undivided loyalty—"no other gods." That the New Testament operates as well on this "first grace, then response of gratitude" pattern confirms again that Yahweh is the gracious God who abounds in love and faithfulness (Exodus 34:6).[4]

### A Guarantee of Yahweh's Presence

The revelation of the name *Yahweh* indicated the promise of his presence with his people. This is guaranteed in the Mosaic Covenant by the tabernacle. The tabernacle is the place of worship and accountability to God. But even more important, there Yahweh "will meet with the Israelites" (Exodus 29:43). He says, "I will dwell among the Israelites and be their God. They will know that I am Yahweh their God, who brought them out of Egypt so that I might dwell among them" (29:45-46).

While God informs Moses about construction of the tabernacle and its furniture, the Israelites make a calf-idol and worship it as the God of the Exodus (Exodus 32). Because of this demonstrated tendency toward disobedience, the Lord proposes that Israel would be better off without him. He will give them the land as promised, but without his presence, for otherwise he will have to judge them more strictly (Exodus 33:1-5).

But Moses recognizes the significance of Yahweh's presence for the choice of Israel as his nation. They not only need the Exodus and the land. To be recognized as uniquely Yahweh's, they must have his presence (Exodus 33:12-16).

Yahweh relents so easily and quickly that we know he also sees his presence as necessary to Israel—not only a presence of judgment, but a presence of compassion, grace, and faithful love (Exodus 34:5-7). Among these people he will do wonders "never before done in any nation in all the world" (34:10).

The book of Exodus closes with the glory of Yahweh coming to inhabit the tabernacle. What privilege! What grace!

### Opportunity to Be a Blessing

What responsibility! A linkup with Yahweh is a powerful opportunity, but also a dangerous one. Judgment always begins at the house of God (1 Peter 4:17). To be a son is always to invite chastening (Hebrews 12:7).

And what was their opportunity as the People of God? "Now if you obey me fully and keep my covenant, then out of all nations you will be my treasured possession. Although the whole earth is mine, you will be for me a kingdom of priests and a holy nation" (Exodus 19:5-6).

A priest is one who intercedes for others. Just as Abraham was God's route for intercession for Abimelech (Genesis 20:7,17), so Israel would be a nation through which the world would find Yahweh.[5] Her success at this, however, is totally conditional. By entering this gracious covenant with Yahweh, she gets favored-nation status. But her own experience of blessing as well as her ability to be a blessing to the world is based on her obedience—as the promises of blessing or cursing in Leviticus 26 so clearly announce.

## UNDERSTANDING THE LAW

### Laws and The Law

To fully appreciate the Mosaic Law, we must compare it with available law codes from the ancient Near East. Many biblical laws resemble those found in earlier codes such as the Code of Hammurabi, the Middle Assyrian Laws, and the Laws of Eshnunna. Common circumstances dictate that many of the same issues be covered. But there *are* differences, and they are significant.

*Biblical law places a primary concern on human life.* The destruction of human life, unless accidental, always requires capital punishment. Other law codes allow monetary compensation, especially in cases involving the death of a lower member of society.[6] The Bible allows compensation only in the case of death by a dangerous animal. Even there, if the bull had the habit of goring, both the bull and the owner must die. The family of the deceased could substitute payment, if they wished.[7] Capital punishment for human life is applied even to animals, continuing the directive of Genesis 9:5-6.

*Biblical law involves "eye for eye, tooth for tooth"* (Exodus 21:22-25). Though it sounds violent, this biblical formula does not advocate barbaric justice, but rather equal justice for all.[8] Those with money do not get off with mere fines. Additionally, the Bible does not allow children to be punished for the wrongs of a parent. In the Code of Hammurabi, if a man strikes another man's daughter and she dies, the murderer's daughter is put to death.[9] Sounds fair . . . unless you were the daughter! In the Bible, the murderer is put to death.[10] A slave receives even better than an eye for an eye if he suffers at the hand of a master: He receives his freedom (21:26).[11]

*Biblical law judges crimes against property more leniently.* Though the Bible judges crimes against people more strictly than earlier laws did, it is less strict than those laws in judging crimes against property. The Mosaic Law normally requires double restitution for theft (Exodus 22:4,7). Hammurabi requires ten to thirtyfold. If the thief cannot pay the restitution, Hammurabi has him killed. Exodus allows him to work it off as a slave (22:3).

If you are a thief, you would rather be one under the Mosaic Law. If you're caught tunneling through someone's mud wall, the homeowner can kill you and ask questions later—but only if it happens at night (22:2-3). Hammurabi will punish you with death day or night, and the hole you made would be filled with your corpse and plastered over.[12] The Laws of Eshnunna let you off with a fine during the day, but requires your death at night.[13] Biblical law regards even the life of a thief as worth something, and tries to protect it!

Without a prison system, options for punishment in the ancient world are fewer; they include capital punishment, fines, and mutilation. In Assyria, a wife can lose her nose or ear for varying degrees of unfaithfulness—no doubt an effective way to cut down on her desirability![14] If you are a surgeon, Hammurabi requires that your hand be cut off if anyone dies under your knife. But the Bible avoids using bodily mutilation as a penalty.

*Biblical Law includes worship practices as part of its law.* Other codes do not, because they are understood to be the product of a king seeking to please his god by formulating just laws. Since Israel's Law is directly from God, there is no distinction between civil and religious law. All law is religious.

"What other nation," Moses asked, "is so great as to have such righteous decrees and laws as this body of laws?" (Deuteronomy 4:8). The question was rhetorical. The answer is obvious.

But it is not enough to see how well the Mosaic Law compares to other law codes. This would be like comparing your farm to one in another country by talking about the type of soil, the annual rainfall, and farm equipment used, but never staying home enough to recognize and enjoy the landscape. If we are to understand the Law, we need to know a little bit about the lay of its land. If we are to understand the Law, we need to study its own inner workings.

**The Lay of the Law**

It is so common to divide the Law into the moral, civil, and ceremonial that many are surprised to find out Moses did not outline it that way!

Actually, the Law comes out in ever-widening circles, as represented in the chart below:

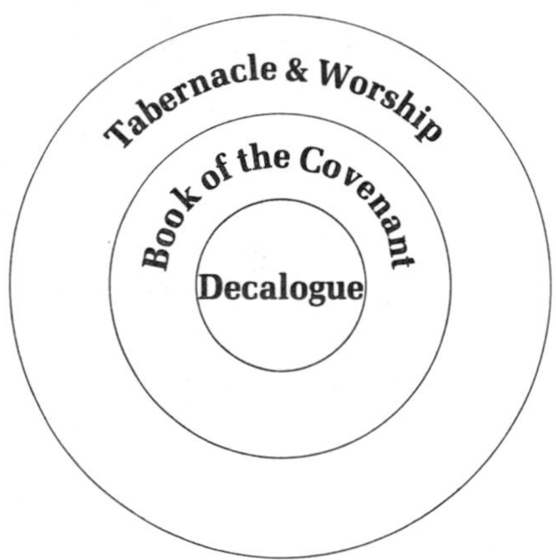


*First comes the Decalogue.* (Exodus 20:3-17). These Ten Commandments are often understood as the abiding moral law which Christians should keep, while the rest of the Law does not apply. This will not work for at least two reasons. First, some of the greatest moral laws are found elsewhere. Christ said the second greatest commandment is: "Love your neighbor as yourself." Reference? Don't look for it in the Ten Commandments. You'll find it in Leviticus 19:18, bumper to bumper with such commands as:

> Do not mate different kinds of animals.
> Do not plant your field with two kinds of seed.
> Do not wear clothing woven of two kinds of materials.

Additionally, not all of the Ten Commandments are absolute moral laws. Clearly, sabbath-keeping is not. It is included in this initial set of laws because it is the *sign of the covenant.* Just as circumcision is the sign of the Abrahamic Covenant, so keeping the sabbath recognizes the true God of creation as Yahweh, the God of Israel (Exodus 31:12-17). It derives not from God's nature, but from his celebration of his creative work as good. Paul, therefore, put the issue of keeping one day sacred in the category of things that each believer could determine on the basis of his own conscience (Romans 14:5-8). No one is to judge another believer by his diet or his observance of sabbaths or other holy days (Colossians 2:16-17).

So the Decalogue does not include all the abiding moral principles found in the Law, and neither are all its commands absolute moral principles. Nevertheless, it is at the very first of the Law because it summarizes the major concerns of the whole of the Law.

If we were to choose one word to summarize these Ten Commandments, it would be *faithfulness.* First, faithfulness to God. No other gods. No idols. No misuse of his Name. Keeping the sabbath is a sign of your commitment to his rule over you.

Faithfulness in relationship to others is the focus of the remaining commands. Parents deserve honor in the family. Faithfulness to your community of neighbors involves not lying, not committing adultery, not stealing, and certainly not murdering. It even involves faithfulness in your motivation. You should not mentally steal your neighbor's wife or anything else that is his.

These commandments give the heart of the rest of the decrees, statutes, and ordinances which make up the national legislation. But wait . . . could we run a country with these laws?

*The Book of the Covenant.* To run a country you need more than stated principles.[15] Should stealing and murder be punished equally? Can coveting be punished at all? The next circle of laws is called the Book of the Covenant (Exodus 20:22—23:19). Here we find the specifics on obligations and punishments needed to implement a just society. It includes what we would call criminal and civil law, as well as detailing basic sabbaths and holy days to be observed by Yahweh's faithful nation. In these chapters the humane and just features of the Mosaic Covenant become clear.

*The Tabernacle.* The rest of the book of Exodus gives directions for the tabernacle as the central worship place where God's presence with Israel was indicated (Exodus 25—40). It represents the unity of the nation around Yahweh.

*Leviticus.* The book of Leviticus is concerned about worship. But Israel's worship is not separate from the rest of life. To keep the decalogue is worship—and these laws are included again in Leviticus (18:20, 19:1-16). At the tabernacle, worship is expressed by sacrifices and offerings which provide the means for fellowship with God, forgiveness of sins, and expressions of thanksgiving and dedication to God (Leviticus 1—7). Physical conditions need to be met—the "clean and unclean" laws (Leviticus 11—16)—to qualify one for worship in the tabernacle and for living among the community. Finally, a more detailed code than the Book of the Covenant includes civil, criminal, and social regulations as part of worship of a holy God (Leviticus 17—25). This presentation of the Law is characterized by Leviticus 20:26—"You are to be holy to me because I, Yahweh, am holy, and I have set you apart from the nations to be my own."

## Kinds of Laws

We still have our questions about the Mosaic Law and the reasons for some of its commands. For instance, why not eat camels—or at least pigs? Why leave the corners of your field uncut? Does the same reason apply to leaving the corners of your hair and beard uncut?

As we have suggested, many types and levels of laws make up a nation's legal code. Some are based on absolute morality and are unchangeable. Some are included for other reasons, yet still serve a useful function in a society. Does it matter if you drive on the right side of the road or the left? In moral principle, no. In practice, yes.

Scholars have been disagreeing for centuries over the reasons for many of the Mosaic laws. I am going to wade in where no angel would dare wet his toe by suggesting a few possible reasons for some of them.

- *Faithfulness in relationships.* We have seen this in the decalogue and it carries through consistently, even in regard to foreigners (Leviticus 19:33). Practical matters of justice—such as honest scales (Leviticus 19:35-36)—fit here as well. Poorer members of the community were not to be forgotten (19:9-10).
- *Respect for blood as representing life given by Yahweh, the Creator.* The blood of an animal must not be eaten (Leviticus 17:10-12). Any animal hunted and killed must have its blood drained out and covered with soil (17:13-14). Human blood must be atoned for. Blood shed by murder must be accounted for by the blood of the murderer.[16]
- *Avoidance of false worship patterns.* Condemned are soothsaying, mediums, tattoos and cuts, sexual rituals, child sacrifice, and even the cutting of the

corners of the beard and hair (Leviticus 19:26-31).[17]

- *Recognition that the earth is the Lord's.* The sabbath year of rest for the land as well as the return of land to families every fifty years recognizes that the Israelites are stewards of his land. Land is not owned absolutely. (Leviticus 25:1-24).[18]
- *Reflecting Yahweh as Creator.* This theme is represented not only in land laws, but also in the bringing of the firstfruits of harvest, and in dedication of the first year of produce from trees. It is represented even in purely symbolic ways. Seeds, animals, and clothing materials are not to be mixed, undoubtedly to reflect in the Israelite's daily life the distinctness of kinds that Yahweh created (Leviticus 19:19). Even the Israelite's fields and his dress said, "Yahweh is the true Creator God." Perhaps some laws proclaiming certain abnormalities (such as skin infections) as unclean were intended to teach that abnormality does not represent Yahweh's original creation.[19] Certainly some of the laws of uncleanness were to protect the community as well (Leviticus 15:1-15).

Though these laws seem complicated to us and impossible to live under, they actually served a positive purpose. By keeping them, Israel would demonstrate her distinctness. The beneficial standards as well as the rich symbolic meaning would continue to communicate her privilege as God's treasured possession (Deuteronomy 4:6-8). Our concentrating on a mass of individual commands misses the true stress on the relationship with God. The key has always been: "If you love

Me, you will keep My commandments" (John 14:15 NASB).

## THE NEW TESTAMENT AND LAW-KEEPING

### Jesus and the Law

In the Old Testament, the Jews never seemed able to keep the Law's most basic requirements. The golden calf routine in one form or another was as regular as rain in Oregon. How is it, then, that when we come to the New Testament we run into a crowd that seems to have taken their law-keeping more scrupulously than Texans take their football? That's good news, isn't it? No, it's more bad news.

Jesus' concern with the nit-picking law-keepers often identified as belonging to the Pharisees' denomination is not that they applied the Law stringently. In fact, he commends their care in tithing even the smallest pieces of produce (Matthew 23:23). His problem with them is that while they exercise great care in parceling produce, they overlook the main thrust. They're like good neighbors in an upstanding community who keep up their yards, have well-behaved kids, have great family loyalty . . . but make their income from owning brothels across town. Or, to use some of our Lord's own picturesque language, they "strain out a gnat but swallow a camel"—neither one a clean animal in Leviticus! Or again, they are "like whitewashed tombs," looking good, but inside are dead men's bones—more uncleanness (Matthew 23:24,27).

Jesus himself is more concerned with people's needs than keeping himself clean. Becoming unclean could happen in any person's daily routine, but certain types of uncleanness, though not sin, could put you out of circulation—and certainly out of the tabernacle or temple area for awhile.

The woman approaching Jesus who for years has been without relief from a hemorrhage is unclean (see Leviticus 15:25-30). She certainly has her nerve grabbing the edge of his robe and so rendering him unclean—without even warning him! No doubt the crowd figures she is in for a tongue-lashing. But Jesus is more impressed with the faith that brought her to dare such a scandal. He pronounces her whole. No longer constantly unclean and unable to go to the temple, she is healed (Mark 5:25-34).

Jesus doesn't avoid contact with the dead either. He crashes funeral parties. This must have given the nit-pickers pause: Is a man unclean when he touches a dead body that becomes alive again (Luke 7:11-16, Numbers 19:11-13)?

They aren't confused, however, about his sabbath-keeping. Here is no debate over mere uncleanness. Nor is it a question about traditions. Here is the very sign of the Mosaic Covenant being transgressed by Jesus on many occasions—or so it seems to them. He and his disciples violate the sabbath by harvesting grain and "threshing it" between their palms as they pass through a field (Luke 6:1-5).[20] Even more energy is expended when Jesus heals a man on the sabbath. And if that isn't enough, Jesus even tells him to carry his bedroll home (John 5:5-8).

Jesus lets them know he keeps the sabbath, but not the way they do. He keeps it the way the priests kept it and the way God kept it. He does good on the sabbath—not work for economic gain. They, too, allow exceptions for the sabbath, but these relate only to animal needs, not human needs (Matthew 12:11-12). Jesus accuses them of not really understanding the sabbath command. It was made for man's benefit (Mark 2:27). It got a man away from his economic concerns, saved him from being a workaholic, saved his household and servants from abuse, and turned his mind toward the Creator God who originated the sabbath.

Because the Pharisees don't understand the Law, they misapply it. They have turned it into outward observance. In a particularly scathing denunciation of the state of Jewish legalism, Jesus points out that fashionably current teaching allows a man to commit mental adultery, deceive his neighbor by the use of misleading oaths, end his commitment to his wife with a piece of paper, get even for any wrongs he suffered, and hate everyone but his friends. The Pharisees have used the Law to achieve their own desires (Matthew 5:17-48). Yet the point of the Law, as stated in Leviticus again and again, is to reflect Yahweh, their God. "Be perfect, therefore, as your heavenly Father is perfect," (Matthew 5:48). "Be holy, because I am holy" (Leviticus 11:44-45, 19:2, 20:26).

The Law, God's gift to Israel, had been turned into a way of gaining points with God. Like all human attempts at earning righteousness, it tried to scale down the holiness of God so man could reach it.

**Paul and the Law**

Paul takes up where Jesus left off. The legalists are a constant migraine for Paul. They dog his footsteps and collar his converts. It is not enough to believe in Jesus, they preach; you must be circumcised and keep the Law.

What makes these false teachers particularly pesky is that their case looked good to new believers. After all, these teachers can declare "The Bible says" and point to Old Testament verses commanding, "Be circumcised," "Don't eat pork," "Keep the Sabbaths and new moons."

In response, Paul has some pretty rough things to say. If you go that route, he says, you better be ready to keep everything perfectly, because "the man who does these things will live by them." He says the law didn't solve sin; it increased it. He says Abraham didn't achieve God's blessing by Law, but by faith (Galatians 3:10-12, 3:6-7).

The tragedy is that Christians by and large believe the legalists correct in their view of the Law. The Law, they say, was a way of earning credit with God. The Law was an impossible bill of goods that God laid on Israel. Before the Law men lived by faith, but afterward they had to operate by rules. All the Law could do was arouse sin.

Did God do that to his people? No! And Paul did not say God had. You see, we have been reading the Law as the legalizers were using it, and in the very way which Paul attacked.

Imagine sitting in an airport lobby and the child next to you shows you a drawing he has found in a book. He has it upside down, but he thinks he is looking at it accurately. He has spotted what looks like a dog in the picture. He says, "Look, a puppy." Your response might be (assuming you wanted to teach him rather than simply humor him), "If that's a puppy, why are these trees hanging upside down?" The child turns back to its mother and says, "Look at the funny trees this nice man showed me." The church has been saying, "Look at the funny Law this nice apostle showed us."

The Law was not a rotten deal for the Israelites. It was the best possible life for God's people in that time and place. It was not a way of becoming God's people; it was the way to reflect and proclaim the true God, Yahweh. Did Paul say it was a rotten deal? No, Paul said *if the legalizers are right* it was a rotten deal. If you look at the picture their way, you will have to keep every last shred of it to be accepted before God. If you look at it their way, something is out of line because Abraham was counted righteous without doing all those things. God accounted to Abraham what he never achieved on his own—remember all those slips?—on the basis of faith.

Paul said, "The Law is just and right and good, but if I'm supposed to keep it for righteousness I'm not going to make it." The Law cannot accomplish that because of the weakness of human flesh. Does that mean the Law was bad? Only if that was what the Law was trying to accomplish. The Law was so good and holy that Paul concedes: "If a law had been given that could impart life, then righteousness would certainly have come by the law" (Galatians 3:21). *But such a law was never given.* No, what the Law could not do and was not designed to do, God did by sending his Son. Atonement by grace has always been the key, and those who read the Law right knew it all along (Galatians 2:15-16).[21]

## The Law's Function

But Paul did make statements about the Law which reflect his own views. The Law is "holy, righteous, and good" (Romans 7:12). The Law was our tutor to bring us to Christ (Galatians 3:23—4:7). The Law was added to the promise (Abrahamic Covenant) "because of transgressions until the Seed to whom the promise referred had come" (Galatians 3:19). The Law was not opposed to the promises of God (Galatians 3:21).

The Mosaic Covenant was good, but it had a temporary function. It did not change God's way of working or make his promise based on works. It was a positive program for a time when things needed to be spelled out, when safeguards were needed to protect Israel from falling easily into Canaanite practices. The Law was like a disciplinarian in charge of your training as a minor. That is a good thing. You need to learn that discipline, those manners, that lesson. When you are older and are disciplined and understand the reasons for manners and lessons, you don't place yourself under the old rules, good as they were. You operate out of your full understanding.

To continue going to bed at nine o'clock every night because that was your parents' rule will keep you in good health, but some things are worth staying up later for. No set of rules will be long enough to cover them, but a mature adult will know what they are. A mature adult will also understand why he had a nine o'clock rule as a child, and will continue to take care of his health even though he is no longer under such a rule.[22]

## The Law as Scripture

So we are not "under the Law" as our operating covenant with God. Paul was opposed to any of his Gentile converts subjecting themselves to the Law either by circumcision or symbolic observances (Galatians 4:10-11, 5:2-3). Why? Because it denies the gospel. It not only signals belief that works are needed to be acceptable to God (5:4), but also denies that Gentiles are on a par with Jews in the body of Christ (3:26-29).

But Paul is not opposed to using the Law for instruction. It was from his pen that 2 Timothy 3:16-17 flowed, affirming that all Scripture, because it is inspired by God, is to be used for teaching. As a converted Pharisee, Paul was certainly aware that the Mosaic Law made up a good portion of those Scriptures, and that all of them from Exodus on advocated obedience to the Law.

Paul doesn't use the Law as a code that the believer is under (covenant), and certainly not as a way of gaining points with God (legalism), but as a source for insight into God's view of life (instruction). The Law is a revelation of God; and if we understand the reasons for the various laws, we can learn the righteous principles being taught.

Paul is not inconsistent when he opposes the Judaizers' use of the Law in Galatians 3:10-12, and then quotes the Law himself, citing Deuteronomy 21:23 to show the meaning of Christ's death for us: "Cursed is everyone that hangs on a tree." Nor is he violating his own principles when he quotes Deuteronomy 25:4 to show that ministers should be paid (1 Corinthians 9:9), or when he uses Leviticus 25:39-42 to conclude that the Lord's redeemed servants should avoid becoming slaves to men (1 Corinthians 7:21-23). Paul's teaching on vengeance comes from the Law (Romans 12:19, Leviticus 19:18, Deuteronomy 32:35). And Paul does not hesitate to remind his converts that honoring parents is a duty that was a special concern of the Law (Ephesians 6:1-3, Exodus 20:12).

The Old Testament, including the Law, was the Bible of the New Testament Church. It was not disposed of as a modern tossable—used once and discarded. Nor was it treated as a museum piece for historic interest only. It was still Scripture. And though all of it was no longer directly applicable, it still could instruct when used with full understanding of its place and purpose.[23]

## ON THE WAY: THE FULFILLMENT OF THE LAW

At the same time Jesus denied any wish to abolish the Law or the Prophets, he also predicted their fulfillment (Matthew 5:17-18). The most minute part of the Law would not pass away "until everything is accomplished." Jesus himself brings the Law to fulfillment in a number of ways.

First, he fulfills the sacrificial system. The sacrifices ordained by the Law could not take away sins (Hebrews 10:3), they had to be continually repeated (Hebrews 7:27), and they were offered by imperfect and finite priests (7:23-28). They were part of a temporary covenant (8:13) that was a picture of the ultimate fulfillment, but they were unable to bring about forgiveness of sins (9:9-10, 10:1-3). For this reason the book of Hebrews calls the New Covenant a "better" and "superior" covenant (8:6). The first or Mosaic Covenant is made "obsolete" (8:13) and applied only "until the time of the new order" (9:10).[24]

Second, Jesus fulfills the righteousness of the Law. Paul declares the whole world guilty before God—the Jew with the Law and the Gentile without it. Some Gentiles were even able to live as righteously as their Jewish neighbors who had God's Law. (Substitute non-Christian and Christian and check your own neighborhood.) The bottom line on earning righteousness is: "No one will be declared righteous in his sight by observing the law; rather, through the law we become conscious of sin" (Romans 3:20).

Paul, however, denies that he is nullifying the Law. He insists that he is upholding or establishing it (3:31). The righteousness of the Law is not established by keeping it for merit before God. That is doomed to failure. The righteousness of the Law is established by receiving the gift of righteousness by faith in Christ (Romans 9:30-33). Christ is the end of the Law (Romans 10:4)—not only because he inaugurated a new covenant to replace it, but because he achieved its righteous standard for all who believe. Christ satisfies the righteous demands of the Law. It is in him that we "become the righteousness of God" (2 Corinthians 5:21).[25]

Our focus is not the keeping of the Law as a merit system, but Jesus Christ himself. Our response is based on gratitude for what God has done in Christ. We love because he first loved us (1 John 4:19). We forgive, because we are forgiven (Ephesians 4:32). We walk worthily because we have been graciously given a special calling (Ephesians 4:1). We honor God with our body because we, like ancient Israel, are bought with a price (1 Corinthians 6:19-20).

No, the Law is not a white elephant. But then, don't feature it as a centerpiece either.

Only Jesus deserves that spot!

# FOR PERSONAL INTERACTION & DISCUSSION

SUGGESTED SCRIPTURE READINGS:

Exodus 20:1-20 and 21:12—22:3
Matthew 5:17-48
Galatians 3:21—4:7

1. Did this chapter change any of your ideas about the Law?
2. If the Law is good, why is the believer not under it today? Is there a difference between being "under the Law" and recognizing the Law as Scripture which is profitable for instruction in righteousness?
3. How do the differences between the laws of Israel and those of her neighbors show the superiority of the Mosaic Law? What guarantee did Israel have about her laws that other nations, including our own, do not have?
4. Do you agree that all legislation is legislated morality? Why is there no distinction between religious and civil law in the Mosaic Law?
5. Was the Mosaic Law intended to motivate by works or by grace? What motive should have prompted those desiring to keep the Law? What is the New Testament motive for obeying God?
6. Why is the Presence of Yahweh important to the Law? Why does Moses reject Yahweh's proposal to give them the land without going with them? Why does Yahweh's Presence with Israel not only indicate his grace toward them, but also demand their responsibility to him? Is this true with all spiritual privileges?
7. What is the primary emphasis of the Ten Commandments? Why do they have this emphasis? How does Jesus' own teaching about the Law agree with this

emphasis? How did the Pharisees violate this emphasis by keeping only the letter of the Law? Can you cite examples from today of external rules receiving more emphasis than spiritual relationships?

8. How is the Law designed to be a proclamation of Israel's Yahweh as the true God? In what ways are believers today to be a proclamation of the God of the Bible?
9. How does Jesus' approach to the sabbath differ from that of the Pharisees? What benefits did the sabbath law bring to man? What other examples show Jesus' rejection of works-religion as an approach to God? What religions today are works-religions? Has the Christian church itself fallen into the trap of works to earn righteousness before God?
10. How do Christians sometimes misunderstand the apostle Paul's view of the Law? Is it the Law Paul rejects, or legalism? What is the Law useful for today?
11. In what ways is the New Covenant a "better covenant" than the old Mosaic Covenant? How has the Law been fulfilled?
12. How is the righteousness of the Law upheld and fulfilled? How can a person who fails to keep the Law achieve righteousness? How does the believer ultimately come to follow the righteous standard God desires (see Romans 8:1-17)?

'IF A MUTUAL LOVE RELATIONSHIP WITH YAHWEH IS THE ENGINE THAT POWERS THE RESPONSE OF OBEDIENCE, THEN MEMORY IS THE FUEL. IF ISRAEL FORGETS THE PAST, THE DYNAMIC OF LOVE WILL BE LOST . . . AND SO EVENTUALLY WILL THE LAND.'

CHAPTER

# 8.

# LIVING THE LIFE

## THE CHALLENGE OF DEUTERONOMY

Back in the sixties when antiwar sentiment was in full bloom, there arose a bumper sticker which announced in clear terms another opinion. It read, AMERICA: LOVE IT OR LEAVE IT.

The book of Deuteronomy introduces us to a far different cultural situation. The children of Israel, a landless people, find themselves standing at the border of the land God had promised to Abraham centuries before. They are entering a land, not leaving it. Taking the land is their top priority. Talk about losing it seems premature at best. And yet Moses, the man of God, delivers a warning about dangers that will ultimately bring God's judgment and the loss of the promised land. Moses shows little concern over the battles ahead with the nations already occupying Canaan. Yahweh is adequate for that. Moses' concern, rather, is over the battle within Israel herself.

*Love* and *Land*—these are the concerns of Deuteronomy. The commands and statutes of the Law as recorded in Exodus and Leviticus may have seemed to the Israelite like so many parts and pieces. In Deuteronomy, Moses pulls the whole apparatus together into a sermon—a sermon which becomes the nation's handbook on land. How should Israel operate in the land? In its way, Moses' handbook is the opposite of that bumper sticker. The modern slogan calls for dedication to a country and asks those who fail to meet that level of dedication to depart. But Moses declares that the one who loves the promised land will lose it.[1] Patriotic commitment to a land or even to nationhood is not adequate. Only full commitment to Yahweh as the one true God will assure his full blessing in the land.

## THE HANDBOOK IN OUTLINE

The book of Deuteronomy is patterned after the vassal covenant treaties we noted previously.[2] The title and preamble come first (Deuteronomy 1:1-5). A course in History 101 follows—not for the purpose of learning names and dates, but to remind Israel of the benefits the King has provided to the people (Deuteronomy 1:6—3:29). Yahweh has cared for them even though they were not always faithful.

> Yahweh your God has blessed you in all the work of your hands. He has watched over your journey through this vast desert. These forty years Yahweh your God has been with you, and you have not lacked anything (2:7).

Included in these benefits are the recent victories over Sihon and Og, kings of Heshbon and Bashan.

After the historical review, Deuteronomy records the basic stipulations of the treaty. These are found in two sets: chapters 5—11, and 12—26. Each set becomes more detailed. Chapters 5—11 highlight the major concerns—those central obligations and attitudes important to relationship with Yahweh. Chapters 12—26 take up the specifics and details of how to live in the land in a way that is consistent with their identity as Yahweh's people.

Critical to treaties of the time was a litany of blessings and curses (chapters 27—28). Blessings come for obedience to the covenant. Curses come as a result of disobedience. Such is Moses' concern about Israel that he gives a final exhortation (29—30). Arrangements are then made for regular public reading and storing of the covenant (31). The Lord's concern about Israel is so great that Moses is commanded to provide a song (32) to remind Israel of God's faithfulness and their own tendency to rebel. For rebellion is what is predicted from these people (31:29). Moses, the superb prophet (34:10-12), then gives his farewell blessing, views the promised land from Mount Nebo, and finishes his course (33—34).

## THE CONCERNS OF DEUTERONOMY

### Love and Covenant

It should no more surprise us that Moses' exhortations follow a covenant pattern than to discover that Mother's Day cards often contain an acrostic poem that spells M-O-T-H-E-R. The very heart of Israel's relationship to Yahweh is one of covenant. The unique contribution of Deuteronomy is Moses' summary of that covenant in terms of one word: *love*. Yahweh has loved them (4:37-38, 7:7-9, 10:14-15) and he chose their fathers, Abraham, Isaac, and Jacob, to receive a promise of blessing. This choice was not made on the basis of achievement or greatness, but simply because of Yahweh's love.

The commitment of Israel to Yahweh also may be summarized by that one word *love*. Because Yahweh, the God of Israel, is the one true God, God's people are to pursue total commitment.[3]

> Hear, O Israel: Yahweh our God, Yahweh is one. Love Yahweh your God with all your heart and with all your soul and with all your strength (6:4-5).

The passage is clear. The type of love we are talking about is not a gushy, surface emotion—but a total involvement which demands complete commitment. Such commitment must begin in the heart—the true inner center of thinking and motives. It must engage the desires and appetites of the life ("soul") and involve all of one's exuberance (strength) in putting that devotion into action.[4]

Unlike modern situational ideas of love, this love for Yahweh is demonstrated by observing his laws. It is joined regularly with phrases like "fearing the LORD," "walking in his ways," and "obeying his commands" (10:12, 11:1, 11:13, 11:22, 30:16, 30:20). But unlike legalistic ideas of obedience, Moses stresses the need for a true inner commitment and devotion to Yahweh. Outer observance is not enough. Even circumcision must go deeper than the skin. It must cut into the heart (Deuteronomy 10:16). This covenant of love brings Israel into relationship with Yahweh. Yahweh himself is their life. It is him they must choose and love (Deuteronomy 30:15-20).

**Love and Yahweh's Uniqueness**

Having a relationship with Yahweh is a unique privilege. The Israelites thought it a bit too unique on occasion. When Yahweh demonstrated his majesty by thunder and lightning, trumpet and smoke at Sinai, he taught them a special fear and awe (Deuteronomy 4:35-36, 4:10-12; Exodus 20:18-21)—so much so that they wanted no more of it! They were not to think of Yahweh as just another god—like the gods of the nations around them. No, Yahweh owns the whole earth (Deuteronomy 10:14).[5] The uniqueness of Yahweh calls for specific response:

- Because Yahweh has no outer form, making images to worship him is forbidden (4:15-20).
- Because Yahweh is the only true God, they must commit themselves totally to him (6:4-12, 4:32-40).
- Because Yahweh is a jealous God, they must avoid worshiping other gods alongside Yahweh (6:13-15, 5:7-9). Yahweh will not be worshiped as one of many.
- Because Yahweh is a God who speaks and answers prayer, Israel has the opportunity to be unique among the nations in wisdom, understanding, and greatness (4:5-8).

- Yahweh fights uniquely for Israel; so when confronting her enemies, Israel must destroy not only the people, but also the images of their gods (7:1-6, 7:21-26).[6]

Among the blessings of Moses at the end of the book is a special comment on the uniqueness of Israel's God:

> There is no one like the God of Jeshurun,
> who rides on the heavens to help you
> and on the clouds in his majesty.
> The eternal God is your refuge,
> and underneath are the everlasting arms.
> He will drive out your enemy before you,
> saying, "Destroy him!" (33:26-27).

Only two verses later the comparison is made with Israel:

> Blessed are you, O Israel!
> Who is like you,
> a people saved by Yahweh?

Because Yahweh is unique, Israel, like no other people, could be unique. Indeed, "Their rock is not like our Rock" (32:31).

> I will proclaim the name of Yahweh.
> Oh, praise the greatness of our God!
> He is the Rock, his works are perfect,
> and all his ways are just.
> A faithful God who does no wrong,
> upright and just is he (32:3-4).[7]

**Love and Remembering**

If a mutual love relationship with Yahweh is the engine that powers the response of obedience, then memory is the fuel. As Blair points out,[8] both Old and New Testaments motivate by two mental activities: hope and memory—focusing on God's promise for the future and remembering God's activities in the past. Israel is about to enter the land and experience another phase of fulfillment of God's promise to Abraham. But if they forget the past, the dynamic for love will be lost . . . and so eventually will the land.

What past events should stir and keep alive their love and commitment?

- God's love for and covenant with Abraham, Isaac, and Jacob and the Lord's choice of them to be his nation (4:37, 7:7-8, 9:5, 10:14-15). This choice, Moses stresses, was not because of their righteousness nor any greatness they possessed. It was purely by grace.
- Their slavery in Egypt and God's deliverance from it (1:30, 4:20, 4:34, 4:37, 5:6, 5:15, 6:12, 6:20-25, 7:8-11, 7:18-19). The deliverance from Egypt was convincing proof of his love for them as well as the basis for their gratitude (7:8-11, 4:20, 4:34, 6:12). It also supported laws that called for kindness to others in need (24:17-18, 10:19, 15:12-15). The ritual of Passover and the Feast of Weeks were specifically designed to put memory on their annual calendar (16:1-12). Their past situation warned against self-confidence, yet gave assurance that God will give them victory in the future (8:12-14, 7:18-19, 20:1).
- God's gift of superior laws by which they could be the marvel of the nations (4:5-14, 4:23).
- The experiences and lessons of the wilderness (1:31, 2:7, 2:36, 3:3, 8:2-5, 8:15-18, 9:7, 9:23, 11:5-7, 24:9). God was teaching them in the wilderness. He taught them the need for total trust and dependence on him for their needs. They learned their own weakness and tendency to rebel.

Be assured the idea here is not the old adage, "Those who will not learn from history are condemned to repeat it." It is more than that. Israel must *identify* with this history, realize God's initiative in coming into relationship with her, and then choose life (Deuteronomy 30:19-20).

This generation has experienced these great events of deliverance (11:1-7). But what of their children? How would a love relationship with God continue? Must their children return to Egypt and be delivered so that they too can know that Yahweh, the true God, is their God?

The importance of memory to love is such that Moses underscores the absolute necessity for teaching the nation's children about Israel's unique history as God's people. Following the central command of Deuteronomy 6:4-5 are these words:

> These commandments that I give you today are to be upon your hearts. Impress them on your children. Talk about them when you sit at home and when you walk along the road, when you lie down and when you get up. Tie them as symbols on your hands and bind them on your foreheads. Write them on the doorframes of your houses and on your gates.

This is total integration of truth to life! Teaching children to remember God's work for his people was not limited to a Sunday school, nor to a few minutes of "quality time." The child's question about the meaning of the commands is to be answered by recalling God's deliverance (6:20-25). Both the law and the experiences of the past must be communicated faithfully to future generations if the land is to be continually enjoyed (4:9-10, 31:9-13).

A friend has a "Memory Board" in his home on which the family displays items showing how God has helped them in the past. This helps to make the truth live for his children. Deuteronomy has even more than this in mind. It wants us to recognize that we were involved in God's deliverances, though witnessed only by former generations. Our memory board should include a cross and an empty tomb. For in these actions he delivered us as well!

### Love and Repentance

But Moses did not expect Israel to succeed in keeping these commands out of a heart of love. He had too much experience with them for that. After all, he even blamed his own failure to obey on their rebelliousness (1:37). "Stiff-necked" is the term that fits these people. "You have been rebellious against Yahweh ever since I have known you" says it all (9:24). Or in even stronger terms,

> Your eyes have seen all that Yahweh did in Egypt to Pharaoh, to all his officials and to all his land. With your own eyes you saw those great trials, those miraculous signs and great wonders. But to this day Yahweh has not given you a mind that understands or eyes that see or ears that hear (29:2-4).

Moses anticipates their rebellion, but Yahweh predicts it. The results of their disobedience are announced ahead of time, acting as red flags to warn that the nation is headed for disaster. Rebellion will introduce, in increasing intensity, plagues, famine, defeat in war, and captivity (28:15-68). This litany of doom is given not to dishearten them, but to warn them and to make them understand the extent of Yahweh's love and commitment. Even when they are in captivity, Yahweh will have compassion on them and return them to the land when they turn with all their heart to him (30:1-10). What a God! They would fail, but he will not. *What a way to love!*

### Love and Land

"There's only one thing that lasts—land." From Scarlett O'Hara to your local real estate broker, so many say it. It's pure paganism and idolatry. The land is Yahweh's. He is its creator and owner. Man lives on it as a steward to oversee and enjoy.

> To Yahweh your God belong the heavens, even the highest heavens, the earth and everything in it (10:14).

But man turns gift into god just as he worships the creature rather than the creator. He fails in that elemental recognition of God—thankfulness.

Israel is about to "inherit" the land as a gift and stewardship from Yahweh (4:21, 12:9, 15:4, 19:10).[9] This land is their inheritance because Yahweh promised it to their forefathers: Abraham, Isaac, and Jacob (1:8, 8:1, 11:9, 26:5). Israel's attitude toward her possession of this land is to be shaped by three truths:[10]

- The land was given as an act of sheer grace (1:25).
- It remains with Israel only as long as they are faithful (11:16-17).
- It is not given because of any prior faithfulness (9:6).

In fact, land presents a new danger that the period in the desert did not. Moses outlines this danger in the central address on major issues and concerns (Deuteronomy 5—11). Following his exhortation on love (chapter 6) and his warning of the danger of mixing with the Canaanite nations (chapter 7), Moses sees the primary danger of land (chapter 8)—*the danger of self-sufficiency*. In the desert, Moses says, God taught you that he was the provider:

> He humbled you, causing you to hunger and then feeding you with manna, which neither you nor your fathers had known, to teach you that man does not live on bread alone but on every word that comes from the mouth of Yahweh (8:3).

Over the years we have heard many comments on "man shall not live by bread alone." Advertisers want you to pile on meat from their deli. Well-meaning preachers suggest that you need not only physical food, but spiritual as well. Yet Moses' point is not the absence of a well-rounded diet, physical or spiritual. The point is that Israel lived in the desert *because God said they would live.* When he spoke they got food. When he decided they would be hungry, they were hungry. All of life is determined by Yahweh's word.

Now they are going into a "good land"[11] that Yahweh has provided according to his word. Yet because Yahweh's provision in the land is not as obvious a gift as it was in the desert, the temptation to draw a faulty conclusion is there:

> You may say to yourself, "My power and the strength of my hands have produced this wealth for me." But remember Yahweh your God, for it is he who gives you the ability to produce wealth, and so confirms his covenant, which he swore to your forefathers, as it is today (8:17-18).

And how must Israel acknowledge that they live by Yahweh's word? By keeping his word, walking in his ways, and fearing him (8:6).

Another bumper sticker surfacing in the sixties repeated a toast by nineteenth-century naval hero Stephen Decatur: MY COUNTRY, RIGHT OR WRONG. To slap one of these on the back of an oxcart in ancient Israel would have been an announcement of rebellion against God. The land is a gift to be held in righteousness, or not at all. Injustice and moral pollution threaten the nation's life in the land (Deuteronomy 16:20, 25:15, 18:9-13).[12] Commitment to land leads to paganism. Commitment to Yahweh means enjoying his land.

## ON THE WAY: COMPLETION OF LOVE AND LAND

### Completion of Love

In a verbal sparring match with the various theological fraternities of his day, Jesus answered each loaded question with a dynamite reply. The noise was still reverberating from such current issues as the church-state debate and the possibility of resurrection, when one scholar threw up a question important only to eggheads in the classroom: "Of all the commandments, which is the most important?" (Mark 12:28).

Jesus gives him the only nonexplosive answer in the bundle. First place goes to Deuteronomy 6:4-5, says Jesus:

> Hear, O Israel, the Lord our God, the Lord is one. Love the Lord your God with all your heart and with all your soul and with all your mind and with all your strength (Mark 12:29-30).

Then, lest anyone misunderstand the unity of this primary command with the other commands, Jesus names the runner-up: "Love your neighbor as yourself" (Leviticus 19:18). This command is not from Deuteronomy, but nonetheless summarizes the spirit of the laws of Deuteronomy which are modeled after the loving care of God himself (Deuteronomy 10:17-19). Not willing to enter a debate which falsely sets these two at odds with one another, Jesus ties them together. The second, though second, follows from the first.

This not-so-theoretical answer by Jesus concerning the heart of the Law brings the only discernable agreement of the afternoon. In fact, the expert not only agrees, but also adds his own footnote (he *is* a teacher!). The footnote, though not novel—the prophets had said as much—must have earned him some raised eyebrows in those sacred temple precincts: "To love him with all your heart, with all your understanding and with all your strength, and to love your neighbor as yourself is more important than all burnt offerings and sacrifices" (Mark 12:33).

Here stands a man who is beginning to perceive the significance of the Law. The Torah of Moses was *instruction in knowing God.* Its center is relationship, not ritual. Its ritual is educational, not magical or manipulative. Its purpose was to picture relational truth and enrich memory, not promote a form of buying off God. God was not interested in bribes (Deuteronomy 10:17). Pagans brought offerings to their deities to encourage divine generosity. Yahweh received thanksgiving offerings from his children for whatever had already been received.[13]

This relational truth of Deuteronomy is not passé. Though there are no certain quotations of Deuteronomy in James 1 and 2,[14] it is interesting to note how much these chapters reflect the central issues of Deuteronomy.

- It is to those who love him that God will give the crown of life (1:12).
- Every "good and perfect gift" comes from the Father of creation who chose us ("twelve tribes," 1:1) as a kind of firstfruits (1:17-18).
- The man who will be blessed is he who not only hears the perfect law, but also does it (1:25).
- Genuine religion is to look after widows and orphans and to keep pure from the world (1:27).
- It is those who are poor that God has chosen to inherit the kingdom promised to those who love him (2:5).

These parallels with Deuteronomy indicate the continuing relevance of these ancient concerns of God. Was the church at Jerusalem thinking Deuteronomy when it made sure there were no needy persons in its midst (Acts 4:34; Deuteronomy 15:4-11)?[15]

Caring Israelites, Deuteronomy said, should make the difference. Though there will always be poor people because of circumstances, the poor should be relieved by those enjoying God's blessing (15:4-11). The promised blessing of abundance on the nation as a whole did not guarantee the physical success of every Israelite. The abundant blessing is corporate, and therefore must be shared.

Did not Paul teach the same in 2 Corinthians 8:13-14 and 9:6-11? Those who blithely quote Philippians

4:19—"And my God shall supply all your needs"—should consider not only that this promise was given because they responded to Paul's need, but also whether the "you" in "your needs" is corporate. The church as a body may well have supply enough for all its needy. Even in the Old Testament God did not evenly distribute either physical or spiritual blessing. He looks for us to be the distributors—distributors of love.

When the gifts have served their purpose of building up one another in love, when there is no more hunger, no more suffering or tears, when all the instruction of Moses and teaching of Paul is swallowed up into perfect knowledge of God, one thing remains supreme—*love*.

**Completion of Torah: Moses and Jesus**

As the book of Deuteronomy closes, it throws a bouquet in Moses' direction:

> Since then no prophet has risen in Israel like Moses, whom the LORD knew face to face, who did all those miraculous signs and wonders the LORD sent him to do in Egypt—to Pharaoh and to all his officials and to his whole land. For no one has ever shown the mighty power or performed the awesome deeds that Moses did in the sight of all Israel (34:10-12).

Moses was the prophet *par excellence*.

Long after this comment, Judaism still believed that none had arisen greater than Moses. Yahweh had given Torah (law, instruction) through Moses.

Of course a replacement had been promised (18:14-22). And though the language is singular, the testing of prophets in the context clearly indicates that the raising up of a prophet could be expected regularly. The danger involved is well illustrated today—"prophets" who can barely manage to predict the sunrise (the event, not the time) still claim to be speaking God's instruction. One church in my locale has actually used 1 Corinthians 13:8 ("Where there be prophecies, they shall fail") to explain why their "prophets" regularly miss the mark.

Duly warned about false prophets, Israel looked for its prophets; but it judged that none matched Moses. Elijah was first runner-up.

The later prophets predicted an Elijah to announce the arrival of Yahweh and his day of refining and repentance (Malachi 3:1-4, 4:1-6), but the people still looked for the prophet to equal Moses. They asked John the Baptist, "Are you the Prophet?" (John 1:21). After seeing Jesus multiply the loaves and fishes, reminiscent of provision in the desert, they remarked: "Surely this is the Prophet who is to come into the world" (John 6:14). Following his other miracles and after hearing his teaching, some concluded: "Surely this man is the Prophet" (John 7:40).

But this same Gospel clears up the uncertainty:

> For the law was given through Moses; grace and truth came through Jesus Christ. No one [including Moses] has ever seen God, but God the only Son, who is at the Father's side, has made him known (John 1:17-18).

Moses, "the servant of God," cannot compete with "the only Son." Moses, who spoke with God directly, had not seen him fully. Yet the Son, who was in the beginning with God and was God, has truly revealed the Father. He is the Word—the revelation—of God. Jesus may say, "Anyone who has seen me has seen the Father" (John 14:9).

When the disciples witnessed that extraordinary meeting of Jesus with Moses and Elijah (Matthew 17:1-5), the cloud of glory once more appeared and the voice of God spoke: "This is my Son, whom I love; with him I am well pleased. Listen to him!" No need for Moses to stay. The God of Moses has sent his Son. Listen to his Torah (Deuteronomy 18:15).

## Completion of Land: "Inheriting The Earth"

David in Psalm 37 urges fellow Israelites not to worry about evil men who seem to be getting ahead in the land. To those fellow Israelites who always find themselves at the mercy of an unprincipled Philistine used cart dealer he advises:

> Trust in the LORD and do good;
> dwell in the land and enjoy safe pasture.
> Delight yourself in the LORD
> and he will give you the desires of your heart.
> (37:3-4)

He counsels them not to worry, but to wait; not to strike out in anger, but to watch for God to finally put things right.

> A little while, and the wicked will be no more;
> though you look for them, they will not be found.
> But the meek will inherit the land
> and enjoy great peace (37:10-11).

Perhaps you recognize that last verse as a New Testament passage. Jesus placed it in the middle of his list of blessings or beatitudes (Matthew 5:5). He was speaking to his disciples to encourage them. Even more so than in David's time, those committed to faithfulness to God had fallen on hard times. Pagan Rome held sway over David's Jerusalem. All was not right. Many Israelites, like the father of John the Baptist, looked for God

> to rescue us from the hand of our enemies,
> and to enable us to serve him without fear
> in holiness and righteousness before him all
> our days (Luke 1:74-75).

Yet the righteous person committed to God does not grab for all he can get. He yearns after the righteous order that God had promised in the land. Jesus says, "He will get it."[16] These descriptions in Matthew 5 are not of different people—one who is poor in spirit, one who is gentle, one who is pure in heart—but are various descriptions from the Old Testament for the righteous person committed to Yahweh. They look ahead to the final installation of peace on earth. Those who are afflicted and brokenhearted—poor in spirit—will receive news of freedom from captivity (Isaiah 61:1). Those who mourn will be comforted because the long exile is over (Isaiah 61:1-2, 40:1-2). Those who hunger and thirst for what really counts will find it (Isaiah 55:1-7).

Is there a new world coming? Yes, there is. In fact, its life is already available. Those who have put their trust in Jesus as God's deliverer already have "eternal life" (John 10:28, 3:36). They are members of the kingdom (Colossians 1:13). They await the return of Christ to see the full implementation of his deliverance, which has come not just for Israel, but for the whole world.[17] "Christ was sacrificed once to take away the sins of many people; and he will appear a second time, not to bear sin, but to bring salvation to those who are waiting for him" (Hebrews 9:28).

**But Until Then?**

We purchased our first house while I was still in seminary. It was a good buy. It put our rent money to use, and in the expanding housing market of the early seventies it sold quickly when we were ready to move on. Moving into that house in Irving, Texas, gave us a sense of permanence. We had a place of our own. That purchase, however, also brought into jarring perspective several Scriptures.

> By faith he [Abraham] made his home in the promised land like a stranger in a foreign country; he lived in tents, as did Isaac and Jacob, who were heirs with him of the same promise. For he was looking forward to the city with foundations, whose architect and builder is God (Hebrews 11:9-10).

Here was a man who never lived in a city with foundations and walls, but in tents. Here was a man whose accommodations showed his faith. He wasn't taking.

He was waiting. The testimony of Hebrews 11:13-14 is significant:

> "All these people were still living by faith when they died. They did not receive the things promised; they only saw them and welcomed them from a distance. And they admitted that they were aliens and strangers on earth. People who say such things show that they are looking for a country of their own."

The New Testament sees believers today as in a similar position to the patriarchs. It is a better position (Hebrews 11:40) because Christ has come and provided redemption, the forgiveness of sins. We have seen the time of fulfillment begin. But we are aliens and pilgrims, for we have "an inheritance that can never perish, spoil or fade—kept in heaven" while we await "the coming of the salvation that is ready to be revealed in the last time" (1 Peter 1:4-5). We are "aliens and strangers in the world" (2:11). Our position is more like Abraham and Israel in the desert than it is like Israel in the land. We are citizens of a kingdom that has not yet been revealed in its fullness.

1 Peter 2:11—3:12 gives instructions on how to live life as an alien. It involves real down-to-earth options. Nothing esoteric here. As C.S. Lewis once observed, it is precisely those who are heavenly minded who are the most earthly good:

> If you read history you will find that the Christians who did most for the present world were just those who thought the most of the next. . . . It is since Christians have largely ceased to think of the other world that they have become so ineffective in this. Aim at Heaven and you will get earth 'thrown in'; aim at earth and you will get neither.[18]

The principle for believers today is: Use the things

of this world, but avoid being entangled in them, because "this world in its present form is passing away" (1 Corinthians 7:31). We may not be limited to living in tents, but our lifestyle should reflect our faith.

The choice: Will we be part of the Now Generation . . . or will we live for the future Kingdom?

# FOR PERSONAL INTERACTION & DISCUSSION

SUGGESTED SCRIPTURE READINGS:

Deuteronomy 6 and 8
Mark 12:28-34
Matthew 5:1-16

1. Why is loving the land such a danger? Who owned the land? What attitudes toward possessions either enhance or diminish love for God today?
2. How does the covenant form of Deuteronomy help to emphasize God's love and grace in his making Israel a nation? How is the idea of love (for God or from God) in Deuteronomy different from either romantic or situational ideas of love today?
3. Why is Yahweh's uniqueness important? Is Christ's uniqueness equally important? How does the comparison of Jesus and Moses stress Christ's uniqueness? What makes him greater than Moses?
4. Why is memory important to faith? Can historic events be part of our own "memory" and understanding of who we are? Would Valley Forge, Gettysburg, and Pearl Harbor be part of the "memory" of an American? What events are most important to your spiritual understanding of your relationship to God?
5. What lessons on parenting are found in Deuteronomy? What are the pluses and minuses of "quality time"? How can Deuteronomy 6:4-5 be practiced in fast-paced, modern society?
6. What sins cause the loss of the land? How do these sins stack up in our culture?
7. What marks the difference between pagan offerings and offerings to Israel's God? How does this relate to bargaining with God?

8. How does a believer live as an "alien and pilgrim"? How should his outlook toward the future relate to his life at present?

PART

3.

# STRUGGLE FOR CONSISTENCY

'THERE IS A BETTER WAY TO LEARN THAN BY HARD EXPERIENCE: *LEARNING BY GODLY HERITAGE*. WALKING IN GOD'S WELL-DEFINED WAYS AVOIDS A LOT OF HEARTACHE.'

CHAPTER

# 9.

# LIVING BY FAITH

## GOD'S RULE IN JOSHUA & JUDGES

"Tibet—a land of contrasts." So reads the travel guide. If travel guides and documentaries are any indication, *most* countries on earth are lands of contrast. One thinks of our own purple mountain majesties and amber waves of grain.

The next biblical books also are lands of contrast. Both chronicle Israel's history in the land prior to the monarchies of Saul and David—but no two books could be so different.

*Joshua is upbeat and joyful.*
Judges is discouraging and depressing.

*Joshua faces difficulties and solves them.*
Judges encounters difficulties and compounds them.

*In Joshua the leader is faithful.*
In Judges the leaders are increasingly inconsistent.

Both books, however, operate on the same principles. These principles begin by recognizing Yahweh as exclusive Sovereign. Everything else follows predictably from there. It's all in the guidebook already provided by Moses. Are you ready for the travelogue?

## THE STRATEGY OF THE BOOK OF JOSHUA

The book of Joshua is laid out according to the strategy of Israel's military campaigns. Joshua's first military goal was to establish Israel in Canaan by taking the whole land, breaking the back of the opposition, and eliminating major political centers. The list of conquered kings and cities in Joshua 12 marks the completion of this effort.

The rest of the book takes up phase two. Having achieved control over Canaan, the land is divided and territory given to each tribe. It is the duty of each tribe to remove the smaller pockets of resistance and finally settle the entire area.

This distinctive strategy is key to understanding the book. Without recognizing this two-stage program, many of the book's statements seem contradictory. For instance, the land is said to have been totally taken by Joshua (11:23), and yet the Lord may say to Joshua: "There are still very large areas of land to be taken over" (13:1). In Joshua 21:44 we read, "The LORD handed all their enemies over to them," and yet in 23:5 Joshua relays to Israel this promise concerning the conquered nations: "God himself *will* drive them out of your way."

The major campaigns of the book's first half also show a distinctive pattern. Jericho and Ai in the center of the land are taken first (6—8). Israel then faces a military confederacy made up of kings to the south. This warfare is triggered by the sly and desperate Gibeonites, who against all odds find a way of changing sides, but then are attacked by their former confederates. With spectacular divine aid, Joshua defeats this southern coalition (9—10). Finally, the great city of Hazor in the north attempts to establish an alliance capable of stopping Israel. The destruction of this formidable force brings to an end any effective military opposition within the land (chapter 11).

Spliced in between these campaigns is the renewal of the covenant at Mount Ebal (8:30-35), as commanded by Moses (Deuteronomy 27). This ceremony reconfirms their commitment to Yahweh as King. The one giving them the land is the God they will follow and obey.

One other feature of the first half of Joshua also is critical: Like a daughter's marriage, there is almost as much importance given to preparation as to execution (no pun intended!). The first five chapters of the book are all preparation. As we shall see, however, they are not incidental. They are vital for communicating the true significance of God's activities.

## UNDERSTANDING JOSHUA AND JUDGES

### God Acting to Accomplish His Plan

As we said earlier, God announced his plan of reversal with Abraham. Beginning with the Exodus, God actively moved to fulfill those promises. He delivered Israel from Egypt. He made her into a great nation. He brought her through the desert, providing for and protecting her. Her recent military victories over Sihon and Og on the east side of the Jordan gave concrete assurance of God's ability.

Were it not for the sheer fear of it, the Israelites on the border of Canaan would feel like kids on Christmas Eve—alive with anticipation, unable to sleep, gloriously expectant. Israel is about to possess the land promised to Abraham, Isaac, and Jacob (Joshua 1:6).

Now the God of Israel no longer works slowly behind the scenes, as in the days of slavery in Egypt; for Joshua and Israel he is gloriously public in fulfilling his promise. In this book the Jordan dries up, perfectly timed to the entrance of the ark-bearing priests into the stream. The walls of Jericho fall in unison with the blast of trumpets and shouts of the people, after they ceremoniously circle the city for a week (Joshua 6). The southern confederation of Amorites is defeated when God sends hailstones and answers Joshua's prayer for extended light (Joshua 10).[1]

These events prove to this first generation of landed Israelites that they are Yahweh's people. They now have their own "Red Sea" experience. Their deliverance *and* their land have been provided by God.

They are further prepared by a series of ceremonies as soon as they enter the land. Circumcision is the first. It would certainly be better military strategy to circumcise all the men while the Jordan still separated them from Jericho. Ask Shechem (Genesis 34). But this ceremony is performed *inside* the land (Joshua 5:1-9). This generation had not been circumcised during its travels in the wilderness. A hint at the reason is given in 5:9—"Today I have rolled away the reproach of Egypt from you." The first generation was faithless in wanting to go back to Egypt, but this generation starts now with a clean slate. Circumcision shows that they recognize the covenant with Abraham (Genesis 17:14). If they are to be Yahweh's people, they must be circumcised.

Second, they observe Passover (5:10). The conquest was timed to parallel the Exodus. *What an anniversary celebration!* Just as Israel had been delivered from Egypt, so God would give her the land.

The next preparation may be labeled a non-event. They sample the produce of the land, and the manna stops (5:12). Remember the lesson of the manna in Deuteronomy 8? Manna in the wilderness was evidence that God was their provider. The provision of food through the more "natural" processes of the land is to be taken as no less a divine blessing. "I Did It My Way" must never enter the Israelite hymnbook.

The observances do not stop there. The first battle itself is a ceremony. For *seven* days *seven* priests march around the city blowing trumpets, carrying the ark of the covenant. On the *seventh* day they circle Jericho no less than *seven* times. Enough sevens for you? If you ask the average Bible reader the significance of seven, he will tell you it is the number of completion. But such abstract notions fail to see the concrete meaning of the text.

How many days are in a week? Where did the Bible first introduce us to the seventh day? The seventh day was the sabbath to be kept as a mark of the Mosaic Covenant (Exodus 31:14-17, 20:8-11). It was the day the true God of creation, having finished that work, rested (Genesis 2:3). Israel's sabbath observance, therefore, declared her the nation of the true Creator God. The numbers here are not mystical, but practical. Taking Jericho is a sacred activity, showing who is God of all the earth.

Jericho is also the *firstfruits* of the land. Just as the first of the crop was Yahweh's, so the first of the cities—with all its livestock and plunder—is his also. *Later* God allows Israel to keep plundered goods and cattle (Joshua 8:2).[2]

Yahweh acts in history to achieve his purpose. At each new step in his program, he miraculously vindicates his message so its significance is not lost (cf. Hebrews 2:1-4).[3] Yahweh could have promised Israel the land, ferried her across the Jordan and had her attack Jericho by normal military strategy. But this might have left a garbled message about the conquest. "Weren't those Jews lucky?" would have been as plausible an opinion as "Yahweh is God of all the earth."

### Moses' Instruction Revisited

If the concerns Moses emphasized on the border of the land were important then, they are doubly important now. Like a good piano sonata there has been a change in movement, but major themes keep appearing.[4]

*Land and Rest.* As in Deuteronomy, the land is an "inheritance" (Joshua 11:23, 23:4-5) given to them by Yahweh (Joshua 1:3-5, 23:16). This partially fulfills the promise to Abraham, Isaac, and Jacob (Joshua 1:6). If Israel obeys, the result will be "rest" (Joshua 21:44-45, 23:1). But if she is unfaithful, God will destroy her from "this good land he has given" (23:15-16).

*Memory.* While experiences of *previous* generations were to be passed on as reminders of God's faithfulness, this generation has its own experience worthy of a special memorial—the crossing of the Jordan on dry ground. Twelve stones are set up to commemorate the event.[5] If the Israelites are to be continuing landholders, they must be continuing teachers. There is a better way to learn than by hard experience—*learning by godly heritage.*[6] By communicating both positive and negative lessons, each succeeding generation will see that the fear of the Lord is truly the beginning of wisdom. Walking in God's well-defined ways avoids a lot of heartache.

*Covenant Obedience.* The book of Joshua is upbeat. Judges is downbeat. This major difference is due to one man, Joshua, who complies with God's instruction to "be careful to obey all the law my servant Moses gave you" (Joshua 1:7). Consistently throughout the book, Joshua shows himself a man of obedience.

The Law of Moses becomes Joshua's constant meditation. One caution here: Meditation in Scripture must not be confused with altered mental states so popular today. Joshua is not trying to sit on the ceiling and pretend he's a golf ball. Meditation for Joshua means a thoughtful study and review of God's instruction so he can put it into practice at the proper time (Joshua 1:8).

Joshua 1:1-9, repeating much of what was recorded in Deuteronomy, anticipates the flow of the book. God's chosen leader, Joshua, gives close attention to the Law (meditates), keeps it totally (turns neither to the right or to the left), and secures the land promised to Israel (good success).[7]

The inspired penman plants a green flag of obedience over and over in the text as he marks how Joshua obeys the Law of Moses (4:10, 8:31, 8:33, 11:12, 11:15, 11:18-20, 11:23, 14:2, 14:5, 14:6-14, 17:4, 20:2-7, 21:1-3, 21:8). Even in "small matters" where the writer does not remind us—such as not allowing a body to hang on a tree overnight (Joshua 10:26, Deuteronomy 21:23)—Joshua is obedient.

Two clear cases of disobedience mar the book of Joshua: the sin of Achan (chapter 7), who takes booty from Jericho which the Lord had claimed as exclusively his; and making a treaty with the deceitful

Gibeonites (chapter 9). The first is neither Joshua's sin nor the rest of Israel's, though it threatens their success. The second sin is inadvertent, though it could have been avoided with more care (9:14). In neither case is the sin allowed to continue and become a pattern.

To Joshua, covenant obedience focused on loving the Lord, just as it did with Moses:[8]

> But be very careful to keep the commandment and the law that Moses the servant of the LORD gave you: to love the LORD your God, to walk in all his ways, to obey his commands, to hold fast to him and to serve him with all your heart and all your soul (Joshua 22:5).

*Rebellion and Land.* Joshua, like Moses, reminds his people that they are still under the threat of cursing should they depart from the Lord (Joshua 23:14-16). They have been blessed under Joshua. In spite of possessing the land, they could call down God's wrath upon themselves.

> If you violate the covenant of the LORD your God, which he commanded you, and go and serve other gods and bow down to them, the LORD's anger will burn against you, and you will quickly perish from the good land he has given you (23:16).

Joshua also warns them about their tendency to rebelliousness.[9]

> You are not able to serve the LORD. He is a holy God; he is a jealous God. He will not forgive your rebellion and your sins. If you forsake the LORD and serve foreign gods, he will turn and bring disaster on you and make an end of you, after he has been good to you (Joshua 24:19).

It is not complexity of commands that will trip them; their own tendency to idolatry will bring down on them Yahweh's jealousy.

## Yahweh Is a Warrior

The notion that God fights for Israel is not original with the book of Joshua. The Exodus itself demonstrated that Yahweh was Israel's military deliverer. Faced with Pharaoh's forces, the people were told, "Yahweh will fight for you; you need only to be still" (Exodus 14:14). The "Song of the Sea" celebrated the victory (15:3):

> Yahweh is a warrior;
> Yahweh is his name.

In Deuteronomy we saw that Yahweh's uniqueness included fighting for Israel. This fighting meant absolute victory and destruction of Yahweh's enemies:

> See now that I myself am He!
>   There is no god besides me.
> I put to death and I bring to life,
>   I have wounded and I will heal,
>   and no one can deliver from my hand.
> I lift my hand to heaven and declare:
>   As surely as I live forever,
> when I sharpen my flashing sword
>   and my hand grasps it in judgment,
> I will take vengeance on my adversaries
>   and repay those who hate me.
> I will make my arrows drunk with blood,
>   while my sword devours flesh:
> the blood of the slain and the captives,
>   the heads of the enemy leaders
>
> (Deuteronomy 32:39-42).

It is Yahweh who will drive out the enemy, encouraging Israel with the shout, "Destroy him!" (Deuteronomy 33:27).

Not only does Deuteronomy assure Israel that Yahweh will fight for her and drive out her enemies, it gives specific instructions on how to wage war:

- The priest initiates the war by reminding them that Yahweh fights for them.

This clearly shows the war's sacred character (20:2-4).[10]

- Cities outside the land need not be entirely destroyed, but attacks on cities inside the land require destruction of all life (20:10-18). This practice is known as the "ban" or *herem*. To put a city under the ban was to devote its occupants to Yahweh for destruction. It is often translated "completely destroyed" or "devoted" (Deuteronomy 20:17, 2:34, 7:2; Joshua 6:17, 8:26).[11] The military camp is to maintain a state of holiness (Deuteronomy 23:9-14), as defined in Leviticus.
- They are specifically to show no pity to inhabitants of the land (Deuteronomy 7:1-2). These wars cannot be explained as cases where man's sinful violence is used by God to accomplish his purpose.[12] God believes they will not want to fully carry out his directions. He warns against pity.

Why does God insist on total destruction or *ḥerem*? Because he doesn't want his favorites to share the land with anyone? No. His "favorite," Abraham, never possessed the land because the inhabitants had not yet reached a level of depravity that *required* their removal (Genesis 15:16). God is not partial. When Israel reaches the same level of immorality, he will treat them in exactly the same way (Leviticus 18:24-28).

So this war of total destruction is first of all a final judgment of God against these nations. God has always reserved this right of judgment. Those who object to it here would object, no doubt, to the Flood (Genesis 6—7) and to the destruction of Sodom and Gomorrah (Genesis 19). This judgment on the Canaanites continues the theme of God as Moral Governor of the universe.[13]

Yet isn't this situation in Joshua different in that human beings—rather than the elements of nature—are the agents of destruction? No doubt this is true. But rulers of state are also required to carry out God's moral laws and punish evildoers (Romans 13:4). So David, as God's king, promises to eliminate the wicked (Psalm 101:8).

Like a child sent to get his own paddle, Israel, by being the instrument of God's moral judgment on the Canaanite nations, is graphically taught its need to obey Yahweh, who indeed is God of the whole earth. And God takes his duties seriously! Israel is warned that failure to remove this cancer of wickedness would eventually bring her own infection and judgment (Deuteronomy 7:1-6, 20:18).

But now let us move from theory to practice. The book of Joshua keys its notion of success to this practice of *ḥerem*. Jericho (6:17, 21), Ai (8:1-2, 26-27), the kings and cities of the southern region (10:25-40), and Hazor and its allies (11:8-14) all receive this radical judgment. Joshua's obedience prompts Yahweh to fight for Israel (10:40-42). And it *is* Yahweh who fights. Before the warfare begins, in a scene reminiscent of Moses at the burning bush, Joshua comes face to face with the commander of the army of Yahweh (5:13-15). *He* will bring victory—not the puny army of Joshua.

At Jericho, Israel is warned that if she does not practice *ḥerem*, she herself will be *ḥerem*—under God's judgment (6:18). At Ai she fights without Yahweh's help because Achan failed to observe the ban. Thirty-six men perish . . . and Joshua is absolutely devastated (Joshua 7). Why? Is thirty-six a high number of men to lose in battle? It apparently is in Yahweh's wars. We search in vain for other casualties.

Another violation of the ban occurs in Joshua 9. The Gibeonites deceive Israel into thinking they are from a distant country. A treaty is made, but three days later the truth is discovered. Caught by their own negligence (9:14), they have already violated the ban by making such a treaty in the Lord's name. Instead, they put the Gibeonites into service to the Levites—"devoting" them to the Lord as nearly as they now can.[14]

Rahab also stands as an exception to the ban. The spies, rightly or wrongly, buy their own protection with a promise of safety for this woman who believes "Yahweh your God is God in heaven above and on the earth below" (2:11-14). Joshua honors this agreement (Joshua 6:17). Like the Canaanite woman who believed strongly enough to press past Jesus' initial refusal (Matthew 15:21-28), Rahab stands as a memorial to a faith not often found in Israel. Could Jesus refuse mercy to such a person when Rahab herself is found in his own family tree (Matthew 1:5)?

Israel under Joshua stands as a memorial to obedience (Joshua 24:31). Because of that commitment to Yahweh, Joshua is able to say at the end of his life, "No one has been able to withstand you. One of you routs a thousand, because the LORD your God fights for you, just as he promised" (23:9-10).

The tragedy of the rest of Israel's history is that no other generation matches this one.

## Deterioration of Commitment in Judges

If the book of Joshua is a flowing stream, fresh and invigorating with direction and power, then in Judges the river turns sluggish and muddy, its polluted water ultimately spiraling down a storm drain.

Judges teaches the same principles Joshua did. But it teaches them as "lessons from the woodshed." Rather than the thrill of victory, the generations living in the time of the judges experience all too often the agony of defeat.

The book starts at the close of Joshua's era, giving a brief but telling overview of progress in taking the land (1:1—2:5). Close to Joshua's own time, there is success.[15] Judah succeeds initially (1:1-18), but later is unable to drive out those who live on the plains and possess chariots (1:19). She practices *ḥerem* (1:8,17), but does she practice it consistently (1:6-7)? Defeats begin to alternate with victories. Bethel is taken and put to the sword (1:22-25), but the tribe of Manasseh is unsuccessful (1:27). When Israel becomes strong she makes slaves of the Canaanites rather than eliminating them (1:28-36). Economics have taken on a higher priority than obedience!

The divine messenger announces the climax to all this "partial obedience" in 2:1-5. Like the proverbial rose, disobedience by any other name smells the same—especially to God. Because Israel has made treaties with the people of the land, God will not remove these nations. Israel will face the result of her sin by daily facing temptation to false worship.

Having given us the bad news, the writer begins again at Joshua's time (2:6-9) and gives us *more* bad news. His concern this time, and through the bulk of the book (chapters 2—16), is to trace in detail the period of the judges and the reasons for Israel's failure to make any progress at fully taking the land.

The writer's theme is not subtle. He announces it clearly (2:10—3:4), then illustrates it with stories of judges and oppressors. To put it bluntly, Israel begins to worship other gods. Oh, they retain Yahweh as one among many; but to the Lord this is the same as forsaking him. The first commandment required worship of Yahweh *alone.*

Their unfaithfulness means Yahweh will not fight for them. In fact, they are under the curse announced by Moses (Judges 2:15, Deuteronomy 28:25). Even when Yahweh provides judges to deliver them, disobedience grows worse following each judge's death (2:18-19).

The conclusion here is the same as in the introductory overview. The Lord will not remove the pagan nations from Canaan because of Israel's disobedience. Now every future generation will have the opportunity to prove whether it will obey as Joshua did (2:20-23), giving exclusive allegiance to Yahweh and obeying him in warfare (3:1-4). Judges 2:23 even hints that Joshua's generation was not allowed to take the full country so that more than one generation would have to be faithful before the land would be totally occupied.[16]

The repetitive and sinfully boring cycle of the book of Judges may be summarized as follows:

SIN: Disobedience to the first commandment by Israel.
SERVITUDE: The nation loses its freedom to its enemies.
SUPPLICATION: Israel cries to Yahweh for deliverance.
SALVATION: Israel is delivered and enjoys temporary peace.[17]

It is not simply that Israel's history goes nowhere. It goes downhill (2:19).

Note the character of the judges themselves. The first is Othniel (3:7-11). He delivers Israel from an outside oppressor. His history is brief, but all we know about him is positive (1:12-14).

From there we move to Ehud, who is brave but who certainly does not go about war in the normal way (3:12-30).

Deborah provides a positive note (chapter 4), but her military commander, Barak, is hesitant to act without her continual support. For his hesitancy, though the Lord gives a mighty victory, Barak is deprived of the honor of capturing the opposing general, Sisera.

The chapters on Gideon illustrate more the Lord's mercy and patience than the quality of the leader (Judges 6—8). Gideon needs sign after sign. His "fleeces" clearly test God's patience. These do not "discover" God's will, but rather are given to encourage a man weak in faith. Under God's careful nurturing, Gideon is finally able to lead a force of only three hundred men in destroying the Midianites, demonstrating how Yahweh desired to fight for Israel.

Deterioration sets in again after Gideon (8:33—10:10). By this time the Lord announces he is tired of delivering Israel only to be forsaken afterward. He will no longer deliver them (10:11-14). The Israelites repent and get rid of their idols (10:15-16).

The last full accounts of judges are those of Jephthah in the east and Samson in the west. Jephthah is not chosen directly by the Lord like earlier judges. Instead, with no promise of deliverance, the leaders of Israel ask Jephthah to be their military commander against the Ammonites (11:4-6). He wants to be recognized as judge if he is victorious (11:7-11). The Lord finally comes to Israel's aid by empowering Jephthah. His history ends, however, with the loss of his daughter and civil war with Ephraim.[18]

While Jephthah delivers east of the Jordan, Samson became judge in the west (Judges 13—16).[19] The writer gives more space to Samson than to any other judge. He was chosen to be judge before birth, so his beginnings rival those of Samuel, Jeremiah, and John the Baptist. Certainly much should be expected from this man. But he is woefully disappointing. He regularly disregards the law, intermarries with the Philistines, and uses his delivering power to carry out acts of incidental vengeance.

God can move his "judge" to action only by stirring him up with personal disappointments in dealings with Philistines. And Samson never does deliver Israel. His last act is still one of personal revenge (16:28) in which God does not deliver even him! The final estimate that "he killed many more when he died than while he lived" is a sad commentary on his life. Even sadder is the fact that his earlier capture brought praise to Dagon which should have been Yahweh's: "Our god has delivered our enemy into our hands" (Judges 16:24).

Why spend so much time on Samson's failure? Because he climaxes the message of Judges. His life matches that of the nation itself. Samson, like Israel, had a special calling, but deserted it to pursue his own desires. His power, though great and bestowed by Yahweh, did not deliver because his life was marked by unfaithfulness to Yahweh and intermarriage with the nations of the land.[20]

In an appendix to the book (17—21), our writer gives another sample of the failure of the period. With two complex stories he illustrates the religious and civil confusion that results from ignoring and disobeying the Law. Rather than following the Law, "everyone did what was right in his own eyes" (17:6, 21:25 NASB).[21] The book of Judges concludes in total contrast to the beginning of Joshua. Joshua meditated on the Law, kept it, and had good success. Israel under the judges was inconsistent and ignorant in her practice of God's word—even in the most basic matters. Judges illustrates the futility and frustration caused by a lack of total commitment.[22]

## ON THE WAY: COMPLETION OF WAR AND REST

### Entering into Rest

The concept of *rest* summarizes the goal of Joshua, as Israel—faithful to the covenant—inherits the land, occupies it, and lives in blessing under Yahweh. The land is the same land promised to Abraham (Joshua 1:6).

This idea of rest is borrowed by the writer to the Hebrews as he exhorts his readers to follow Jesus. Jesus is greater than Moses and has become the author of our eternal salvation. Jesus will bring us into the glory God first planned for man by overcoming the barrier to that glory—death, the penalty for sin (Hebrews 2:9-10; 3:1-6).

But the writer fears that some of his readers, though they have heard the good news, will not be allowed to enter God's rest because of their rebellion (Hebrews 3:15, quoting Psalm 95). They may become like those who died in the desert, having sinful, unbelieving hearts (Hebrews 3:16-19). For hearing the message is not enough—it must be accepted by faith (4:1-2).

The author of Hebrews, like John Bunyan in his *Pilgrim's Progress*, sees believers as pilgrims on the way to rest. Those who truly believe will successfully make it through the pilgrimage and enter that rest (4:3).

But there is an apparent difficulty. Psalm 95 tells about the failure of the first generation under Moses, and calls on Israel in David's time to "kneel before the LORD our Maker"—so they may experience God's rest. Why is David offering the possibility of rest if Joshua has *already* given them rest? The answer of Hebrews: "If Joshua had given them rest, God would not have spoken later about another day. There remains, then, a Sabbath-rest for the people of God" (4:8-9).[23]

Earlier, the writer of Hebrews pointed out that God put everything under man, yet man never achieved perfect rule on earth. This rule awaits its fulfillment in Jesus (Hebrews 2:5-9). Now the writer points out that in spite of the success and "rest" of Joshua's generation, rest was never fully achieved—as our own study of Joshua shows. Actually, other temporary or partial experiences of rest occur later than Joshua (2 Samuel 7:1, 1 Kings 5:4), yet the full and continuous experience (2 Samuel 7:10-11) of the promise to Abraham was never accomplished.[24] That promised, undisturbed blessing of being Yahweh's people and enjoying Yahweh's rest is still a future, ultimate goal (Hebrews 4:11).[25]

We look for a heavenly country as did the patriarchs (Hebrews 11:15-16). Our promise brings us to Mount Zion, the heavenly Jerusalem, the city of the living God—where God is present along with myriads of angels and the spirits of righteous men awaiting resurrection. Jesus, who has made it all possible, is also there (12:22-24).

Abraham looked forward to this city "whose architect and builder is God" (11:10). And where was Abraham expecting this city? Hebrews 11:9 identifies the "promised land" as the very area he was tenting in![26] That Abraham was looking for a "heavenly country" does not mean he expected it to be extraplanetary! Hebrews 6:4 indicates some have tasted "the heavenly gift," but this gift is not *in* heaven. It is *from* heaven.[27] The Jews often used the word "heaven" to refer to God. To receive a heavenly city or a heavenly country is equivalent to saying its "architect and builder is God" (11:10). It has been prepared by God (11:16).

This already-prepared city will be a part of the New Creation, the new "heaven and earth" (Revelation 21:1-2).[28] With its coming, "rest" will be finally achieved in all its dimensions—for such rest was never possible apart from fellowship with God and loving him with all the heart, soul, and strength. This new cosmos will be characterized by righteousness (2 Peter 3:13). But the most important thing about this new city, country, and final rest is that we will finally have "come to God" . . . and "to Jesus" (Hebrews 12:23-24). "The dwelling of God is with men" (Revelation 21:3).

**Jesus Is a Warrior**

The completion of rest is achieved in the same way—though on a wider scale—as Yahweh commanded Joshua. Because of its "holy war," Joshua has not been a popular book:

> Many can remember how Joshua the warrior used to figure as a hero-saint in sermons and in Bible stories for the young. The present writer recalls a picture in a Bible for children portraying the general equipped with Greek helmet and a combination Greek and Roman suit of armor, kneeling before the Prince of the Lord's host in front of a very Roman-looking Jericho. That seemed quite as it should be! Today, however, Joshua presents a problem . . . . The present writer holds entirely with those who reject the War-God concept. To his mind God is not, and never was, what Joshua thought Him to

> be. He never led an armed force into Canaan, and He leads no armed force today.[29]

We can agree entirely with those who do not believe any nation on earth today is justified in taking territory and eliminating its inhabitants on the basis of a special call of God. Neither is the church today called to rule any physical land. The Christian college group which walked all around the campus of a secular university had, I hope, something else in mind besides walls falling down.

The New Testament, however, does predict a time of future warfare and judgment at the return of Christ. Just as God brought judgment in the Flood, and to Sodom and Gomorrah, and in ancient Canaan, so also has he promised judgment in the future. Judgment too must have its fulfillment.

The scene of Revelation 19:11-16 graphically portrays Jesus engaged in Holy War at his return.

> I saw heaven standing open and there before me was a white horse, whose rider is called Faithful and True. With justice he judges and makes war. His eyes are like blazing fire, and on his head are many crowns. He has a name written on him that no one but he himself knows. He is dressed in a robe dipped in blood, and his name is the Word of God. The armies of heaven were following him, riding on white horses and dressed in fine linen, white and clean. Out of his mouth comes a sharp sword with which to strike down the nations. "He will rule them with an iron scepter." He treads the winepress of the fury of the wrath of God Almighty. On his robe and on his thigh he has this name written: KING OF KINGS AND LORD OF LORDS.

In the battle that follows, all the troops of the kings of the earth "were killed with the sword that came out of the mouth of the rider on the horse" (19:21).

This is just what was requested by the martyrs who earlier called out to God: "How long, Sovereign Lord, holy and true, until you judge the inhabitants of the earth and avenge our blood?" (Revelation 6:10). Is it right for saints in God's presence to call for vengeance? Isn't this kind of vengeance an Old Testament concept which Jesus rejected in teaching us to love our enemies?

Not in the least. The New Testament teaches, like the Old, that vengeance belongs to God alone (Romans 12:19, Deuteronomy 32:35), and that we must "leave room for God's wrath." We are not to avenge ourselves. But God is just and holy in his judgments (Revelation 16:5-7). He is the Avenger.

> God is just: He will pay back trouble to those who trouble you and give relief to you who are troubled, and to us as well. This will happen when the Lord Jesus is revealed from heaven in blazing fire with his powerful angels. He will punish those who do not know God and do not obey the gospel of our Lord Jesus. They will be punished with everlasting destruction and shut out from the presence of the Lord and from the majesty of his power on the day he comes to be glorified in his holy people and to be marveled at among all those who have believed (2 Thessalonians 1:6-10).

*Then* Christ will rule. *Then* there will be rest. What a land of contrast!

# FOR PERSONAL INTERACTION & DISCUSSION

SUGGESTED SCRIPTURE READINGS:

Joshua 1:1-9
Judges 2:8—3:5
Hebrews 3:16—4:11, 11:8-16, and 12:22-29

1. What are each of the two parts of Joshua about? Why may the Lord have wanted each tribe to take its own territory? Were they successful?
2. What areas of disobedience characterize Judges, but not Joshua? In your estimation, how much of our own spiritual failure is due to direct disobedience, how much to difficult circumstances and trials, and how much to confusion over the will of God?
3. Do you think the failure during the period of the judges could have been avoided if God would have provided more supernatural occurrences, like the Jordan River crossing or the collapse of Jericho?
4. How does Samuel's judgeship illustrate the failure of being only half committed to God? Why does a life like this fail to bring honor to God?
5. How is the true Creator God celebrated and honored in the taking of Jericho?
6. What is the meaning of *meditation* in Scripture (as in Joshua 1:8)? What is the goal of meditation? How is the goal achieved?
7. How does the idea of "Yahweh Is a Warrior" tie in to divine justice? How will this idea of divine judgment have its fulfillment?
8. What does *rest* mean? Why is the need for peace and rest a commonly felt need among us? How is this need met by Jesus? How is rest related to fellowship with God? Is this true on a personal level as well?

'CREATIVITY IS NOT A VIRTUE WHEN USED TO TWIST TORAH. THE KING IS TO BE A STUDENT OF SCRIPTURE WITH A LOVE FOR ITS GOD-INTENDED INSTRUCTION. HE IS NOT TO BECOME A LOOPHOLE HUNTER WHO FINDS ARGUMENTS TO JUSTIFY HIS OWN DESIRES.'

CHAPTER

# 10.

# MODIFICATION TO MONARCHY

## A KING FROM AMONG YOUR OWN BROTHERS

It's being the last employee hired when the economy begins to slide.

It's motoring along a lonely stretch of road at night when the car starts to sputter.

It's discovering you're wearing your pajamas to church (a recurring dream I had as a youngster).

It's trying to steer with a vise-grip on the steering hub.

*It's insecurity.*

Helen Keller said about security, "It is mostly a superstition. Security does not exist in nature, nor do the children of men as a whole experience it. . . . Life is either a daring adventure or nothing."

We all like to hear rags-to-riches stories. But what we enjoy most is the "to riches" part. Vulnerability, like chicken pox, is given a wide berth.

The children of Israel felt vulnerable. As disjointed tribes they faced raiding parties from outside the land and settled, skilled enemies from within. The Philistines were better organized and better equipped than Israel.[1]

The system of judges had been tried and found wanting. Or more accurately, as G.K. Chesterton once said about the Christian ideal, it was "found difficult, and left untried."[2] Israel had operated under a pure theocracy on a national level. God directly intervened to raise up leaders for the whole nation when necessary.

The book of Samuel (First and Second Samuel to us) is about the move to monarchy—the change to kingship. Surprises are in store, however. No one ever invented a system of security apart from God. Even God can't. But then, he knows better than to try.

## SCOPING OUT SAMUEL

The book of Samuel is a repository of favorite Bible stories: the tale of Samuel's birth, the account of the Philistines' trouble when they capture the ark, the heroism and true friendship of Jonathan, and certainly the defeat of Goliath by the "boy" David. Often, however, these favorites have been torn from their surroundings. Treated as individual snapshots without regard to the total landscape, their larger significance often is missed.

After Judges we need a break. With an even dozen judges, it was hard to keep the players straight without a scorecard. In Samuel there are only three main participants: Samuel, Saul, and David. But don't dispense with the scorecard just yet—there are a number of lesser players who have a lot to do with the final score.

### The Barren Woman—1 Samuel 1-2

One of these participants is a barren woman, and with her the story opens. Here is a woman emotionally in rags. Though her husband loves her, he has taken another wife—no doubt because she has given him no children. Her rival mocks her, much as Hagar did Sarah. To put it in a word, Hannah feels *vulnerable*.

But this is just the kind of case in which God has shown his power in the past. He has produced a whole nation from a barren womb—in fact, from a whole succession of them (Genesis 11:30, 25:21, 29:31). Hannah's distress leads her to cry to the Lord and dedicate her offspring to exclusive service to him. This response—the response the Lord wanted from the whole nation—leads to the birth of the last judge: Samuel.

Hannah's experience and her prayer (2:1-10) exalt the Lord as the one who

> . . . raises the poor from the dust
> and lifts the needy from the ash heap;
> he seats them with princes
> and has them inherit a throne of honor (2:8).

The unique Lord of Israel *is* security. He is the Rock of safety. *"There is no Rock like our God"* (2:2).

**Samuel, Prophet and Judge—1 Samuel 3-7**

After that quick introduction to the Lord's ability to deliver, we are returned to the shocking reality of Israel's dismal state. This is nowhere more obvious than in the very center of Israel's worship of Yahweh—the tabernacle. Under current priest Eli and his boys, Samuel joins a situation at the Lord's tent which could not be more disgusting. Eli's sons violate the rules of sacrifice to satisfy their own tastes, threaten violence against faithful worshipers, and introduce Canaanite sexual abominations (2:12-17, 22-25).

In the midst of this loathsome disobedience, God raises his leader from infancy to manhood, marking Samuel's progress against the continuing failure of Eli's sons (2:11, 2:18-21, 2:26, 3:1-21).

We all are familiar with the story of Samuel sleeping in the tabernacle, hearing the voice of the Lord, and three times rousing Eli to ask what he wanted before finally being told to answer the Lord the next time. It is a dynamic and positive story for children, though I have since forgotten what direct relevance it could have for them. No doubt children are told that here was a good boy who did what he was told. Perhaps they are advised to consider that voices they hear might be from the Lord! Or, more likely: "Listen to God." But I fear that often the real significance of the event is missed.

This is not an incidental story, but the beginning of a great career. This is Samuel's first experience as a prophet of God. The fact that all of Samuel's words came true—remember the test for a true prophet—prompted Israel to recognize again that here was a prophet in their midst (3:19-21; cf. 3:1).

Not only is Samuel a prophet, but he becomes a judge. The capture of the ark and its history in Philistine territory (chapters 4—6) show that God does not need Israel to vindicate himself as the true God. Rather, *they need him*. With Eli and his sons dead, deliverance from the Philistines may begin. Samuel in his role as judge achieves one of those mighty deliverances in which Yahweh himself fights for Israel (chapter 7).

But now Samuel's final and most famous task begins—to take Israel into its monarchy. Samuel is God's kingmaker (chapters 8—12). Not that Samuel likes the job. He considers the elders' request for a king a personal slap in the face; worse than that, so does Yahweh (8:6-8, 12:13-19). Yet the idea of a king in Israel isn't new: Jacob predicted the rising of the king's ruling scepter in the tribe of Judah (Genesis 49:10), regulations for the king were given in Moses' handbook (Deuteronomy 17:14-20), and Hannah's prayer spoke of Yahweh strengthening his king (1 Samuel 2:10).

The people, however, request a king in a desire for visible security. They have no hope that Samuel's sons will follow as faithful judges (8:1-3), and they don't want to wait until the next invasion for a deliverer to arise. Better to have a permanent king who will fight their battles (8:19-20). Their failure to completely trust Yahweh for safety will mean higher taxes to support a defense complex, a costly central bureaucracy, and a draft to establish a standing army (8:10-18). What a price to pay for lack of faith!

Yet it is not an absolute evil, though these people ask out of evil motives. Yahweh will give them their king, and that king is Saul (1 Samuel 9-11). Saul seeks out the prophet to help him find his father's donkeys, and ends up with the throne.

### Saul as King

Saul is privately anointed, then publicly proclaimed by the Lord's direction. Like the judges before him, he is empowered by the Spirit of God to deliver from an oppressor (1 Samuel 11). This initial victory leads to complete acceptance of Saul as king.

Saul is a successful king. He defeats Israel's enemies, freeing them from outside oppression (14:47-48). He worships Yahweh, not idols (14:35, 15:31), and expels mediums and spiritists from Israel (28:3). David praises him for having brought economic prosperity as well (2 Samuel 1:24).

But our book is interested not so much in King Saul's general success as in why he and his line were removed from kingship. So 1 Samuel 13—15 focuses on two particular failures:

- not following instructions to wait for Samuel to offer a pre-battle sacrifice;[3]
- and not carrying out *ḥerem* against the Amalekites as commanded by the Lord through Samuel.

Both these failures show that Saul has a mistaken notion of kingship—one that Yahweh will not bear. The notion: that like other ancient kings, Israel's king would be an absolute monarch—that his rule would be law.

No, Israel already has a law given by God, not developed by the king. Also, Yahweh speaks through prophets. That word is higher than the king. Moses specifically warned about the king considering himself above the Law (Deuteronomy 17:18-20). Rather, like Joshua, the king was to be a student of the Law that he might obey it. Torah is higher than king. Prophet is higher than king. Both are Yahweh's instruction.[4]

For Saul's first disobedience to Samuel's instruction, Saul loses the right to pass on the kingship to his sons (13:13-14). At his second failure to carry out orders, he loses his own right to the throne (15:26).[5]

**David as King**

Because Saul no longer is God's choice for king, Samuel immediately anoints David (16:1-13). Not only that, the Spirit who empowers the king comes upon David and leaves Saul (16:13-14).

*King without a Throne: 1 Samuel 16—31.* David, though unknown publicly as king, begins to carry out his task. Why the story of David and Goliath? For David, like Saul and the judges before him, divine appointment is proven by a great delivery. *That* is what the story of David and Goliath is all about. It is about faith—but the faith of Israel's new and unknown king, rather than a little boy who has enough faith to go around killing giants like an Old Testament Jack-and-the-Beanstalk.

The old king, no longer empowered by God, is not leading his nation into battle and expecting great deliverances. He is huddling in his tent, trying to figure out a way to answer the challenge of Goliath. He is willing to try even a strapping youth (not a little boy) who rejects the tall Saul's armor, not because it is too big, but because he is not used to it.

David wins his initial victory as king but no one recognizes its full significance. David's continuing success, however, alerts Saul to the truth (18:5-8). When David does not die in battle against great odds, Saul tries to kill David directly. The rest of 1 Samuel finds Saul chasing David around the wilderness of Judah. It is a time for David to learn security in the midst of vulnerability (Psalm 4:8). Saul becomes increasingly unstable as he tries to fight against the word of judgment through Samuel.[6]

*David as the Model King: 2 Samuel 1—10.* After Saul's death, David is quickly anointed king over Judah. Saul's surviving son reigns over the rest of the tribes, but the real power behind his throne is his general, Abner. David conducts this struggle without animosity. He laments the deaths of Saul and Jonathan (2 Samuel 1). He congratulates the men of Jabesh Gilead who rescued Saul's body from further dishonor (2:4-7). He punishes the murderers of Saul's son who thought David would reward them (chapter 4). The one blot on his record is the death of Abner who was visiting to arrange terms of peace (3:12-37).

When Jimmy Carter was president, the press loved to call his contingent of advisers "The Georgia Mafia" because of the number of former associates he brought to Washington from his home state. The writer of 2 Samuel clearly explains that a "Bethlehem Mafia" surrounds David. Most readers miss it, however, because they don't recognize the names.

For instance, who is Zeruiah (2:18)? No, Zeruiah is not a man's name, but the name of David's sister (1 Chronicles 2:13-16). The three "sons of Zeruiah" are David's nephews. Joab is one of these. He has fought for David in the wilderness and has become David's general. Though totally loyal to David (and to himself—we are never sure in which order), Joab with his brother are a challenge for the king throughout the book. The king often sees them as thorns in his royal side (3:39, 16:10, 19:22). Joab's murder of Abner incenses David. He calls a curse on Joab's house and personally mourns the death. Somehow he is able to avoid a "Davidgate" crisis as the rest of Israel recognizes that Abner's death was Joab's personal vendetta and did not involve the king.[7]

After being anointed king over all Israel, David scores immediate successes against Israel's enemies. He conquers the secure Jebusites at Jerusalem and whips the Philistines, who take their best shot at nipping this rising monarch before he blooms (5:6-25).

David establishes Jerusalem as his capital and moves the ark of the covenant there. His desire to build a permanent temple for the Lord is refused, but he receives a promise that more than compensates for the immediate disappointment (chapter 7). Yahweh gives David more military successes (8:1-14, 10:1-19), and David does what is "just and right for all his people" (8:15). This includes even the house of Saul and Jonathan, as David seeks to show kindness to their remaining heir (chapter 9).

*A Sword in David's House: 2 Samuel 11—20.* The inspired account of David's faithfulness and the blessing of God comes to a screeching standstill in chapter 11. The story of David's reign now turns on the noisy hinge of David's monstrous sin. Ask any pagan about King David and the immediate association will be "Bathsheba." Though David establishes a rule of justice unexcelled in future generations, his name will live in infamy for this startling succession of sins against Yahweh.

Nothing is held back from us in this chapter. God's record is honest. David's sin was not a sudden slip, but a conscious decision. He saw her bathing—an innocent enough accident, given the geography of Jerusalem and the height of the king's palace. But he inquires. He sends for her. He sleeps with her. Here David has taken to himself the rights of an absolute monarch and violated the Law. He has coveted another man's wife and committed adultery with her (Exodus 20:14,17, Deuteronomy 5:18,21).

In time she informs David that she is pregnant. A practical problem develops. Her husband, Uriah, has been out fighting David's wars and will know the baby is not his. David develops a series of plans to cover his sin.

*Plan #1*: Call Uriah home from battle. He will sleep with his wife. When the baby comes he will believe it is a bit premature. This plan fails because Uriah's sense of duty puts David's to shame. Uriah will not play when his comrades are still in the field.

*Plan #2*: Get him drunk. Uriah's sense of duty will be lowered and he will go home. Failure again: Even drunk he is more honorable than David.

*Plan #3*: Have him die in battle. Then David will marry Bathsheba and not be discovered. This plot is successful only because it depends on Uriah's honor: He carries his own death message to the front and never takes a peek. David's nephew Joab can be counted on to keep the secret.

There it is—the raw power of the typical ancient king whose word is law.[8] "But the thing David had done displeased Yahweh" (2 Samuel 11:27). God's verdict is short and stunning.

God sends the prophet Nathan to the king to arouse that deep sense of justice which in David had been derailed. In the case of a rich man stealing a poor man's only lamb so the rich man wouldn't have to cut into his own reserves, David sees the issue clearly. He bursts out with the self-condemning verdict, "The man who did this deserves to die!"

This fierce indignation evaporates when he learns *he* is the rich man. Had David lived in the twentieth century his rationalization no doubt would be, "We couldn't help ourselves. God wants us to be happy, doesn't he?" But he acknowledges his guilt.

God decides not to kill David, but the sword will now interrupt the peace of his house. The sacredness of his own marriages will be violated. His sin was secret. His penalty will be public (2 Samuel 12:7-12).[9]

The sword touches the rest of David's reign (chapters 13—20). The happy blessedness of rule is gone. With this sin David has lost all control over his own family—for what can he say to his sons when their lusts run rampant?

Amnon wants his half-sister Tamar and gives in to his lust. Absalom, brother of Tamar, takes revenge by killing Amnon. Absalom's desire for revenge probably is heightened by the fact that Amnon is firstborn. Absalom has his eye on the throne, and sees himself as next in line. Not willing to wait, he attempts a coup against his father. He is initially successful, but a civil war ensues in which Absalom loses his life. As David grieves over Absalom, he wishes instead that his own life had been demanded for his sin:

> O, my son Absalom! My son, my son Absalom!
> If only I had died instead of you—
> O Absalom, my son, my son! (18:33).

*Final Matters: 2 Samuel 21—24.* To round out David's reign, other events and records are added at the story's end.[10] Two psalms are included here, both celebrating Yahweh as the Rock, much as Hannah did at the beginning. The king learns that his strength is not in his standing army (chapter 22), but in Yahweh the deliverer.

The second of these psalms (23:1-7) constitutes David's last words. It focuses on two truths: the beauty of a righteous reign, and the promise of God to David for a continuing dynasty. There are the pillars of Israel's kingship.

## THE CONCERNS OF SAMUEL

### The Nature of Kingship

The people were premature in demanding a king. Their motives had been evil. But the choice of Saul was God's opportunity to make the main point right at the beginning. Israel's king was a sub-regent: a ruler under God. Yahweh is Israel's king and always had been (1 Samuel 12:12). The human ruler was, in fact, no more than a permanent judge over all Israel. Like the judge, the king was directly selected by God and was vindicated by victory over Israel's oppressors. The king was, therefore, not an absolute monarch. He was subject to Yahweh's word. No matter how great the pressure, no matter how fine the rationalization (and Saul makes us feel sorry for him on both counts), kingship demanded obedience.

By making clear with the very first king that this principle was not to be qualified or compromised, Yahweh etched into Israel's history a lesson for all future kings. They are implementers of law, not originators. Creativity is not a virtue when used to twist Torah. The king is to be a student of Scripture with a love for its God-intended instruction. He is not to become a loophole hunter who finds arguments to justify his own desires.[11]

Do not feel too badly about Saul. When he does not submit to God's judgment, he reaffirms the rightness of God's sentence. What should he have done as rejected king? Resign and return to his farm. He had lost his office, but he could still be right before God and live as any other Israelite. The real injury to Saul was self-inflicted. He tried to hold on to what was no longer his.

David too, like Joshua, must study the law in order to apply it. Moving the ark on a new cart (2 Samuel 6), though considered proper in Philistine culture

(1 Samuel 6:7), was not the way Yahweh had instructed. The Levites were to carry the ark with poles inserted in the rings on its side (Exodus 25:10-16). Even Levites who touched the ark would die (Numbers 4:15). David had clearly learned his error before moving the ark again (2 Samuel 6:12-15).

David's sins against Uriah and Bathsheba were also sins against Yahweh.[12] These were certainly no less sins than those of Saul. David's sins were more than personal violations of the Law; they were the use of the kingship itself to stand above the Law. So why was David's line not removed from office?

The only possible answer is 2 Samuel 7:8-16—the Davidic Covenant.

**The Davidic Covenant**

Clearly 2 Samuel 7 is the charter that plots the future of kingship for Israel. The Abrahamic Covenant plotted the future of God's program to ultimately bless the world. Through one man, Abraham, all the world's nations would be blessed (Genesis 12:3). This blessing would come through his descendants who were to receive the land of Canaan (Genesis 17:7-8). These descendants became a nation at Mount Sinai under the Mosaic Covenant. Now, within this nation, David's line is fixed as the line of rulers.

The scene of 2 Samuel 7 finds David desiring to establish a central worship place at Jerusalem by building a permanent temple to replace the movable tent of worship. Yahweh responds that he has never implied that he wants such a "house." Rather than allow David to assist him, he will assist David. He will establish David's "house" as the perpetual ruling line over Israel. This guarantee is based not on the presence of a temple, but on the promise of Yahweh himself.

The promise includes:

- David's name made great (7:9).
- An undisturbed place for Israel and rest from enemies (7:10-11).

- The establishing of David's line as rulers over his kingdom forever (7:16, 22:51; Psalm 89:28-29).
- A special Father-son relationship between Yahweh and the king (2 Samuel 7:14; "You are my Son," Psalm 2:7; "my firstborn," Psalm 89:27).
- Sin would bring punishment (2 Samuel 7:14), but no removal of the line of kingship as in Saul's case (7:15; Psalm 89:30-33).

As in the other covenants, enjoyment of the promise is conditioned upon obedience, but the promise itself is eternal (cf. 2 Samuel 23:5).[13]

**The Uniqueness of Yahweh**

David's response (7:18-29) revives the theme of Yahweh's uniqueness. Yahweh has been unique as Israel's delivering God (7:22-24). David has known this from the past. But now he can only exclaim,[14]

> Who am I, O Sovereign LORD, and what is my family, that you have brought me this far? . . . Is this your usual way of dealing with man, O Sovereign LORD? (7:18-19)

Yahweh is unique in his gracious promises. By his grace he already has established Israel as his people (7:24). Now by his grace he is establishing the Davidic line.

But this has been the proclamation from the beginning of Samuel. Hannah recognized this sovereign action of Yahweh:

> The LORD brings death and makes alive;
>   he brings down to the grave and raises up.
> The LORD sends poverty and wealth;
>   he humbles and he exalts.
>
> He raises the poor from the dust
>   and lifts the needy from the ash heap;
> he seats them with princes
>   and has them inherit a throne of honor. . . .

> It is not by strength that one prevails;
> those who oppose the LORD will be shattered
> (1 Samuel 2:6-10).

Samuel was raised up from a barren womb. David, though the youngest of Jesse's sons, was chosen king. But the real shock comes in 2 Samuel 12:24-25 with the second son, Solomon, born to David and Bathsheba:

> Yahweh loved him; and because Yahweh loved him, he sent word through Nathan the prophet to name him Jedidiah [loved by Yahweh].

Solomon would be the son to follow David on the throne and build the temple for the Lord.[15] Yahweh is a God of grace.

Students often ask, "What would have happened had Saul not disobeyed? How would the King have then come from Judah (Genesis 49:10) if God had continued Saul's kingdom forever (1 Samuel 13:13)?" Questions like these, which try to understand God's ability to control history using even the sinful choices of men, are beyond human understanding.

Anyway, I have a more interesting question. What would have happened had David not sinned with Bathsheba? Would there have been no Solomon? And further, how could God choose Solomon—the product of a marriage which never should have been—over other sons?

> The LORD is compassionate and gracious,
> slow to anger, abounding in love.
> He will not always accuse,
> nor will he harbor his anger forever;
> he does not treat us as our sins deserve
> or repay us according to our iniquities.
> For as high as the heavens are above the earth,
> so great is his love for those who fear him;
> as far as the east is from the west,
> so far has he removed our transgressions from us
> (Psalm 103:8-12).

## ON THE WAY: COMPLETION OF KINGSHIP

### The Promise Continued

Psalm 2 vividly captures the Davidic promise in action. The psalm begins by picturing rebellion against Yahweh and his anointed ruler or "messiah." What reaction is there to this rebellion? Yahweh derisively laughs, and gives his answer: He names his king, the one he has installed on Mount Zion in Jerusalem (2:4-6).

This Davidic king in Zion now speaks: "He [Yahweh] said to me, 'You are my Son; today I have become your Father'" (2:7). Here the language of 2 Samuel 7 is used. David and his line have been installed as Yahweh's kings. And how is this significant? At the king's request, Yahweh will give victory in putting down attacking nations. Ultimately Israel will possess "the ends of the earth" as nation after nation rebels against Yahweh's rule and is defeated (2:8-9).

The kings of the earth must not kick against God's ordained order. With wise insight, they must submit to Yahweh and his king before it is too late (2:10-12).

If God's intention of universal rule for his anointed king is not clear enough from Psalm 2, then Psalm 72 should solve the matter.

> He will rule from sea to sea
> and from the River to the ends of the earth.
> The desert tribes will bow before him
> and his enemies will lick the dust.
> The kings of Tarshish and of distant shores
> will bring tribute to him;
> the kings of Sheba and Seba
> will present him gifts.
> All kings will bow down to him
> and all nations will serve him (72:8-11).

Even when Yahweh's chastening hand came as promised upon sinful Davidic kings, and even when Israel went into exile, *the promise itself held firm.* In

David's line "rascals there may be, but the blessing would never be revoked from the family."[16]

> This is what the LORD says: "If I have not established my covenant with day and night and the fixed laws of heaven and earth, then I will reject the descendants of Jacob and David my servant and will not choose one of his sons to rule over the descendants of Abraham, Isaac and Jacob. For I will restore their fortunes and have compassion on them." (Jeremiah 33:25-26)

**New Testament Completion**

Christians often read the New Testament as if its Old Testament quotations about Christ are referring *only* to him. This frequently is not the case. For instance, when we read Hebrews 1:5 and see 2 Samuel 7:14 quoted, we might assume that

> I will be his Father
> and he will be my Son

was a direct quotation about Jesus. Students are quite surprised the first time they read the very next phrase in 2 Samuel 7: "When he does wrong, I will punish him with the rod of men." Could this passage be speaking of the *perfect* Son of God?

As often as not, the New Testament quotations reflect the *completion* of God's promises in Christ. Christ is predicted throughout the Scriptures (Luke 24:27), but he is not necessarily *directly* predicted in all the Scriptures. Nor is he hidden there in some mystical or allegorical way. All of these lines of promise and great themes of the Old Testament ultimately meet in Christ.

If it was true for the Roman Empire that "all roads lead to Rome," it is also true for Scripture that "no matter how many promises God has made, they are 'Yes' [fulfilled] in Christ" (2 Corinthians 1:20).

How is the promise to David and the theme of kingship fulfilled in Christ? On this the New Testament is very clear. Check out these facts:

- Jesus was born in the line of David (Matthew 1:1-17, Luke 2:4, Romans 1:3).
- He rode into Jerusalem in the predicted manner, and accepted the acclamations of those who saw him as the son of David who would save them and introduce the coming kingdom (Mark 11:2-10, cf. Psalm 118:25-26, Zechariah 9:9).
- On the cross he experienced the same persecution from which David asked God to deliver him. Both David and Jesus were apparently forsaken by God into their enemies' hands (Matthew 27:46, Psalm 22:1), were mocked for believing God would deliver them (Matthew 27:43, Psalm 22:8), were physically pinned down by their enemies (Matthew 27:35, Psalm 22:16), had lots cast for their clothing (Matthew 27:35, Psalm 22:18), were thirsty and received sour wine to drink (Matthew 27:48, Psalm 22:15 and 69:21), and were delivered (Matthew 28:6, Psalm 22:22-24). Could these parallel circumstances happen just by chance, or is God trying to tell us something?
- His resurrection from the dead fulfilled Psalm 2:7—"You are my Son; today I have become your Father" (Acts 13:32-33). For though Jesus was always the Son of God in his divine nature, here we are speaking of the announcement by Yahweh concerning his rule as David's heir.
- His ascension to heaven marked the beginning of a period predicted in Psalm 110:1—"Sit at my right hand until I

make your enemies a footstool for your feet" (Acts 2:32-36). In the resurrection and ascension, God has exalted Jesus to the position of Lord and Christ (Messiah, Anointed King—Acts 2:36 and 5:31, Hebrews 1:3-13).

- His reign over the nations on earth—when he "will rule them with an iron scepter" (Psalm 2:9)—is yet future. It will be implemented at his return to earth (Revelation 19:15, 12:5).

Like a well-synchronized multi-projector slide presentation, each phase clicks off. And so the hope of Israel for a Davidic king to give them what was promised is "Yes" in Christ Jesus. His rule not only will be over those of physical Israel who put their trust in him, but will extend from sea to sea and to the ends of the earth.

Security *is* to be found in The King after all!

"Amen. Come, Lord Jesus."

# FOR PERSONAL INTERACTION & DISCUSSION

SUGGESTED SCRIPTURE READINGS:

2 Samuel 7
Psalm 2
Acts 2:29-41

1. What was it about the "pure theocracy" that made the Israelites feel vulnerable? On the other hand, what advantages did this government have for the people? What sort of "securities" should a believer pursue or not pursue?
2. What is the story of David and Goliath really about? Will every giant fall if we just believe it? What about the martyrs in the Roman Colosseum?
3. Why is it important to understand that the word of God was higher than the king's word in Israel? Why did Saul end up in such a pitiful spiritual and psychological condition after he is rejected as king? How do these principles relate to human response to God today?
4. How does David's special treatment of his nephews bring him difficulty?
5. Identify some poor decisions of David in the first part of 2 Samuel. If David is not perfect in his judgment, why is he so blessed? Why is the sin with Bathsheba such a disastrous sin, if David has made mistakes before yet continued to be blessed?
6. What effect did David's sin with Bathsheba have on his family? In what ways do we lose credibility with our own families? Is there any way this credibility can be regained?
7. What promise kept David's line from losing the kingship? How does this promise meet its ultimate fulfillment? How does God mark out Jesus so no one can miss the fact that he is the promised King? How will those who are wise respond to the King?

'LIKE THE KINGS OF OLD, MANY TODAY TRY ALL KINDS OF NOSTRUMS TO GAIN SECURITY: AN IMPROVED ECONOMIC THEORY, A MORE HIGHLY SKILLED MILITARY, SURVIVALISTIC PRACTICES. BUT THERE IS A MORE BASIC YARDSTICK THAT DETERMINES HUMAN EVENTS . . . AND ULTIMATE DESTINY.'

---

CHAPTER

# 11.

# NATION HEADING FOR JUDGMENT

## THE THEOLOGY OF KINGS

The repetition is deafening. Over and over the Scriptures pronounce the verdict. Like a skillful surgeon doing an exploratory operation, the divinely inspired author dissects the near-corpse of Israel to find the cause of her fatal malady. Again and again, as he examines each organ, he discovers a spreading cancer.

The body politic of Israel is not doomed because of a minor slip in dietary regulations or other miscellaneous commands. Nor is the root problem to be found in unwise economic theory or insufficient military capacity. No, the root cause is moral and religious. *Israel sinned.* And her sin is not slight, but basic. As the author-prophet looks at Israel's kings, he announces his diagnosis with boring regularity:

> He committed all the sins his father had done before him; his heart was not fully devoted to the LORD his God, as the heart of David his forefather had been (1 Kings 15:3).
>
> He walked in all the ways of Jeroboam son of Nebat and in his sin, which he caused Israel to commit (1 Kings 16:26).

> He did evil in the eyes of the LORD, because he walked in the ways of his father and mother and in the ways of Jeroboam son of Nebat, who caused Israel to sin (1 Kings 22:52).
>
> He did not turn away from the sins of Jeroboam, which he had caused Israel to commit (2 Kings 10:31).
>
> He did evil in the eyes of the LORD, just as his fathers had done (2 Kings 23:37).

## The Downward Track to Judgment

In an unexpected place the downward track to judgment begins. The seeds of destruction take root in the soil of blessing, during the reign of Solomon, that illustrious son of David. The author of Kings highlights for us the glory of Israel during Solomon's reign. And glorious it is! After Solomon secures his throne against the double treachery of Adonijah (1 Kings 1—2), he offers no less than a thousand burnt offerings to Yahweh at Gibeon (1 Kings 3:4). Yahweh appears to him on that occasion and offers to Solomon whatever he wishes. The scene is the closest the Bible gets to a genie-out-of-the-bottle opportunity, and Solomon is equal to the occasion. Therein lies the greatness of his reign.

Having enough insight already to see the seriousness of his responsibility as king, Solomon asks for more wisdom. He asks for it not simply to be the wisest man on earth, but so he could fairly judge his people (3:9), as illustrated in the case which follows of the two harlots (3:16-28). *That is what is so pleasing to God.* Solomon doesn't ask for himself at all, but for others' benefit—those for whom he is responsible as the shepherd of Israel.

King Solomon lifts Israel to its peak of fame—only in music and battle is David more famous. Truly the golden age of Israel has arrived (10:14,21).

At the center of his kingly accomplishments is the building of the temple of Yahweh in Jerusalem. Solomon's majestic prayer at the dedication of that sanctuary acknowledges Israel's mission to spread belief in Yahweh. Solomon calls on God to accept this sanctuary as a house where prayers are answered and mercy is granted (8:22-61). As a result, God again appears to Solomon (9:1-9). He accepts the temple as his own, but warns that obedience is still required to receive his blessing. He will not save Israel from judgment just because his temple is here. This warning has prophetic significance, for those in Jeremiah's day will say "The Temple, The Temple," and place their hope in the faulty notion that God would never destroy it.

Ultimately all this blessing becomes a mere foil for disappointment. Solomon's marriages with foreign women lead to his spiritual downfall. By allowing them to go to the "shrine of their choice" to worship, Solomon introduces false worship on Israelite soil. The women finally are able to turn him from his view of God's uniqueness (8:60) to worshiping other gods along with Yahweh (11:4-8). For this defection, God takes the ten northern tribes from Solomon and gives them to one of his servants, Jeroboam, the son of Nebat.[1]

## A RATING SCALE FOR KINGS

For the military, college football, and top tunes, it's *rankings*.

For students, restaurants, and eggs, it's *grading*.

For TV programs, movies, and automobile tires, it's *ratings*.

It's hard to imagine modern life without our "scale from one to ten." Weekly and monthly tabloids ask couples to rate their marriages based on their answers to twenty or fewer questions. Entire magazines exist to rate consumer products. But these are not the first. In the book of Kings we discover an ancient rating scale as the prophet-author evaluates Israel's rulers. Four types of sins emerge as the pulse of each reign is measured.

### The Sin of Jeroboam

Every king of the ten northern tribes is charged with the "sin of Jeroboam." Like a greasy-spoon diner that repeatedly fails the state health inspection for the same violation, the kings of the northern tribes refuse to reverse this policy of Jeroboam and save their kingdoms. And what is this sin which meant a rating of failure?

Jeroboam has God's word that his line will continue on the throne in the north under one condition: obedience (1 Kings 11:38). But Jeroboam believes in good politics more than God's promise, and reasons away the promise out of fear that the northern tribes might want to return to the Davidic king. He concludes that if his people worship in Jerusalem they might have a nostalgic desire to return to those days of glory as a unified nation. So as far as Jeroboam is concerned, unified worship has to go. At Bethel and Dan he sets up two substitute places of worship and introduces images to represent Yahweh—golden calves no less. Shades of Aaron!

But Jeroboam's attempt to save his kingdom is the very thing which loses it, and judgment is announced (14:7-16). No king of Israel has the spiritual sense to eliminate this unacceptable worship—and every dynasty after Jeroboam meets its doom because of it (1 Kings 16:2-3; 2 Kings 10:30-31, 15:8-12).

**The Sin of Canaanitism**

Solomon's idolatry is the initial step in turning Israel toward the sins of the Canaanites, who had been expelled from the land for their debauchery and idolatry. His son Rehoboam, who had an Ammonitess for a mother, cancels any progress made since the period of the judges. In his reign, the Canaanite sins committed by Judah include the building of high places of false worship with sacred pillars and Asherim poles, and reintroduction of male prostitutes as part of worship.

> Judah did evil in the eyes of the LORD. By the sins they committed they stirred up his jealous anger more than their fathers had done (1 Kings 14:22).

Later kings not guilty of this false worship are said to be "like David" (1 Kings 15:11-14; 2 Kings 18:3, 22:2; cf. 1 Kings 15:5).[2]

**The Sin of Ahab**

Also deserving a negative rating is the sin of Ahab. Ahab follows his father Omri to Israel's throne after the fall of Jeroboam's line. His father is generally more well known than he in ancient Near Eastern history; but in the Bible, Ahab is the more prominent.[3] The reason is infamous.

> He not only considered it trivial to commit the sins of Jeroboam son of Nebat, but he also married Jezebel daughter of Ethbaal king of the Sidonians, and began to serve Baal and worship him. He set up an altar for Baal in the temple of Baal that he built in Samaria (1 Kings 16:31-32).

Don't miss the full significance of this action. If other kings allowed images to represent the Lord and even allowed false worship, Ahab was first to introduce another god as Israel's official deity. Will Yahweh be robbed of his inheritance? Will he be displaced by Baal under the strong-willed pressure of Jezebel on her wimp of a husband, King Ahab?

**Worship at High Places**

One final sin is noted by the inspired writer: the failure to limit sacrifice to the temple in Jerusalem. This is not a disabling sin. A king could commit this sin and still be labeled "good" by our writer-guide. But an approved king might find a postscript on his reign: "The high places, however, were not removed, and the people continued to offer sacrifices and burn incense there." This is the postscript for Jehoshaphat (1 Kings 22:43) and for Asa (1 Kings 15:9-14).

At first glance, it might seem that these men allow the worship of other gods at high places. But Asa had removed Canaanite worship and idols (1 Kings 15:12-13). These were high places on which *Yahweh* was worshiped! Note carefully our writer's observation on Solomon in the early part of his reign: "Solomon loved the LORD, walking in the statutes of his father David, except he sacrificed and burned incense on the high places.

And the king went to Gibeon to sacrifice there, for that was the great high place; Solomon offered a thousand burnt offerings on that altar" (1 Kings 3:3-4 NASB).

Sacrifice to Yahweh at other than the tabernacle or temple was common following the overrunning of the tabernacle at Shiloh (1 Samuel 4; 7:6, 7:9, 7:17, 9:12-13, 10:8). God's desire, expressed in the Law, was that one central location be used for sacrifice (Deuteronomy 12:1-14).[4] His acceptance of the temple made it clear that all sacrifice and incense was to be offered at Jerusalem (1 Kings 9:3, 8:10-11).

Every king of Judah who receives a "good" rating has that rating qualified by his failure to limit sacrifice to Jerusalem—until we come to Hezekiah. This is what the writer says of him:

> Hezekiah trusted in the LORD, the God of Israel. There was no one like him among all the kings of Judah, either before him or after him. He held fast to the LORD and did not cease to follow him; he kept the commands the LORD had given Moses. And the LORD was with him; he was successful in whatever he undertook (2 Kings 18:5-7).

Hezekiah rates first among the kings in trusting God. Therefore he is not satisfied to eliminate Canaanite idolatry. Halfway obedience is not his style.

Only one other king has as good a rating: Josiah (2 Kings 23:25). But Manasseh, Josiah's grandfather, reigned so long and committed so many abominations that God already has determined to send Judah into exile to Babylon (2 Kings 23:26). When Josiah finds the book of the Law in the temple, the exclusive worship of Yahweh becomes national policy. The idols occupying the temple are destroyed. False worship is rooted out of the land along with Canaanite practices. Josiah even goes to Bethel and destroys the high place set up there by Jeroboam (2 Kings 23:15-16).

What is the key to rating a king? For this too we may go back to the reign of Solomon. This king, who so pleased God by asking for wisdom, had written, "The fear of Yahweh is the beginning of wisdom" (Proverbs 9:10). Or we could look at Solomon's prayer and dedication of the temple. There we find showcased the view of God which pervades the book of Kings. The God of Israel is unique when compared with the "gods" of other nations (1 Kings 8:23). In fact, there is no one else (8:60). And Israel's mission is to be a testimony of Yahweh (8:43,60). Israel's temple should be a house of prayer for all people (8:41-43).

But because Yahweh is a unique God, Israel must be a unique people. Unlike Josiah, the good king who came too late, Israel did not love Yahweh with all its heart and all its soul and all its might (Deuteronomy 6:5, 2 Kings 23:25).[5]

And what of the temple of Solomon, which was to be the central worship place? "I will reject Jerusalem, the city I chose, and this temple, about which I said, 'There shall my Name be'" (2 Kings 23:27). A sad final commentary on such an illustrious and glorious beginning!

**Final Ratings**

The author of Kings has given us a spiritual assessment of each ruler of both the northern (also called Israel and Ephraim) and the southern (also called Judah) kingdoms. Like a rating scale in a tour guidebook, he has carefully graded each reign. If a king has avoided all the pitfalls above, he receives what we might call a four-star rating. This is the highest possible. Only two kings receive it: Hezekiah and Josiah.

None of the nineteen northern kings repent of the sin of Jeroboam. Bethel becomes the primary sanctuary in the north and images are worshiped there. Jehu, that military man so violent that Elisha commands his messenger to flee as soon as he has anointed him king, is given a reward of five generations on the throne because he eliminated the sin of Ahab (official Baalism) from Israel. But because Jehu's zeal for Yahweh does not extend to eliminating the false image worship at Bethel, he is not given the seal of divine approval.

Eight kings of the southern kingdom (Judah) receive some commendation:

Asa removes the false high places and demotes his idolatrous grandmother (1 Kings 15:11-15).

Jehoshaphat follows his father Asa's example in freeing the land from idolatry, yet like his father does not limit sacrifice to Jerusalem (1 King 22:43).

Joash, the boy king, is faithful as long as he is under the tutorship of the priest Jehoiada (2 Kings 12:1-3; 2 Chronicles 24:2,17-25).

Amaziah "did what was right . . . but not as his father David had done" (2 Kings 14:3). This indicates a failure during his reign to stay completely free from idolatry (cf. 2 Chronicles 25:14).

Azariah, also called Uzziah, and his son Jotham are rated as good, though Uzziah is stricken with leprosy as a judgment for trying to be his own priest and burn incense (2 Kings 15:1-5, 32-35; 2 Chronicles 26:16-21).

Finally come Hezekiah and Josiah, who are more faithful than all the kings before them.

On the other side of the coin are those kings who give the body of Israel its greatest case of ptomaine poisoning. Clearly King Manasseh deserves his "most-wicked" rating. The list of his sins is foul and sickening. Among them:

- He introduces child sacrifice, killing even his own son.
- He uses the temple for false worship and idols.
- He practices astrology.
- He consults mediums and spiritists.

Our author declares the "Midnight Reign of Manasseh"[6] as the seal of Judah's doom. She will be exiled. Even Josiah's fine rule cannot reverse the impact of his grandfather's wickedness.

In the northern kingdom, Ahab and his sons are viewed as a profound threat to Israel. They not only continue the sin of Jeroboam, but they introduce Baal worship from Phoenicia as the official religion. This threat and the importance of eliminating it make the reigns of

Ahab and his sons significant as the setting for the ministry of Elijah and Elisha, prophets of Yahweh.

## THE SIGNIFICANCE OF ELIJAH AND ELISHA

### The Contest with Baal

Among all the drama surrounding the Old Testament prophets, one event is certain to capture the imagination of both children and adults: the contest on Mount Carmel between Yahweh's prophet Elijah and the prophets of Baal (1 Kings 18). The backdrop is the reign of Ahab and his foreign queen, Jezebel. Under her painted thumb, Ahab not only allows her to worship Baal on Israelite soil—as Solomon had done with his foreign wives—but also cannot resist her desire to enthrone Baal as the official sovereign god of Israel. For disobedience to the Mosaic Covenant, Ahab's territory already is suffering from lack of rain. This judgment of drought was outlined in Deuteronomy 28:23-24. Elijah announces it (1 Kings 17:1) so there can be no doubt about its purpose as a judgment from Yahweh.

The contest on Carmel, suggested by Elijah, will test whether Yahweh or Baal is to be God of Israel (1 Kings 18:20-46). Whose God can light his own sacrifice? A pitiful scene follows. The prophets of Baal gyrate, wail, and cut themselves in ultimate devotion. Elijah taunts them with scornful sarcasm. Perhaps their god has stepped out for the moment. Perhaps he is hunting. He is such a difficult fellow to get hold of! He seems unavailable for the moment.[7]

But the contest is unfair! Elijah makes it so. An old, disused altar to Yahweh is rebuilt using twelve stones to represent the nation Yahweh formed. Twelve jugs of water are poured over the sacrifice to make it nearly impossible to light.

With only one climactic call to Yahweh the contest is won. It's over. As King Ahab watches, the prophets of Baal are executed as false prophets and the people declare, "Yahweh, he is God." Elijah intercedes for the land and awaits the rain. Then, tasting the thrill of this victory for his God, he outraces Ahab to Jezreel to witness the final scene of the elimination of Baal in Israel. Ahab will announce to Jezebel the result of the contest. The kingdom will be secured again for Yahweh.

But it doesn't turn out that simple. Not until many more years and one prophet later will Baalism be eradicated from Israel's royal court.

Though most Bible students recognize the theme of Elijah's victory on Carmel, it remained for Leah Bronner in her study of Canaanite Baal epics discovered at Ugarit to demonstrate that nearly everything Elijah and Elisha did was devoted to showing that Yahweh was stronger than Baal.[8] Note each of the following teachings about Baal and how it was clearly disproven in the actions of Elijah and Elisha:

| *Teaching about Baal* | *Action of Elijah & Elisha* |
|---|---|
| Baal controls the rain (He "rides upon the clouds"). | Rain stops and starts at Elijah's word. |
| Baal is the god of fertility and vegetation. | Israel suffers famine due to lack of rain, yet Elijah and Elisha are able to provide increased oil and grain. |
| Baal has power over fire and lightning. | Yahweh, not Baal, lights his sacrifice, Elijah calls down fire on the king's troops (2 Kings 1:10-12), and a chariot with horses of fire precedes his departure by whirlwind (2 Kings 2:11). |
| Baal controls life, including power over barrenness, sickness, and death. | A son is provided to a barren woman, healings take place, and resurrections occur. |

Baal is disproven. If only Israel—all twelve tribes—would learn to follow Yahweh, the Most High God. Why will you die, O Israel, when the truth is clear before you? Why do you leave the God who loves you and is able to care for you? Why do you forsake Yahweh, the God Who Is Present to fulfill his promises, for gods who are always unavailable?

*Why do we?*

**Violation of Covenant Law**

The worship of Baal was, of course, a violation of the Mosaic Covenant (Deuteronomy 5:6-10, 6:4-5). When Yahweh is not recognized as sovereign, there will be additional violations of his justice. Other gods do not provide righteous laws. Other nations' kings make laws and are the law. This was not to be with Israel. Yahweh is the only absolute ruler. Even the human king in Israel is subject to his Law.

Nowhere else is this difference between Israel and the surrounding nations better illustrated than in the reign of Ahab. The story of Naboth's vineyard is not given simply to entertain and excite. Dramatic though it is, it is more important as a demonstration of the level to which Israel had fallen under Ahab and Jezebel. 1 Kings 21 narrates the incident.

Ahab wants Naboth's property because it would make a good vegetable garden near his palace. Naboth, completely within his rights under the covenant, refuses to sell since this property had been allotted to his ancestors and handed down according to the Law. Ahab, wimp that he is, heads for home dejected.

Jezebel marvels that there is a problem. Certainly kings get what they want, don't they? That's how eminent domain works back home in Phoenicia! Using the power of the throne, Jezebel arranges for Naboth's unjust death and secures the property for Ahab. Ahab goes down to take possession and lay out his vegetable plot, only to meet disappointment again. The plot is occupied by the persistent prophet. Elijah declares that it will be the king's inheritance that is destroyed! Ahab's line will be exterminated. No males will survive Yahweh's judgment.

### Care for the Faithful

With covenant justice taking a back seat, the ministry of the prophets to those in trouble becomes critical. God's care is shown through these prophets' concern for the needs of the faithful. A jar of oil is multiplied for a woman to redeem her sons from slavery (2 Kings 4:1-7). A barren woman is provided a son (4:8-37). A poisoned stew is rendered harmless (4:38-41). Food is multiplied to feed a crowd (4:42-44).

## THEMES FOR THE EXILE

But what have these major emphases of Kings to do with the book's purpose? Is this book just a chronicle of God's power, mighty in his prophets yet unable to change the course of the nation? Both Israel and Judah are carried off into captivity. Did God fail? Is it all over? After Elijah fails to see Baal worship exterminated by the Mount Carmel victory, is his disappointment the whole story? "Take my life; I am no better than my ancestors" (1 Kings 19:4). "Nothing is going to change," he seems to say.[9]

For the discerning reader in captivity, the book of Kings provides answers full of meaning and hope, answers based squarely on the Mosaic Covenant and its significance.

### The Land

We have already seen the importance of the land of Canaan as part of God's promise. Deuteronomy clearly outlined the conditions for any generation enjoying the blessing of that land. Kings also is a book about land . . . about being expelled from the land.

Most nations believed being expelled from their land meant their god was weaker than the god of the conquering nation. But the exiles from Israel are to learn exactly the opposite. It is not that Marduk of Babylon is more powerful than Yahweh, but that Yahweh himself is driving out his people, just as he promised. The covenant has been violated and the land has been polluted. Yahweh is a God of promise. He promised to bring them in, but he also promised to take them out if they befouled the land as the nations before them did (Leviticus 18:24-28). He is keeping his promise.

**Yahweh Is Sovereign**

Yahweh showed he was more powerful than Baal and that he could sovereignly destroy Baalism in Israel even when the majority had not repented. The discerning reader will learn that Yahweh is in sovereign control even in exile.

Some Israelites thought their security was in the temple (Jeremiah 7:4-8). Some found their security in the very Law they were breaking (Jeremiah 8:8-9). But, like Habakkuk, the nation must learn that "The righteous will live by his faith" (Habakkuk 2:4). Only faith in Yahweh is adequate. The ruins of temple, Jerusalem, and land prove it (Habakkuk 3:16-19). *The God of Elijah still lives.*

**Yahweh Is Gracious**

After reading the book of Kings, the thoughtful Israelite could not question Yahweh's justice in punishing Israel. In fact, he might wonder why it had not come earlier—especially if he had also read Deuteronomy.

The predicted judgments of Deuteronomy had come time and time again. There was lack of rain, famine, destruction by invaders, lack of peace. Prophetic announcements had warned of apostasy. Exile to Assyria for Israel (722 B.C.) and to Babylon for Judah (606-586 B.C.) came after prolonged patience. Like an overanxious mother watching both the door and the clock, God waited and waited before declaring the situation hopeless.

But even in exile there is hope. Hints of God's continuing commitment appear like beacons throughout the book. Solomon's prayer dedicating the temple asks God to hear them even in exile (1 Kings 8:46-52). God leaves a tribe for the Davidic ruler because of his promise to David that there would be a lamp in Jerusalem (1 Kings 11:12-13 and 11:36; 2 Kings 8:19). Will he let that lamp go out forever? The final scene of the book is the release of King Jehoiachin from prison. Could God still be at work?

## The Need for Repentance

Our author is no mere academician writing a multi-volume treatise on the fall of an empire, like Gibbon's on Rome. He writes to achieve a *response*. He selects those events which show what has gone on in Israel's history so that his readers-in-exile may understand what their hope is—and also what their responsibility is.

The nation in exile, reading this history, can have no doubt concerning the cause of their calamity. Neither can they have any doubt concerning their only hope. Solomon's request, coming at the peak of God's blessing, clearly states the hope of Yahweh's people when they sin:

> If they have a change of heart in the land where they are held captive, and repent and plead with you in the land of their conquerors and say, "We have sinned, we have done wrong, we have acted wickedly"; and if they turn back to you with all their heart and soul in the land of their enemies who took them captive, and pray to you toward the land you gave their fathers, toward the city you have chosen and the temple I have built for your Name; then from heaven, your dwelling place, hear their prayer and their plea, and uphold their cause. And forgive your people, who have sinned against you; forgive all the offenses they have committed against you, and cause their conquerors to show them mercy (1 Kings 8:47-50).

It is when they turn with "all their heart and with all their soul" that God may have compassion and return them to the land (cf. 1 Kings 8:33-34). The people must turn back to the standards laid out by Moses (Deuteronomy 6:4-5). Repentance is their hope.[10]

Josiah provides the model of how one should act when under God's judgment:

> Neither before nor after Josiah was there a king like him who turned to the Lord as he

> did—with all his heart and with all his soul and with all his strength, in accordance with all the law of Moses (2 Kings 23:25).

This noble king's decision to "walk after the LORD, and to keep His commandments and His testimonies and His statutes with all his heart and all his soul" (23:3 NASB) reminds the Israelite of the way back prescribed by the Law:

> When you and your children return to the LORD your God and obey him with all your heart and with all your soul according to everything I command you today, then the LORD your God will restore [return] your fortunes and have compassion on you and gather you again from all the nations where he scattered you (Deuteronomy 30:2-3).

## ON THE WAY: NEW TESTAMENT COMPLETION

### Mistaken Identity?

No doubt it's happened to you. A child grasps the leg of your slacks as you are shopping, and begins to come with you. How to minimize the shock when he discovers that you are not "Daddy"? As we open the pages of the New Testament, the Jewish people were not looking for "Daddy;" but they were expecting Elijah.

It should not surprise us, then, that when John the Baptist preached repentance in preparation for the Kingdom, questions about his identity were raised. The last prophet of the Old Testament, Malachi, had predicted a future Elijah who would rebuke the Israelites for their disobedience. This is like saying, "You will have another, final warning before judgment." The ministry of this coming Elijah? "He will turn the hearts of the fathers to their children, and the hearts of the children to their fathers; or else I will come and strike the land with a curse" (Malachi 4:6).

Israel must repent and return to the true faith of Abraham, Isaac, and Jacob, or the land will again come under God's judgment. For though some have returned to the land from captivity, the kingdom of David has not been restored. They are ruled by Gentile kings.

John rejects the idea that he is Elijah (John 1:21). Indeed, Jesus affirms that the predicted Elijah had not yet come (Matthew 17:11). Yet in the same breath he adds, "But I tell you, Elijah has already come, and they did not recognize him, but have done to him everything they wished" (17:12). They can experience Elijah's ministry by accepting the message of John the Baptist and repenting. But the officials of Israel—like the house of Ahab—will not repent. Once more it will be necessary to say to Jerusalem: "Your house is left to you desolate" (Matthew 23:37-39).

### A Greater Identity

If John the Baptist is not Elijah, is Jesus? Some think so (Matthew 16:14). Certainly there are reasons for thinking he is. Notice the similarities in ministry and miracles between Jesus and Elijah and his successor, Elisha—resurrections, provisions of food, and control over natural forces.

The Gospel of Luke particularly is interested in a comparison between Elijah-Elisha and Jesus. Luke includes the prediction that John the Baptist comes "in the spirit and power of Elijah" (Luke 1:17), but he focuses most on works and sayings of Jesus that compare to those of Elijah and Elisha:[11]

- Jesus ruffles the feathers of those in his hometown synagogue, pointing out that Elijah went to a Phoenician widow's house rather than a Jewish home, and that Elisha healed a Syrian leper, Naaman, though Israel had its full share of lepers. The synagogue is angered by this scarcely veiled suggestion that Israel was in a state of unbelief similar to that in Elijah and Elisha's day (Luke 4:25-30).
- He resurrects a young man and gives him back to his widowed mother, as well as

another child who is dead before he arrives (Luke 7:11-16, 1 Kings 17:17-24, 2 Kings 4:1-37).

- He feeds a multitude and has twelve baskets left (Luke 9:12-17, 2 Kings 4:42-44).
- Moses and Elijah talk with Jesus on the mountain following his announcement that some standing there would not see death (Elijah's experience) before seeing the kingdom (Luke 9:27-31).
- Jesus' disciples, enthusiastic about the dramatic aspects of Elijah's ministry, want Jesus to allow them to call fire down from heaven on an inhospitable Samaritan village (Luke 9:54, 2 Kings 1:10-12).
- Jesus refuses to allow a potential disciple to join him if he must go and say goodbye to his parents. And then, using the very imagery of Elisha's plow, he declares: "No one who puts his hand to the plow and looks back is fit for service in the kingdom of God" (Luke 9:61-62, 1 Kings 19:19-21).

Seeing only a nice set of parallels, however, would be to miss the point. Jesus is not just another great prophet like Elijah. He is greater than Elijah and Elisha. A second trip through these passages is in order.

- In Luke 4 Jesus announces himself not as Elijah, but as the Servant of Yahweh who was to come (4:17-21).
- In the cases of resurrection, Jesus does not pray for resurrection as Elijah and Elisha did, but commands it.
- Elisha's multiplication of food fed about one hundred men. Jesus feeds five thousand.
- On the mountain with Moses and Elijah, Jesus is identified as the chosen Son whose instruction should be followed.

- Finally, if you want to follow Jesus but desire to go back to say goodbye to your parents, you receive not a mild rebuke—as did Elisha—but a removal of the opportunity. Those who do not immediately snatch the opportunity to follow Jesus have no true perception of who he is. Jesus is not Elijah. He is the Son. Those who follow him have true insight given from the Father (Luke 10:21). Theirs is the highest privilege:

"Blessed are the eyes that see what you see. For I tell you that many prophets and kings wanted to see what you see but did not see it, and to hear what you hear but did not hear it." (Luke 10:23-24)

Like the kings of old, many today try all kinds of nostrums to gain security: an improved economic theory, a more highly skilled military, survivalistic practices.

But there is a more basic yardstick that determines human events . . . and ultimate destiny.

# FOR PERSONAL INTERACTION & DISCUSSION

SUGGESTED SCRIPTURE READINGS:

1 Kings 9:1-9, 11:1-13,
and 18:20-46
Luke 9

1. Why is Solomon's request for wisdom so pleasing to God? What kinds of requests would be similar today?
2. How did Solomon's reign start Israel down the track to judgment? How was Jeroboam's sin similar? How can "good politics" (substitute "economics," "business," etc.) get in the way of following God's word? Why does this temptation work so often?
3. Why is the sin of Ahab a more serious threat than other sins? How do the ministries of the prophets Elijah and Elisha meet this threat?
4. Who are the two best kings and what makes their reigns distinct? What is the key to rating a king? What is the key to rating each of us today?
5. How does Yahweh show himself as the only true God in the book of Kings?
6. Where must the believing Israelite find his security? Could an Israelite know why his nation failed? What is the remedy to failure?
7. How is Jesus shown to be a greater person than Elijah? What greater response is required? What greater benefits are given?

'ANCIENT WISDOM DOES NOT DISTINGUISH BETWEEN THE SACRED AND THE SECULAR, THE SCIENTIFIC AND THE MORAL. IT IS ALL THE WISDOM OF GOD. WE NEGLECT SUCH WISDOM AT OUR OWN RISK.'

CHAPTER 12.

# PRUDENT LIVING

## WISDOM FOR LIFE

Every nation has its proverbs, maxims, parables, and other forms of wit and wisdom—ways to express the marrow of life with graphic intensity. These "pithy grabbers" are meant to bring home plain truth with the force of a sledgehammer. Common sense and not-so-common insight are wedded to practical instruction for life.

Who does not smile at the double portrayal of laziness in Proverbs 26:14-15?

> As a door turns upon its hinges,
> so a sluggard turns on his bed.
>
> The sluggard buries his hand in the dish;
> he is too lazy to bring it back to his mouth.

Who does not recognize the practical insight in these snatches of life?

> A cheerful heart is good medicine,
> but a crushed spirit dries up the bones
> (Proverbs 17:22).
>
> Even a fool is thought wise if he keeps silent,
> and discerning if he holds his tongue
> (Proverbs 17:28).

That last proverb may be the nicest way ever devised of saying, "Shut-up!"

"Fish and visitors stink in three days."[1]

Yes, that is Benjamin Franklin, not the Bible. But Solomon had his finger on the same truth twenty-seven centuries earlier:

> Seldom set foot in your neighbor's house—
> too much of you, and he will hate you
> (Proverbs 25:17).

On the other hand, friendly letters or those with a check enclosed are always welcome.

> Like cold water to a weary soul
> is good news from a distant land
> (Proverbs 25:25).

## BIBLICAL WISDOM

But biblical wisdom isn't limited to helpful or witty observations about everyday life in the same mold as Ben Franklin or Erma Bombeck. Its net takes in a larger catch. Its purpose is not mere "observations on life," but *how to live life.* Along with the bits and pieces of getting along, making a living, and conducting oneself appropriately, are the weightier matters of commitment to God, good and evil, reward and punishment, and life's pitfalls.

### The Torah Connection: The Fear of the Lord

To some, the books of wisdom (Proverbs, Ecclesiastes, Job), seem unrelated to the history of Israel and her faith in God. In Proverbs, sacrifice is mentioned less than a handful of times, the temple or tabernacle not at all, and references to Yahweh's covenant with Israel are nonexistent. Job and Ecclesiastes score about the same. How can the Old Testament include books about living life with so little teaching in matters so central to Israel's faith and history?

The answer, like the sluggard's dish, is readily at hand. That it is not immediately recognized is due to the failure of modern readers to have dipped their hand into the dish of the Law. The central phrase, "The fear of Yahweh," is the umbilical cord which unites Proverbs to the nourishing Law.[2]

The importance of this phrase to the wisdom books is clear.[3] In an opening section, we learn that the Proverbs are

> "for attaining wisdom . . .
> discipline . . .
> understanding . . .
> prudence . . .
> knowledge . . .
> discretion."

And what is the first item—in fact, the absolute prerequisite—for this training?

> The fear of the LORD is the beginning of knowledge,
> but fools despise wisdom and discipline (1:7).

The phrase occurs no less than fourteen times in Proverbs, proclaiming the only approach for wise living.

Job, in the first chapter of that book of wisdom, is described by Yahweh as "blameless and upright, a man who fears God and shuns evil" (Job 1:8). This initial pitch by God opens up a long season for Job when Satan refuses to acknowledge the strike: "Does Job fear God for nothing?" he asks (1:9). The book not only vindicates Job and God, but suggests there are reasons for life's circumstances that man cannot know. This lack of knowledge, however baffling, is no basis for unfaithfulness to God. The wise man will recognize that God is wiser than himself and will believe God has a purpose for even the difficulties of life. The Law says the same thing:

> The secret things belong to the LORD our God, but the things revealed belong to us and to our children forever, that we may follow all the words of this law (Deuteronomy 29:29).

And Ecclesiastes, though different in tone, is no different in conclusion:

> Now all has been heard;
> here is the conclusion of the matter:
> Fear God and keep his commandments,
> for this is the whole duty of man (12:13).

This is not just his conclusion, but a refrain scattered throughout the book. Added to all the emptiness and senselessness the Preacher finds in life is man's total inability to understand the meaning of all that happens to him. Yet the theme rings clear:

> In many dreams and in many words there is emptiness. Rather, fear God (Ecclesiastes 5:7 NASB).

> Although a sinner does evil a hundred times and may lengthen his life, still I know that it will be well for those who fear God, who fear Him openly (Ecclesiastes 8:12 NASB).

What is meant by "The fear of the LORD?" The concept is well developed in the Torah. It first occurs in Genesis 20:11. Abraham has passed off Sarah as his sister because he thought, "There is surely no fear of God in this place, and they will kill me because of my wife." Abraham thought they had no moral standards, so he lowered his to match. Later, Abraham's own commitment to God is vindicated when he is willing to obey God at the cost of his own son. "Now I know that you fear God" is the verdict (Genesis 22:12).

The idea is found most often in Deuteronomy, where it is coupled with other expressions like "walk in his ways," "keep his commands," "serve the LORD," "love him," and "follow him" (4:10, 5:29, 6:13, 6:24, 8:6, 10:12, 10:20, 13:4, 17:19, 28:58, 31:12-13). How does a person fear the Lord?

> These are the commands, decrees and laws the LORD your God directed me to teach you to observe in the land . . . so

> that you, your children and their children after them may fear the LORD your God as long as you live by keeping all his decrees and commands that I give you (Deuteronomy 6:1-2).

The "fear of the LORD" is not limited to a *feeling* of reverence and awe. *It is a commitment to the LORD by following his instruction.* It is a response of faithful obedience to the LORD by subjection to his revealed will. It would be impossible for the Israelite to fear the Lord without instruction in the Law (Deuteronomy 31:12-13).[4]

Proverbs is not a popularized substitute for the Law—a kind of primer for those too negligent to learn Torah.[5] Rather, it is a supplement. As Kidner so graphically puts it, "There are details of character small enough to escape the mesh of the law and the broadsides of the prophets, and yet decisive in personal dealings. Proverbs moves in this realm."[6]

An example of this finer mesh which Proverbs supplies can be discovered by comparing it with the Law on the subject of adultery. The Law, of course, condemns it. The person who fears Yahweh will keep clear of it. Proverbs instructs the young man to do exactly that; but it also prepares him by practical description for the temptation that may come:

> Do not lust in your heart after her beauty
> or let her captivate you with her eyes,
> For the prostitute reduces you to a loaf of bread,
> and the adulteress preys upon your very life
> (6:25-26).
>
> The lips of an adulteress drip honey,
> and her speech is smoother than oil;
> but in the end she is bitter as gall,
> sharp as a double-edged sword
> (5:3-4).

Not only is the young man told to stay away from a woman like that, he is warned of practical consequences.

A man who commits adultery lacks judgment;
whoever does so destroys himself.
Blows and disgrace are his lot,
and his shame will never be wiped away;
for jealousy arouses a husband's fury,
and he will show no mercy when he takes revenge.
He will not accept any compensation;
he will refuse the bribe, however great it is (6:32-35).

Only fools turn in at that tempting call of folly:

Stolen water is sweet;
food eaten in secret is delicious! (9:17)

Such men are ignorant of the consequences:

Little do they know that the dead are there,
that her guests are in the
depths of the grave (9:18).

Rather than the illicit, captivating theft of what is another man's, the ideal of marriage and its joys are fully and unashamedly recommended.

May your fountain be blessed,
and may you rejoice in the wife of your youth.
A loving doe, a graceful deer—
may her breasts satisfy you always,
may you ever be captivated by her love (5:18-20).

This combination of the Mosaic Torah, graphically supplemented by the torah (instruction) of the wise parent,[7] is designed to fully implement the fear of the LORD.

To fear the LORD is to hate evil (8:13).
The fear of the LORD adds length to life (10:27).
He who fears the LORD has a secure fortress,
and for his children it will be a refuge (14:26).
The fear of the LORD is a fountain of life (14:27).
Better a little with the fear of the LORD than
great wealth with turmoil (15:16).

The fear of the LORD teaches a man wisdom (15:33).
Through the fear of the LORD a man avoids evil (16:6).
The fear of the Lord—that is wisdom, and to shun evil is understanding (Job 28:28).

### The Creation Connection

But Proverbs goes beyond putting feet to the commands of the Law. It also develops the truth of creation. Genesis 1—2 taught the creation of an orderly and beautiful world. Proverbs teaches the creation of an orderly and beautiful life. If Yahweh is Creator, man must learn to live in harmony with the order that the Creator ordained.[8] This is wisdom indeed!

We might be surprised to read this description of the man celebrated as wiser than all others of the east: "He described plant life, from the cedar of Lebanon to the hyssop that grows out of walls. He also taught about animals and birds, reptiles and fish" (1 Kings 4:33). Solomon would have enjoyed some of my children's favorite questions: "Dad, why did God create slugs?" followed quickly by "Why mosquitoes?" "Why flies?"

I quickly gulp down the temptation to ask, "Why questioning kids?" The answer is too obvious: "To keep parents on their toes."

There are proverbs which deal with planting and reaping, with diligence, with the poor as God's creatures. Lessons of wisdom are borrowed from the ant and badgers. Ancient wisdom does not distinguish between the sacred and the secular, the scientific and the moral. It is all the wisdom of God. A skilled craftsman is wise because he has learned his trade well. A man is wise when he has learned to live skillfully according to God's order. Wisdom was the "craftsman" at the Creator's side when he created the world, and the discerning man will live in harmony with it (Proverbs 8:22-36). We neglect such wisdom at our own risk.

The Proverbs warn of attitudes and actions that cause a man to literally destroy himself. "Envy rots the bones"

(14:30). Pride brings disgrace (11:2). "Food gained by fraud tastes sweet to a man, but he ends up with a mouth full of gravel" (20:17). "The evil deeds of a wicked man ensnare him" (5:22).

The belief that Yahweh created an orderly world joins the fear of the LORD as a major emphasis of wisdom teaching. Yahweh is Creator and is still in charge of the world. It is man's duty to live in harmony with Yahweh's rule as Creator. Wisdom was Yahweh's possession at the creation and it is by wisdom that creation took place (8:22-31).[9] It is man's duty to discover this wisdom and to operate according to it (8:32-36).

> Blessed is the man who listens to me,
> watching daily at my doors, waiting at
> my doorway.
> For whoever finds me finds life
> and receives favor from the LORD (8:34-35).

### The Life Connection

Reduced to essentials, most truths are marvelously simple. Proverbs recognizes this. When all the scrambling is over, it comes down to *life* or *death*. There are only two tracks. Track one is the way of the wise, the way of the righteous, the way of prosperity, the way of life. Track two is the way of the fool, of the wicked, of poverty, and of death.

Wait a minute! Isn't that oversimplistic? Doesn't Solomon know, as Job did, that some wicked enjoy prosperity? Doesn't he know that some righteous are poor? Doesn't he know that some good men die young, and evil men die old?

I just had a look at the obituary column of our local paper. There were the requisite number of deaths of older people. Then there were deaths of younger men. One death was from a motorcycle accident when the driver lost control of his vehicle. A second man flipped a car on an empty freeway at 3 A.M. A third young man died from an apparent overdose of sleeping pills; his wife had been drunk and in a car wreck the night before. A fourth was stabbed by a friend, drugs the apparent motivator. Finally, a young lady died after an extended illness.

Notice anything? All but one of these younger deaths, possibly two, were due to disregard of wisdom in the conduct of life. They took the track of death and they got there—early.

When we lived in Texas—and it's not much different in Oregon—there was still a vestige of the old frontier shoot-em-up approach in and around bars in the early hours of the morning. The TV news carried the inevitable results the next day.

In other words, you have a better chance of living if you are in bed at what my mother used to call "a decent hour." It seems that even on the purely physical plane, a person who follows these principles is likely to live a longer and "better" life.

Sure, Proverbs knows there is no mechanical guarantee about these formulas. Some good people die young. You and I both could name some. The righteous have their setbacks (Proverbs 24:16). The wicked often do so well that the righteous are tempted toward envy (24:1-2, 23:17, 3:31). But like our own folk wisdom recognizes, those people are "living on borrowed time." They are swimming against the tide. The odds will catch up with them.

It is not merely odds that will catch up with them. It is Yahweh himself, who oversees his creation. He brings vengeance on those who violate his people living in harmony with him (Proverbs 16:5, 17:5, 29:26). He assures of judgment and of retribution. It is Yahweh who is to be trusted. And though Proverbs concentrates on present life, true life is not limited to the here-and-now. Just as some people experience death even while yet alive, so life is more than mere existence. The life entered now through submission to Yahweh does not end at death. Death and the grave are for those who live in the realm of folly. For the righteous—and for no one else—there is a future (12:28).[10]

Apart from God's revelation, can we prove that this divine order exists? Reading obituaries helps, but we also have to recognize (as the book of Ecclesiastes does) that if we want absolute proof—and perfect sense—in this world, we are not going to find it.

Ecclesiastes does more than point out that "life isn't a bowl of cherries." If you want everything in life to make sense, says the Preacher, forget it. As earthdwellers, we don't have heaven's perspective—and we cannot have it. For us, "the creation was subjected to futility [vanity, meaninglessness]" until it is fully redeemed by God (Romans 8:20-21 NASB).[11]

If Proverbs encourages us to live positively in the light of divine revelation, Ecclesiastes warns us against requiring full explanations. From the human vantage point, time and chance happen to us all (Ecclesiastes 9:11).

But one rule also applies to all. It stands unchanged throughout:

> Fear God and keep his commandments,
> for this is the whole duty of man.
> For God will bring every deed into judgment,
> including every hidden thing, whether it
> is good or evil
> (Ecclesiastes 12:13-14).

## ON THE WAY: WISDOM FULFILLED

### Jesus and Proverbs

Jesus' sayings and parables about the essence of life have lost none of their punch, though delivered almost two millennia ago. Consider these:

> Blessed are the poor in spirit, for theirs is the kingdom of heaven (Matthew 5:3).

> Where your treasure is, there your heart will be also (Luke 12:34).

> Which of you, if his son asks for bread, will give him a stone? (Matthew 7:9).

A man's life does not consist in the abundance of his possessions (Luke 12:15).

Neither do men pour new wine into old wineskins (Matthew 9:17).

If a blind man leads a blind man, both will fall into a pit (Matthew 15:14).

Such simple observations on life cut through to issues that continue to confront us. Are we living for this life or the next? Is God really good? Are the concerns for food and clothing ultimate concerns, or distractions? Is the landscape dotted with counterfeits who lead ignorant men to destruction?

Like Proverbs, Jesus teaches trust in the Creator God. "Solomon in all his splendor" could not match the natural dress of the lilies (Matthew 6:28-29). For Jesus, like Solomon's Proverbs, there are only two tracks: life or death. One path is worn wide by the multitude who take it. The other path has become narrow and hidden so that few find and follow it (Matthew 7:13-14).

### The Wise King

The name *Solomon* was known not only for royal splendor and proverbs, but stood also for the idea of the wise king—in spite of his failures in old age. It was Solomon who knew enough to ask for wisdom to judge God's people rightly.

Yet Solomon did fail. He failed in the very fear of the Lord which he knew wisdom required. He first permitted, then catered, to idolatry. He also took full advantage of his kingly position to surround himself with all the trappings of empire—in spite of the warnings of Deuteronomy (17:16-20).

God dumped Rehoboam, Solomon's son, from ruling over all Israel because of Solomon's idolatry. The people rejected him because of oppressive taxation. Solomon, they said, had "put a heavy yoke on us, but now lighten the harsh labor and the heavy yoke he put on us" (1 Kings 12:4). Rehoboam promised more of the same. Exit ten tribes.

Such was the wisdom of Solomon. Renowned, but inconsistent. Dazzling, but short-lived. Remarkable for its life-insight. Profoundly puzzling in its demise. Like a fourth of July rocket it lit up the sky, but soon disappeared in smoke and vapor.

Yet Isaiah predicts a future king in David's line who would be perfect in his wise rule:

> The Spirit of the LORD will rest on him—
> the Spirit of wisdom and of understanding,
> the Spirit of counsel and of power,
> the Spirit of knowledge and of the fear
> of the LORD—
> and he will delight in the fear of the LORD
> (Isaiah 11:2-3).

The King with these qualities will provide Israel with a ruler who will do what no king has managed to date—bring perfect justice and peace (Isaiah 11:3-9).[12]

Like a child trained to hear the summons to come home, the words of Jesus in Matthew 11:28-30 must have raised the head of many a Jewish listener:

> Come to me, all you who are weary and burdened, and I will give you rest. Take my yoke upon you and learn from me, for I am gentle and humble in heart, and you will find rest for your souls. For my yoke is easy and my burden is light.

No burden of oppressive kingship here. Jesus' rule would liberate.

Jesus not only claims a wisdom for ruling that Solomon could not match, but asserts his exclusive rights to the franchise:

> All things have been committed to me by my Father. No one knows the Son except the Father, and no one knows the Father except the Son and those to whom the Son chooses to reveal him (Matthew 11:27).

His followers, pictured as "little children" compared to those considered "wise and learned" (11:25), receive his invitation to "find rest for your souls" (11:29).

Again, the Jewish listener would not miss the reference to Jeremiah 6:16 (emphasis added):

> Stand at the crossroads and look;
> ask for the ancient paths,
> ask where the good way is, and walk in it,
> and *you will find rest for your souls.*
> But you said, "We will not walk in it."

The Israelites of Jeremiah's time were rejecting God's way, though they offered sacrifices. God was not impressed.

> What do I care about incense from Sheba
> or sweet calamus from a distant land?
> Your burnt offerings are not acceptable;
> your sacrifices do not please me
> (Jeremiah 6:20).

In spite of experiencing the judgment of exile which Jeremiah proclaimed, nothing has changed. Israel had lapsed back into mere external and outward worship. Jesus, like Jeremiah, calls them back to the wisdom of the good way—the ancient path of true relationship to Yahweh. One greater than Solomon has come (Mattew 12:42) with wisdom and relief. Because he is "gentle and humble in heart" (Matthew 11:29), he will rule his people in the fear of the Lord without arrogance and rebellion. Will they reject the wise King?[13]

### The Worthy Lamb

When the announced wise King becomes a sacrificial lamb upon a Roman cross, the hopes of those expecting relief and rest seemed dashed. How can rule be reconciled with sacrificial death?

A scene in Revelation 4—5 brings the two themes together in dramatic clarity. Called up into heaven to see the future, the apostle John finds himself viewing

God's throne room. Almighty God, surrounded by groups of creatures, is worshiped as the Holy and Sovereign Creator (4:1-11). But a drama develops before John's eyes which interrupts this praise and brings activity in heaven to a halt. The Almighty holds the scroll of destiny, but no one in all creation is found who is worthy to approach the throne and open this scroll which will unravel the scenes necessary to bring history to its climax. John is visibly shaken and weeps at this setback, but is told someone has been found who is worthy.

> The Lion of the tribe of Judah, the Root of David, has triumphed. He is able to open the scroll and its seven seals (5:5).

But when John looks, he sees no glorious triumphant King. He sees a Lamb that looked as if it had been recently sacrificed! This lowly, bloody Lamb is permitted to take the scroll. The creatures closest to the throne begin a new song soon to be joined in chorus by a myriad of angels:

> Worthy is the Lamb, who was slain,
> to receive power and wealth
> and wisdom and strength
> and honor and glory and praise! (5:12).

The message is clear. Jesus triumphed in crucifixion—as a sacrificial lamb. God's plan may proceed toward its grand climax because he died. The Lamb who was slain is worthy to reign—to receive the power and wealth and wisdom of office.

> And with your blood you purchased men
> for God from every tribe and language
> and people and nation.
> You have made them to be a kingdom and priests
> to serve our God, and they will reign
> on the earth (5:9-10).

**Jesus Is Wisdom**

It is no wonder Paul identifies *Christ crucified* as God's power and wisdom (1 Corinthians 1:18-31). In contrast to the best that human wisdom can do, Jesus is God's plan for human redemption. This plan looks like foolishness to earthbound philosophers. How can man comprehend a plan so based on love and servitude that his own deliverance and restoration is achieved by the death of the very "Lord of glory" (2:8)? How foolish to give up position to serve! How foolish to serve than be served!

*But how redemptive!*

> The foolishness of God is wiser than men, and the weakness of God is stronger than men (1:25 NASB).

Worthy is the Lamb who is "our righteousness, holiness, and redemption" (1:30). His death and resurrection have cleared the track that leads to life. He "has destroyed death and has brought life and immortality to light through the gospel" (2 Timothy 1:10).

The Way of Wisdom is complete.

# FOR PERSONAL INTERACTION & DISCUSSION

SUGGESTED SCRIPTURE READINGS:

Proverbs 1
Isaiah 11:1-9
Matthew 11:25-30
Revelation 5
1 Corinthians 1:18-31

1. How do biblical proverbs compare with our own proverbs? How are they similar? What makes them different?
2. Is the wise person the one with all the answers? What lesson about life does the book of Job teach? How does this relate to wisdom?
3. In what way is the message of Ecclesiastes similar to that of Job? What do all three books (Job, Ecclesiastes, Proverbs) all recommend as the wise approach to life?
4. What is the fear of the Lord? What other ideas are similar to it? How does it relate to the Law?
5. What does Proverbs advise about sex and marriage? Is this true to life? Is Proverbs prudish?
6. How does knowing wisdom tie in to creation? Does belief in a Creator provide an assurance of an underlying order to life? What good is a belief in such a basic order?
7. What is the way of life and the way of death in Proverbs? Is Proverbs too optimistic in its description of the life of the righteous person? How does Ecclesiastes present the other side of the coin and balance an overly optimistic reading of Proverbs?
8. Why are temporary setbacks not finally important to the writer of Proverbs? How does this come through in Jesus' teaching?

9. Why is the rule of Jesus considered a "light yoke"? How does it differ from that of previous kings?
10. How does the scene in Revelation 4—5 tie Jesus' sacrificial death into his rule as the wise and worthy king? How does the route of sacrifice differ from conventional, earthly wisdom? How does it complete true, divine wisdom?

PART

# 4.

# RESTORATION AND HOPE

Not unlike Sherman's march to the sea, Nebuchadnezzar's destruction of Judah and Jerusalem left the land in shambles—so much so that Jeremiah pictured Palestine as returning to the earth's original chaotic state: "formless and empty" (Jeremiah 4:23-26).

As the Jews were evacuated they apparently were gathered for transport at Ramah, near enough Rachel's tomb for the prophet to picture that mother of Israel "weeping for her children and refusing to be comforted, because her children are no more" (Jeremiah 31:15).

The Jews, nevertheless, prospered in the land of their captivity. Though not free, they were not prisoners either. They were allowed to have their own community organization and elders, and could build houses, farm, and earn a living.[1]

The Babylonian empire soon developed its own problems. After King Nebuchadnezzar's death the sprawling empire deteriorated rapidly, helped along by the rise of Cyrus the Mede to head the Persian empire. In the autumn of 539, Babylon fell without a struggle. She had been weighed on God's sovereign scales and found too slim on justice (Daniel 5:27).

This Cyrus, Isaiah had predicted, would be brought to power by Yahweh himself to return God's exiled people, allowing them to rebuild Jerusalem (Isaiah 45:1-6,13).

The new Persian policy toward captive peoples was more humane than any of its predecessors. The Assyrians, who captured northern Israel in 722 B.C., had not only exiled nations but also replaced them in their land with other displaced peoples—a kind of international shell game. This resulted in foreigners populating the region of Samaria. These people, after a number of disastrous episodes, decided to worship Yahweh as well as their own gods (cf. 2 Kings 17:24-41). The Babylonians, the next world power after Assyria, had maintained puppet governments and exacted tribute; but an especially rebellious territory like Judah would be taken into exile. The Persians under Cyrus reversed all this. They returned captive peoples to their own land and restored the worship of each nation's gods. This was good insurance for kingand empire. How better to earn the favor of so many gods?

Such is the scene when a few Jewish survivors return from exile to restore their community in Jerusalem and Judah, as recorded in the books of Ezra and Nehemiah.

'RACHEL STILL CRIES. SHE CRIED WHEN THEY WENT OUT UNDER NEBUCHADNEZZAR. NEARLY SIX CENTURIES LATER, SHE STILL IS WEEPING. AND IN MATTHEW'S DAY, JEREMIAH'S REPORT OF ISRAEL'S SUFFERING IS YET BEING FULFILLED.'

CHAPTER

# 13.

# A PEG IN THE HOLY PLACE

CONCERNS OF EZRA AND NEHEMIAH

My first three years of academics took place in a one-room schoolhouse. My mind has preserved mental snapshots of those rows of desks—each row to the left representing a year of progress. Central heating was supplied by a single stove in the rear of the room.

When the winds of progress inevitably prevailed, our school consolidated with a larger district in the nearest town. Eventually the property was sold, but whatever plans the buyer had went awry. Brush grew up in the playground. The merry-go-round broke down. The building deteriorated.

Not long ago, several of us returned to that site of earlier misadventures. Thirty years had taken its toll, but we entered and tried to match our memories to the scene before us. The room was much smaller than our childhood eyes recalled—especially the cloakroom where my sister, Janet, spent many exiled hours learning in isolation away from people-oriented distractions. Most difficult to match, however, was our remembrance of a clean, tidy, orderly room with the shambles lying before us. Though we fully expected such conditions, a sense of depression clouded our homecoming mood.

How much worse it must have been for Israel's first returning exiles. No drop-in visit here. Like pioneers, they left security for a new, yet old, land. They were not on a brief nostalgic journey. They were returning to stay and to restore the worship of Yahweh in Jerusalem. How the rubble must have depressed them!

## RETURNS AND REFORMS

### The Exiles Return—538 B.C.

Actually, the books of Ezra and Nehemiah record three returns. The first return follows the edict of Cyrus, which allows the Jews to return to their homeland, supplies them with the captured temple treasures, and calls for neighborly contributions to the project so the temple may be restored (Ezra 1). The Jews who returned worked under Zerubbabel, a descendant of King David, to restore sacrificial worship (Ezra 3) and rebuild the temple.[2]

Opposition to the project from other residents and local officials brought the project to a standstill for fifteen years (Ezra 4:1-5, 4:24).[3] One protest too many, however, reversed the trend. King Darius, recently come to the throne of Persia, ordered a search of the archives and found a memorandum outlining Cyrus's original decree. Officials were then ordered to aid the project by supplying expenses and sacrificial animals. The threat of finding oneself impaled on a beam from his own destroyed house encouraged cooperation (Ezra 6:11).

### Ezra—Priest and Scribe

The initial return did not involve Ezra at all. Ezra 7 introduces us to this unique man. The time is nearly eighty years after the first return and nearly sixty years after the temple's completion.[4] Ezra desires to teach Israel to live according to the Law of Moses so God can bless and fully restore Israel (Ezra 7:1-10). King Artaxerxes, the reigning Persian, also has an interest in the Jews obeying "the Law of your God" as well as "the law of the king" (Ezra 7:25-26): If he did not allow the God of the Jews to be worshiped properly, what might this God do against the king of the Persians (Ezra 7:23)? Artaxerxes knew how to cover all the bases!

Ezra didn't have to be much of a detective to find abuses of the Law among the returned community. Intermarriage with heathen neighbors was epidemic—not only among the people in general but even among leaders and priests. The rest of the book of Ezra chronicles Ezra's successful yet painful effort to reverse this trend which threatened to wipe out the Jews as a distinctive people for Yahweh (Ezra 9—10).

**Nehemiah the Governor**

Nehemiah comes next, thirteen years after Ezra, in the book which bears his name and contains a personal account of his own experiences. Nehemiah occupied the close and trusted position of King's Cupbearer, yet his life-interest was not personal advancement but the welfare of Jerusalem and the returned exiles. The news that Zion's faraway city walls were still in ruins left him nearly despondent. Always a man of prayer, he turns to God. He admits Israel's wickedness, but focuses on God's promise of deliverance and prays for success. Always a man of action, he successfully seeks from Artaxerxes a leave of absence along with supplies for rebuilding the wall of Jerusalem (Nehemiah 1—2).

Like Zerubbabel, Nehemiah faces opposition from surrounding peoples and officials. In his case the threats are more physical than legal. Sentence prayers to his God carry him through the personal abuse and potential discouragement which threatened completion of the project (4:4-5, 4:9, 5:19, 6:9, 6:14). Jerusalem's wall is complete in fifty-two days despite ridicule ("If even a fox climbed up on it, he would break down their wall of stones!" 4:3), attempt at assassination ("Come, let us meet together . . . on the plain of Ono," 6:2-3), and fifth-column intrigue (6:10-13).

Like Ezra, Nehemiah was concerned about the spiritual health of the Jews. The rest of the book focuses on spiritual reforms (Nehemiah 8—13). The upcoming national festival in the seventh month provides an opportunity. Appropriately enough, Ezra's reading of the Law of Moses is the fuse that lights the reform (8:1-9). The immediate response is a full celebration of the very feast they are attending, the Feast of Booths, following precisely the Law's instruction (8:13-17). Next comes confession of Israel's repeated failure before a faithful and just God (9:5-37). The people recognize their need to be faithful to the Mosaic Law before God can fully remove the punishment of exile. They covenant together to do just that (9:38—10:39). Leaving nothing to chance, they list their most frequent failings:

- intermarriage with heathen peoples
- failure to keep the sabbath
- failure to provide for the needs of temple worship
- failure to recognize God's right to the firstborn
- failure to tithe

Talk about specific application! How often is spiritual growth dependent on our willingness to be specific and honest about weakness? This profitable time together ends with arrangements for sufficiently populating Jerusalem, the dedication of the finished walls, and the exclusion of Ammonites and Moabites from the community (11:1—13:3). The people go home and Nehemiah reports back to Artaxerxes. All is well.

Or is it? When Nehemiah returns he finds that promised reforms have been neglected (chapter 13). The influential Tobiah, governor of the Ammonite province, has been given a room in the temple itself![5] Temple supplies were neglected and the Levites had returned to their own fields to support themselves. Men worked on the sabbath, marketing their goods right in Jerusalem. To top everything, people had reverted to square one and were intermarrying with heathen peoples. Nehemiah, the man of prayer and action, strengthens his resolve by prayer and forcefully acts to stop these practices once again.

Surely these men—Zerubbabel, Ezra, and Nehemiah, along with the prophets Haggai, Zechariah, and Malachi—made their impact on the community of returned exiles. The very existence of these books shows that the Jews recognized their concerns as God's own concerns. The lesson for this people (and any people) is found in another book written for the exiles. The word spoken first to Asa needs to be heard again: "If you seek him [Yahweh], he will be found by you, but if you forsake him, he will forsake you" (2 Chronicles 15:2).

## UNDERSTANDING EZRA-NEHEMIAH

### The Good Hand of God

Many supernatural events assured the Israelites they were God's people. Yahweh had vindicated himself in Egypt, had brought them through the Sea, had miraculously fed them in the desert, had brought them across the Jordan, defeated the Canaanites, and delivered them innumerable times since. If their time of punishment in Babylon—predicted as seventy years (Jeremiah 25:11-12, 29:10-14)—was indeed over, then expectation must have been high that Yahweh would intervene.

And intervene he did. "The LORD moved the heart of Cyrus king of Persia" (Ezra 1:1). Unlike Yahweh's ancient acts of deliverance, his actions in these books take place behind the scenes. He is the sovereign God of history who can bring things to pass without showing his hand. It is enough that God names Cyrus as the deliverer in advance (Isaiah 44:28—45:7). Though no cloud of glory and no pillar of fire by night led these people, they nonetheless enjoyed fulfillment of his word (Isaiah 40:8).

The negro spiritual has it, "He's got the whole world in his hands." Just so, Ezra and Nehemiah recognize Yahweh's ability to bring to pass his will. They also recognize Yahweh's involvement in their own work when they are committed to his plan.

At every step where they desire to glorify God in their plans and a green light shows up, they perceive the hand of God. Does Ezra want to go to Jerusalem to teach the Law? He seeks permission from the Gentile ruler

Artaxerxes. Permission is granted. This is "the hand of the LORD his God" (Ezra 7:6, 7:27-28).

Does Nehemiah want to help reestablish Jerusalem and Judah in the land of promise—a place where his heart is, though his feet stand in faraway Susa? He prays that God might allow it. He tells his desires to the king. Permission and more is granted. It is "the gracious hand of my God upon me" (Nehemiah 2:8,18).

It is this God of heaven who moved the heart of Cyrus, and who moved the hearts of those who returned under Zerubbabel, and who put it in the heart of Nehemiah to act for Jerusalem (Ezra 1:1, 1:5; Nehemiah 2:12, 7:5; cf. Ezra 8:18).[6] It is this same God who protects his people—whether from the perils of desert travel or from plotting officials (Ezra 8:21-23, 8:31, 4:5, 9:9; Nehemiah 4:15, 4:20, 6:16).

The returnees no doubt could have wished for "instant success" and "instant fulfillment" of all the prophecies about God's ultimate salvation after exile—just as today many look for "instant maturity" and "instant perfection" through some new method or quick fix. Even at the original entrance to the land, God tested Israel's response and faithfulness. Here, too, he would test her faithfulness—not in great battles, but in a struggling situation when his own activity seems not so spectacular.

**Doing It Right**

Every youngster needs to learn about doing it right. My father did his best to teach me about the right use of tools. I was most impressed with this lesson after I used one of his wood chisels to lop the head off a small metal bolt. Let's just say Dad got my attention that day.

Israel too needed the lesson of doing it right. Her neglect in following the directions of the Law had been total and nearly fatal. Hear the confession of Nehemiah:

> I confess the sins we Israelites, including myself and my father's house, have committed against you. We have acted very wickedly toward you. We have not obeyed the commands, decrees and laws you gave

> your servant Moses (Nehemiah 1:6-7; cf. 9:13-37, Ezra 9:6-7).

The reason for failure was recognized. So was the solution:

> Remember the instruction you gave your servant Moses, saying, "If you are unfaithful, I will scatter you among the nations, but if you return to me and obey my commands, then even if your exiled people are at the farthest horizon, I will gather them from there and bring them to the place I have chosen as a dwelling for my Name" (Nehemiah 1:8-9; cf. Deuteronomy 30:1-10, 1 Kings 8:46-51).

This accounts for the primary emphasis in these books on obeying the Law of Moses. Far from being a new emphasis, this insistence on obedience for blessing takes us back to the basic principles of Israel's founding.[7] Just as she was oppressed in the period of Judges because of disobedience, so now exile had come. The solution is the same. She must turn back to Yahweh.

And emphasis it is! On every page we are told that things are being prescribed "in accordance with what is written in the Law of Moses the man of God" (Ezra 3:2), or "according to the command of the God of Israel" (6:14; cf. Nehemiah 8:1, 8:14), and "according to what is written in the Book of Moses" (Ezra 6:18; cf. Nehemiah 8:15). Ezra is recognized as "well versed in the Law of Moses" and had "devoted himself to the study and observance of the Law of the LORD, and to teaching its decrees and laws in Israel" (Ezra 7:6, 7:10-11). It is the "wisdom of God" which he possesses (7:25-26).

The people recognize their sin as disregarding "the commands you gave through your servants the prophets" (9:10-11) and as unfaithfulness to God (10:2). How to set right the violation? "Let it be done according to the Law" (10:3).

Based on the Law, usury was stopped, intermarriages with pagan peoples were dissolved, uncertified priests were excluded from temple duty, and pledges were given to live lives consistent with commitment to God (Nehemiah 5:6-12, 7:64, 10:29-39). But the close of the book leaves in doubt whether the people will consistently obey. At Nehemiah's return from Persia he finds many of these same violations occurring. So the book's final concern is, Will God's people open themselves to the blessing of full restoration through obedience, or won't they?

**Separation and Opposition**

Another primary emphasis of Ezra-Nehemiah is the need to be a separate and distinct people. Intermarriage with peoples not exclusively devoted to worship of Yahweh would dilute and destroy true worship (Ezra 9:1-2). This is not a matter of pure blood lines. Israel's history is dotted with those descended from other nations—Rahab and Ruth being two conspicuous examples. The concern is not with pure ancestry, but with a pure people. There is a vast difference. Anyone can join this people, as Ezra 6:21 indicates, but to marry pagan peoples is to compromise faith with Yahweh. Solomon's foreign wives stand as a warning against this folly (Nehemiah 13:26-27). Divorce seems like a tragic and difficult option. But when God's directives have been disregarded, people often find themselves in a no-win situation. Their initial sin has made it impossible to cleanse themselves without causing more pain and suffering.

The questions the Corinthians asked the apostle Paul about their "mixed marriages" may well have been raised by reading Ezra and Nehemiah. They wanted to know whether marriages between believers and unbelievers should be dissolved (1 Corinthians 7:1, 7:12-16).

Paul says, "No." He concludes that their situation is exactly the opposite of the Old Testament. In Ezra's day the presence of an unbeliever in the marriage made the whole family "unclean" before God. But under the progress of the gospel, Paul says, it is just the reverse. The unbelieving spouse and the children are counted as "clean" or "sanctified" because of the believing mate. Why should this be? A moment's reflection shows the difference.

In the Old Testament to marry an unbeliever was to defect from God. But this is far from the Corinthian situation. Paul had brought the gospel to the Corinthians. Many now believed and had come into relationship with God. Being tied to unbelieving mates does not indicate their movement away from God. Rather, their belief shows positively that God is at work in their family. No sin caused these "mixed marriages." They became "mixed" because salvation came to their house.

Just as intermarriage with surrounding peoples is prohibited by Ezra-Nehemiah, so is cooperative worship. While these peoples claim to worship Yahweh, they do not worship him exclusively as the Law required (Ezra 4:1-3). These people were transplanted into Samaria by Assyria at the fall of the northern kingdom of Israel. They "worshiped the LORD, but they also appointed all sorts of their own people . . . as priests . . . . They worshiped the LORD, but they also served their own gods" (2 Kings 17:32-33). This is not true worship at all, as the historian of Kings points out (17:34-41).

Such "exclusiveness" as that demonstrated by Ezra and Nehemiah invariably brings opposition. It seems much nicer and not so narrow to teach that "there are many routes to heaven" or that people are "all worshiping the same God in their own way." This is all very polite, but it will hardly do for proof. Biblical history and the Jewish exile speak against it.

### The Great, Mighty, and Awesome God

To many an exiled Jew it may have seemed God had "gone underground"—like a spy who cuts off all normal contacts. But this is not how Nehemiah views him. Nehemiah's prayers reveal a message about God that illumines everything else. Yahweh, God of heaven, is "the great and awesome God, who keeps his covenant of love with those who love him and obey his commands" (Nehemiah 1:5). Yahweh, Creator of all, is he who made a covenant with Abraham to give his descendants the land

(9:7-8). His keeping this covenant shows his righteousness (9:8). Yahweh is a forgiving God, gracious and compassionate, even in the face of rebellion by his people (9:16-19, 9:30-31). He did not "put an end to them or abandon them" (9:30-31). Yahweh is faithful and just. "In all that has happened to us," Nehemiah prays, "you have been just; you have acted faithfully, while we did wrong" (9:33). Yahweh is "the great, mighty, and awesome God, who keeps his covenant of love" (9:32). If they are in distress, it is not Yahweh's fault. The God of heaven has moved kingdoms for them.

### Prayers of Remembrance

Nehemiah's view of God explains his many prayers. The awesome God is able to come to his aid and is willing to involve himself with a people who recognize their failings and call upon him.

Did Nehemiah invent the sentence prayer? We find them spread throughout the book. In a number of them Nehemiah asks God to remember him, a request based on Nehemiah's understanding of God's justice. Nehemiah follows the prescription of the Law: "Do not seek revenge" (Leviticus 19:18). Vengeance is the Lord's (Deuteronomy 32:35). When Nehemiah is abused he commits it to God and asks him to carry out justice (cf. Romans 12:19).

On other occasions Nehemiah asks God to remember his efforts. Sometimes, due to the indifference of others, a believer's work is unsuccessful and sometimes even misunderstood. Nehemiah knows God alone is judge of our efforts. It is encouraging in difficult times to be able to commit such things to him (cf. 1 Corinthians 4:1-5).

### A New Exodus?

How do Ezra and Nehemiah view the situation of the returned exiles? Do they see the return from Babylon as a second Exodus, such as that predicted in Isaiah 40:1-11? Opinion is divided. Certainly some events suggest a parallel with the original Exodus—such as neighbors giving money to the returning Jews (Ezra 1:4) and the problem of intermarriage (Ezra 9:1-2; compare Moses' warnings in Deuteronomy 7:1-4). Certainly the celebration of the Festival of Booths (Nehemiah 8:13-17), which recalled God's leading through the wilderness, would encourage the people to reflect on the first Exodus. These worshipers also had crossed a desert and entered the land. And in that great prayer of Nehemiah 9, the Exodus is labeled front-page news: "You made a name for yourself, which remains to this day" (9:10).

But in all this is not one clear indication that they saw themselves in a second Exodus.[8] In fact, the "parallels" make totally different points. Even the Feast of Booths is stressed not to suggest a new Exodus, but to show their joyful compliance with the Law as read by Ezra. There are clearer parallels to Solomon's temple building (cedars from Lebanon, begun in the second month, Davidic worship, and the nearly duplicated chorus; Ezra 3:7-11, cf. 2 Chronicles 5:13) than to the Exodus.

If Ezra-Nehemiah does not proclaim a second Exodus, how does it view Israel's situation? The answer is clear and shows why they are unwilling to fully identify with a new Exodus. They are slaves (Ezra 9:9). They are subjects to a foreign king, the king of Persia. As much as God has moved his heart to aid them, they have not been freed as a people. The land is not theirs. The Davidic king is not on the throne.

What has God done for them?

> But now for a brief moment grace has been shown from the LORD our God, to leave us an escaped remnant and to give us a peg in His holy place, that our God may enlighten our eyes and grant us a little reviving in our bondage. For we are slaves; yet in our bondage, our God has not forsaken us, but has extended lovingkindness to us in the sight of the kings of Persia, to give us reviving to raise up the house of our God, to restore its ruins, and to give us a wall in Judah and Jerusalem (Ezra 9:8-9 NASB).

They have a "peg" in Jerusalem. The word means "tent-peg" and refers to the place a wanderer pitches his tent.[9] God has given them an opportunity, something of a start—and Ezra is concerned that their renewed sin might wipe out this beginning: "Would you not be angry enough with us to destroy us, leaving us no remnant or survivor?" (Ezra 9:14).

The prayer of Nehemiah 9 arrives at the same bottom line:

> But see, we are slaves today, slaves in the land you gave our forefathers so they could eat its fruit and the other good things it produces. Because of our sins, its abundant harvest goes to the kings you have placed over us. They rule over our bodies and our cattle as they please. We are in great distress (9:36-37).

The judgment begun at the exile has not been fully lifted. But they have a beginning. The Lord has moved the heart of Cyrus. The temple is rebuilt. They have their peg in the holy place.

## ON THE WAY: COMPLETION OF EXILE

Remember Jeremiah's picture of Rachel weeping for her children as they were marched off to exile? Matthew uses this scene in an entirely different connection. In Matthew 2 we find Herod, not Nebuchadnezzar, persecuting the Jews. In an effort to eliminate any competition, Herod orders a pogrom against the Jewish lads of Bethlehem. All boys two years of age and under are to be butchered, so Herod can eradicate the one born "king of the Jews" (2:13-18, 2:2).

Jesus escapes, but others die—as they often have under Pharaohs and Herods and Hitlers. The massacre of Bethlehem, Matthew says, fulfilled the words of the prophet Jeremiah.

> A voice is heard in Ramah,
> weeping and great mourning,

Rachel weeping for her children
  and refusing to be comforted,
because they are no more (Matthew 2:18).

But how can the deaths of these children of Bethlehem fulfill Jeremiah's words when Jeremiah was speaking of the Babylonian captivity over five centuries earlier (Jeremiah 31:15)?

The answer shows that Matthew views the return from exile in precisely the same way as did Ezra and Nehemiah.

As we noted in our discussion of the Exodus, Matthew uses Hosea 11:1—"Out of Egypt I called my Son," a verse speaking of Israel's exodus from Egypt—to show that Jesus is Israel's representative who will fulfill God's purposes for his people. Jesus will bring in the new and final Exodus. What God did for Israel at her beginning, he will bring to completion through his Son. This New Exodus would bring Jews back from their exile in Babylon and elsewhere and restore them to the land and nationhood (Isaiah 49).

Is it then surprising that in this same context Matthew again uses a verse referring to Israel's history, and teaches its fulfillment in Jesus? In the account of the Bethlehem massacre, Matthew quotes Jeremiah 31:15 to remind the Jews they still await restoration from the captivity Nebuchadnezzar began. His use of this verse indicates that, like Ezra and Nehemiah, he believes the Jews are *still slaves* under Gentile rulers.

The Babylonian captivity was replaced by the rule of Persia. Cyrus allowed a contingent to return and rebuild the temple, but full restoration was not achieved.

The next king of the hill was Alexander the Great of Greece, conqueror of the then-known world. After Alexander's early death and the division of his empire, the Jews rebelled against a despised Seleucid ruler, Antiochus IV. For a brief moment this revolt of the Maccabees gave Judea its freedom. But it produced no lasting kingdom. The Jews soon found themselves under Pax Romana—Roman "peace."

Herod, Caesar's local stand-in, appears as the latest of a long series of Gentile rulers. As Ezra confessed,

> We and our kings and our priests have been subjected to the sword and captivity, to pillage and humiliation at the hand of foreign kings, as it is today (Ezra 9:7).

That confession would hold equally good for any Jew of Jesus' day.

Rachel still cries. She cried when they went out under Nebuchadnezzar. Nearly six centuries later, she still is weeping. And in Matthew's day, Jeremiah's report of Israel's suffering is yet being fulfilled.

But Jeremiah did not tell us about Rachel's crying to predict unending persecution for the Jews. In fact, he uses this grim picture as a backdrop for sketching a brighter day.

Rachel will not always cry, says Jeremiah, because Yahweh will *never* abandon his people. Rachel's children will return and be restored, and God will give them a New Covenant more effective than the one given after the original Exodus. This covenant will produce in them a new heart—and Yahweh will never again have to chasten his people with judgment (Jeremiah 31:16-37).

Jesus, the promised Messiah, will complete the New Exodus—full restoration from the captivity of Babylon. Even now his herald is calling, "Repent, for the kingdom of heaven is near" (Matthew 3:2). This John the Baptist, Matthew says, is the messenger Isaiah predicted who would announce the New Exodus.

> A voice of one calling in the desert,
> "Prepare the way for the Lord,
> make straight paths for him"
> (Matthew 3:3, Isaiah 40:3).

Rachel's crying must cease. As surely as Jeremiah predicted Jewish suffering under captivity, he predicted future relief and restoration. Matthew says, "It's beginning. The King has arrived."

The King is coming, the King is coming,
I just heard the trumpet sounding and now
His face I see!
The King is coming, the King is coming;
Praise God! He's coming for me![10]

# FOR PERSONAL INTERACTION & DISCUSSION

SUGGESTED SCRIPTURE READINGS:

Ezra 9
Nehemiah 1—2
Jeremiah 31:5-34
Matthew 2:1-18

1. How does understanding that there were three returns from exile help put the books of Ezra and Nehemiah into proper perspective?
2. What are the specific sins which trouble the people at this time? What would you think would be the specific sins that would be listed if God were evaluating his people today?
3. Why is not the attitude of excluding foreigners not simply a racist approach to salvation? What is the New Testament attitude toward separating from unbelieving married partners? Why the difference?
4. How does God's activity in this period differ from his great acts of salvation in earlier periods? Which approach compares to our own time? How do the attitudes of Ezra and Nehemiah toward God's oversight help us in our own outlook on life?
5. What about the attitude of these men toward sin?
6. Consider the "instant success" syndrome. What would you desire that God provide for your life? Have you prayed about it? Is it something that brings glory to God and fits his purposes for life? Must God answer immediately, or are you willing to wait for doors to open?
7. How does effort relate to prayer? What is to be our attitude when our efforts are misunderstood or opposed by others?

8. How does the hope of a New Exodus tie in to the return from Babylon and to Jesus? Why is Rachel crying? Is she still crying?

'AREN'T THESE VISIONS
ENOUGH TO STIR EVEN
THE DULLEST OF HEARTS?
THERE IS A FUTURE FOR
JERUSALEM! AND IN THAT
ULTIMATE HOPE THERE IS
FORGIVENESS AND A
FUTURE FOR US ALL.'

CHAPTER

# 14.

# THE SECOND TEMPLE

HOPE IN
HAGGAI
&
ZECHARIAH

"Hope deferred makes the heart sick." So Solomon tells us in Proverbs 13:12. Unrealized hopes sack marriages, ruin careers, prompt suicides, and make midlife crisis a household term. To bet your life on someone or something and then lose is more than demoralizing. It can cripple.

The prophets Haggai and Zechariah are called to minister to people who began with elevated hopes and dreams. This first group of returning exiles gave up what had become, surprisingly enough, a comfortable life in captivity. With the words of the prophets in their minds and hearts, they headed home to the land of promise. The earlier predictions of exile by Jeremiah and others had not been popular; but now the people could claim the brighter prophecies of restoration (Jeremiah 30:18—31:40). Riches did not await them, but they could be the first generation to reenter the land and see God work. In Israel's history they could stand like those of Joshua's generation and see Yahweh do great and mighty things for them.

Yet it was not to be. As we saw in the last chapter, the initial attempt to rebuild the temple was halted for fifteen years by opposition from non-Jewish residents and officials. The work barely had begun. Unlike Joshua's generation, the Jews had no command from God to exterminate the other peoples in the land, nor were they enabled to do so. They came not with might or with power. They came by permission of Cyrus.[1]

Disillusion set in. Cynicism found fertile soil. Energies were turned to the business of making a living. Hope was placed on a dusty shelf to be reconsidered when more time was available. Enter Haggai and Zechariah.

## HAGGAI, PROPHET OF PRIORITIES

### Misplaced Priorities

Haggai is first to face the lethargy of the people. Some were saying, "The time has not yet come for the LORD's house to be built" (Haggai 1:2). Not good enough, says Haggai: "Is it a time for you yourselves to be living in your paneled houses, while this house [the temple] remains a ruin?" As often happens, living has become so important that living for a purpose has been pushed to the back of the bus.

Take stock, says Haggai; what have you accomplished? Haven't you noticed that you've been caught in that most desperate of circles—the direct pursuit of things? What have you gained? You always seem to come up short. Your moneybag is full of holes. Has God been trying to tell you something (1:5-6)?

The God who provided manna to that first generation is blowing away the crops of this one. Why? Because they put their comfort ahead of spiritual priorities. The temple still lies in ruins.

Their delay in rebuilding the temple cannot be compared to debate today over building a new and larger sanctuary for a local assembly. Today's questions are merely issues of propriety, convenience and seating. But having a temple meant proper worship according to God's revealed word. Not having it meant neglecting the ceremonies that announced God's forgiveness and care.

If those responsible for rebuilding the temple have doubts about timing, they need doubt no more: Haggai's message to Zerubbabel the governor, Joshua the high priest, and the people is, "'I am with you,' declares the LORD" (1:13). With this the people resume work on the temple.

**A House with a Future**

After building is resumed, each message from Haggai is increasingly positive. Do some feel like quitting because this temple, built from recycled rocks and common timber from nearby mountains, doesn't have the glory of Solomon's temple? Then they should know that God himself will make the temple a place of splendor, with gold and silver from the nations. Not only splendor, but peace will finally come to this place—a peace never finally established even under the man of peace who built the first temple (2:1-9; cf. 2 Samuel 7:11-16).

**Blessing Begun**

When will God begin to bless them? God could not bless them with an incomplete temple in their midst. "The ruined skeleton of the Temple was like a dead body decaying in Jerusalem and making everything contaminated."[2] Even what was offered on the altar was considered defiled by God.[3] But now that they had begun to build, God's word to them is, "From this day on I will bless you" (Haggai 2:19).

**Another House with a Future**

With each prophecy Haggai alternates between present and future perspectives.[4] His final prophecy (2:20-23), like the second (2:1-9), looks to the future fulfillment of God's promises. The "signet ring" of kingship will return to the descendant of David. The son of David, Zerubbabel, is now only a governor under King Darius of Persia, but it will not always be so. Yahweh "will overturn royal thrones and shatter the power of the foreign kingdoms." As at Israel's beginning, *Yahweh will again fight for Israel.* The house of David, like the house of God, has been chosen for future greatness.

Haggai performs his task well. His messages get the people going. Straightforward and hardhitting, he deals with the immediate problems of lethargy and defeatism. He holds up the twin banners of the house of God and the house of David and starts the people marching.

## ZECHARIAH—VISIONS OF HOPE

Zechariah delivers his first message one month before Haggai's last recorded words—appropriately so! He takes up and enlarges on what Haggai had begun. With broader brush strokes and greater depth of field, he paints a picture of the future that God's people can ponder again and again. Haggai gave them the sketch. Zechariah gives them the oil.

### Zechariah's Purpose

But first, Zechariah gives a message that is direct and definite. "Return to me, declares Yahweh of Hosts, and I will return to you" (1:3, my translation). This initial message sets the tone for all the rest. Right from the start, God's people must recognize there are no guarantees for this generation. If they do not avoid the evil practices of their fathers who were taken into exile, they can expect the same judgment. Their fathers are dead, as are even the prophets who brought God's message; but God's message itself came to pass.

Haggai tackled immediate problems to get the temple started. But Zechariah wants to probe deeper. The people must realize that building the temple will not guarantee that the promises will be fulfilled. Unless they consistently follow the Lord, they cannot expect the hopes of this book to begin unfolding in their lifetime.[5]

### Zechariah's Visions

One night, two months after Haggai's last message, Zechariah enjoys little sleep. He is kept alert by a series of complex scenes that pass before his red eyes. They are not the result of indigestion, nor should they be equated with the "visions" of leaders today. No, Zechariah's visions are appropriate to a prophet: They are revelations from God. Exciting ideas do not qualify. Zechariah is not merely "pumping sunshine" or using modern motivational techniques. Only divinely inspired revelation can produce truly inspired living.

This one-night screening has some eye-catching features. Along with horses and chariots are a man with a measuring line, a woman in a basket, a flying scroll, a priest in dirty duds, and a golden menorah with automatic oil feed.[6]

But what can it mean? These visual messages click off a number of crucial concepts. The visions begin and end with patrols which survey the earth and report back to the angel of the Lord (1:7-17, 6:1-8). The theme: Yahweh controls history and nations. He has judged Israel for her sin, now he will judge the nations. This is further spelled out by the second vision in which four craftsmen demolish four "horns" which stand for the nations that exiled Judah and Israel (1:18-21). But Jerusalem itself has a great future (2:1-13). The man who would measure Jerusalem is to inform Zechariah that the city will be larger than ever before—so large it will not be walled. But she will not need walls. Yahweh, as in the days of the Exodus, will provide a wall of protecting fire around his people.[7] Yahweh's presence will cause other nations to become his people too.

A vision of the filthy high priest introduces another theme (3:1-10). Looking more like a bum than God's high priest, Joshua's clothes picture the sin of Israel. Satan would demand punishment, but God announces grace. He will take away Israel's sin in a single day through his future servant, the Branch. Not only will her sin be removed and forgiveness granted, but justice will be guaranteed as the scroll of the Law flies throughout the whole land (5:1-4). This aerodynamic billboard searches out and removes the very sins that the Law placed under a curse. In this way the hidden apostasy of individuals would not be allowed to bring failure to the nation. Wickedness itself, pictured as a woman—perhaps a figurine idol—would be removed from Israel and sent back to its source, Babylon (5:5-11).[8]

In addition to the high priest, a civil leader named Zerubbabel is brought into the visions (4:1-14). The golden menorah, the seven-stemmed lamp of the temple, represents Israel as God's light. Two olive trees joined to the lamp supply it with golden oil. These stand for the two anointed offices of priest and king, represented by Joshua and Zerubbabel (heir to the throne of David). God will use these two functions to sustain his people. Even now in this "day of small things" (4:10), when it seems as if nothing spectacular is happening, God's Spirit is at work. Completion of the temple will be the first step in the ultimate success of God's program.

### A Crown in Jerusalem

This focus on priest and king is reaffirmed in a following message (6:9-15). Here a crown is made and placed on the head of Joshua, the high priest. Joshua again symbolizes the future servant, the Branch. The Branch—a name already used in Jeremiah 23:5 and 33:15 for the coming Messiah of David's line—will take his place on the throne. "He will be a priest on his throne" (Zechariah 6:13). So the two offices of priest and king will become one in the Messiah. To place a crown on the head of Zerubbabel would signal rebellion against the Persian throne.[9] But this was not the time for rebellion. God would work by his Spirit at the proper time, without military might or power. Yet even now these prophets do not hesitate to predict the restoration of David's throne.

Aren't these visions enough to stir even the dullest of hearts? The Jews would not always be under the Persian throne. David's line and Israel's worship will last until even the nations themselves join Israel. God will pardon their sin and remove evil from among them. There is a future for Jerusalem! And in that ultimate hope there is forgiveness and a future for us all.

### Feast or Fast?

Like a newsreel between two special features, chapters 7 and 8 lie between Zechariah's visions and prophecies—and answer a rather mundane question about keeping fasts. Four yearly fasts had been started by the Jews to mourn the fall of Jerusalem.[10] "Should these fasts continue?" a delegation from Bethel asks the priests (7:1-3).

Glad you asked, says Zechariah. God has something to say about that. This little question provides an opportunity to reemphasize the main features of God's message through Zechariah. Check them out:

- Their fasting was over their own loss and not over the sin which caused that loss. They will need to start to do justice, not mourn God's righteous judgment of past failure (7:4-14).
- Jerusalem will be reestablished as God's great city complete with aged people and playing children (8:3-6).
- There will be a greater return of Israel to the land (8:7-8).
- Because rebuilding the temple has started, God will be able to bless them if they are careful to reverse their former injustice in the land (8:9-17).
- Periods of fasting will be changed into times of rejoicing, and other nations will want to worship at Jerusalem because of the news of God's blessing on Israel (8:18-23).

Jerusalem, the temple, God's blessing, returning to God, and conversion of the nations are all reaffirmed in answer to a question about fasting! Jesus provided an additional answer: When the Messiah himself is present, no one fasts (Mark 2:19).

**Two Final Oracles—Zechariah 9-14**

There was upheaval in the empire before Darius was firmly established on the Persian throne. Undoubtedly the Jews hoped God would use this confusion to break up the empire and allow his people to begin their life again as an independent state. But it was not to be. The first vision (1:8-17) contained the discouraging report that all was quiet. When would God begin to move the political situation for the restoration of his people? These last two prophetic messages glimpsed the future of Israel leading to a time of ultimate peace and fulfillment.

Someone has said that God has not shown each of us our future because we would not be prepared to accept it all at once. Reading Zechariah 9—14 is like that. Ultimate blessing is here, but so are rough times—the kind of times synonymous with the area of the world known as the Middle East.

Much like Psalm 2, these oracles predict the Lord's victory over the nations. The nations will gather against Jerusalem, but God will use her to judge them (12:1-9). The surrounding peoples will be conquered (9:1-8), and many, like the Jebusites of David's time, will become part of Israel (9:7). It is Yahweh who fights for them again (9:14-17). The final battle for Jerusalem will bring Yahweh himself to the Mount of Olives to aid Israel and bring plagues on the rebellious nations (14:2-15).

Reading Zechariah 9—14 is much like singing a musical round. Half the fun is recognizing the repeated lines as they enter at alternate places. Just so, these prophetic episodes are not traced chronologically. Again and again, themes are repeated—yet modified.[11] Zechariah gives us not an event-by-event calendar of the future, but pictures of events like pages in an album. Each page is dedicated to a particular slice of the future.

One such page is God's action to deliver Israel from the nations while at the same time using her to cause many nations to recognize the true God. Another page includes snapshots of the Messiah. Like other Old Testament prophets, Zechariah does not separate events of Jesus' first coming (to suffer) from his second coming (to reign). Examples of both are found on the same page.

One great picture of the future Messiah is that of Zechariah 9:9-10. The righteous Messiah comes with salvation—a king who enters Jerusalem riding a purebred donkey. He is not arrogant as other shepherds of Israel have been (another theme of these prophecies—11:15-17, 13:2-6). Here is one who humbly follows Yahweh's word (cf. Isaiah 66:2). This scene, of course, pictures Jesus' triumphal entry into Jerusalem; yet verse 10 awaits fulfillment at the Second Coming.

Another Messianic scene is found in 13:7-9. Following the discussion of false prophets (13:2-6), Yahweh's own shepherd is introduced. But astonishingly enough, Yahweh calls on his sword of judgment to kill his shepherd. Moreover, Yahweh calls this shepherd *My Associate* (NASB; NIV: "who is close to me"). This word translated "associate" is used elsewhere only in the Law of Moses where it is translated "neighbor" or "brother." ("Do not have intercourse with your *neighbor's* wife," Leviticus 18:20.) It looks at an equal, a comrade, a fellow-citizen with equal standing.[12] The Messiah, the man equal in standing with Yahweh, will suffer Yahweh's righteous judgment. Again, readers of the New Testament will recognize that Jesus applied this verse to himself. In his crucifixion God brought judgment on his own Shepherd, that a fountain might be opened to cleanse us from sin and impurity (Zechariah 13:1, Matthew 26:31).

## THE OUTLOOK OF THE POST-EXILIC PROPHETS

Our overview of the themes of Haggai and Zechariah makes plain the outlook of the prophets after the exile: The house of David and the house of God, so tightly combined in the original Davidic Covenant (2 Samuel 7:11-16), are still the hope of the future. "Then suddenly the Lord you are seeking will come to his temple; the messenger of the covenant, whom you desire, will come" (Malachi 3:1). Yahweh's presence with the nation once again, predicted in Ezekiel 44:4, is her only hope of restoration and salvation.[13]

The other concern is like the old chorus sung by Sunday school children: "Will you be ready when Jesus comes?" Malachi, after announcing the coming of Messiah to his temple, continues: "But who can endure the day of his coming? Who can stand when he appears? For he will be like a refiner's fire or a launderer's soap" (Malachi 3:2). Zechariah's call for repentance is reissued by Malachi. Unfaithfulness to the temple and injustice to fellow Israelites still predominate.

But make no mistake about the *Cause* of their salvation. Yahweh of Hosts (or armies) is his name. This is the favorite name for God in these books (translated "LORD Almighty" in the NIV). This name is appropriate in worship settings where "hosts" refers to the angels who surround God's throne (Isaiah 6:1-5). It is also used for God's power to deliver through heavenly armies of angels (Psalm 46:7, cf. Joshua 5:14). Yahweh of Hosts is the awesome God they are to worship and to whom they look for deliverance. He is in control of all the earth, which his angelic army patrols.

Hope has been proclaimed, but there is a gauntlet to run. The returned exiles may despise "the day of small things"—no glory, no fire, no military victories—yet there is a great future for Judah and also for Ephraim (Zechariah 10:6-12), neither of which were yet fully restored. The temple project is the first signal that God would restore his people. If they return faithfully to him, they can be part of a great movement leading ultimately to the promised kingdom under the restored line of David. Perhaps a Jew of Zerubbabel's time could have seen it as Paul did: "I consider that our present sufferings are not worth comparing with the glory that will be revealed in us" (Romans 8:18). It sure beats finishing life with a bag full of holes!

Israel's King is our King. We are citizens of his kingdom. Our project is not a temple made with hands. But if we are going to make our lives count, we had better know how to build (1 Corinthians 3:10-17).

## ON THE WAY: THE DAY OF SALVATION

As Jesus rode that purebred donkey into Jerusalem, he was riding an animal favored by ancient kings but long since supplanted by the horse as the steed of choice. His kingship was recognized by the crowd that accompanied him with shouting (Matthew 21:1-11):

> "Hosanna to the Son of David!"
> "Blessed is he who comes in the name of the Lord!"
> "Hosanna in the highest!"

Did not the prophet say to shout at this event (Zechariah 9:9)? And what did they shout? None other than the words of Psalm 118:25-26.

What is it about this psalm which singles it out for use on such an occasion?

Psalm 118 celebrates a great event—an unexpected victory over the enemies of Israel who are pictured as swarming around Israel's leader like bees. The celebration makes its way to the temple where the leader asks entrance to give his thanks to Yahweh (19-21). He is allowed to enter and offer his praise (22-24), praise that begins with a proverb: "The stone the builders rejected has become the capstone." The praise continues, "The LORD has done this, and it is marvelous in our eyes. This is the day the Lord has made; let us rejoice and be glad in it."

What could he mean by the rejected stone becoming the capstone? The capstone finishes the building (Zechariah 4:7). Because the leader is entering the temple, this saying must be about the temple itself—most likely the second temple.[14] A stone from the rubble of Solomon's temple, rejected earlier by the builders, is found to be just the right stone for the final, honored spot.

What could the leader mean by applying this proverb to himself? He sees his situation as parallel. He was rejected and yet now has been elevated to a place of honor. Verses 17 and 18 of the psalm confirm this:

> I will not die but live,
> and will proclaim what the LORD has done.
> The LORD has chastened me severely,
> but he has not given me over to death.

Because the leader in Psalms is usually the king of David's line and represents the people of Israel in his actions, the conclusion of Perowne seems most likely:

> They [Israel] had been despised by their heathen masters, but now, by the good

> hand of their God upon them, they had been lifted into a place of honour. They, rejected of men, were chosen of God as the chief stone of that new spiritual building which Jehovah was about to erect.[15]

Israel had been counted out. Declared a national has-been. Washed up on the sands of time. Yet her captivity was not an end, but a beginning. She may celebrate her deliverance in the language of those kings that Yahweh delivered before her. But she must also *pray* for deliverance (118:25), because she has not yet seen Yahweh's full salvation:[16]

> O LORD, save us;
> O LORD, grant us success.

In the same way, the Jews of Jesus' time still looked for salvation, though they were living in the land of their forefathers with the temple completed and some of the riches of the nations adding to its splendor. Yet Yahweh's full salvation had not yet come. They are subjects, no longer of the Persians, but of the Romans.

**Hosanna**

"Hosanna!" the crowds shouted as Jesus headed toward the temple. This cry repeats the Hebrew words in Psalm 118:25—"Save now." Here comes the King! They expect him to deliver. Only later did they recognize that the words true of Israel once before would also be true of Israel's final King: "The stone the builders rejected" is the one God places at the top of the building.

Peter boldly declares of Jesus, "He is the stone you builders rejected, which has become the capstone." This means "Salvation is found in no one else, for there is no other name under heaven given to men by which we must be saved" (Acts 4:11-12).

**The Day**

> This is the day the LORD has made;
> let us rejoice and be glad in it
> (Psalm 118:24).

Christians sing these lines today as if they speak of each new day provided by God. "Let's rejoice in another day God has given us" is the common thought. But Psalm 118 is not exhorting us to find something joyous about every day. It is speaking of a special day of victory when God delivers. Yahweh makes such a day by his intervention. A day of victory! A day of celebration! The psalm looks and prays for another such day—a day of ultimate salvation.

Isaiah 49 predicted that kind of day for the exiles. Not only will Yahweh's Servant restore the tribes of Israel, but he will be "a light for the Gentiles, that you may bring my salvation to the ends of the earth" (49:6). God says to Israel,

> In the time of my favor I will answer you,
> and in the day of salvation I will help you (49:8).

In Christ, that day of salvation has arrived! Paul declares, "God was reconciling the world to himself in Christ, not counting men's sins against them" (2 Corinthians 5:19). As Christ's ambassadors we implore others, "Be reconciled to God." Reconciliation is possible because "God made him who had no sin to be sin for us, so that in him we might become the righteousness of God" (5:20-21). Quoting Isaiah 49:8, Paul concludes: "I tell you, now is the time of God's favor, now is the day of salvation" (2 Corinthians 6:2).

We, my friends, are living in the day of salvation! Christ has come and provided light not only to the Jews, but also to the Gentiles. Rejected by rulers, he nonetheless is God's answer. We await his return to complete all that the prophets have spoken; but today we may celebrate.

Sing it with me:

> This is the day that the Lord has made,
> We will rejoice and be glad in it!

# FOR PERSONAL INTERACTION & DISCUSSION

SUGGESTED SCRIPTURE READINGS:

Zechariah 9:9-17
Psalm 118
2 Corinthians 5:17—6:2

1. How did changing priorities keep the returned exiles from fulfilling their original purpose? What unhealthy priority took first place? Is this a common problem? Illustrate it from your own experience.
2. What dual promise and hope are held up in the book of Haggai? Why are these so important to these people?
3. How does Zechariah's basic message differ from Haggai's? What possible misconception does he correct? What response does he want from the people?
4. How do the visual images in Zechariah clarify what God will do for his people?
5. What is the message about Yahweh's Shepherd? How does he compare with the other shepherds of Israel? What specifics about this Shepherd tie in to Jesus?
6. What is the "day of salvation"? What is meant by "now is the day of salvation" (2 Corinthians 6:2)? What glorious message does this make available? What should our response be?

‘ALREADY WE ARE IN “THE LAST DAYS” SPOKEN OF BY THE PROPHETS. WE ARE IN THE TIME OF FULFILLMENT. THE AGE TO COME IS HERE; YET IT IS NOT FULLY REVEALED. ALREADY . . . BUT NOT YET.’

---

CHAPTER 15.

# ON THE WAY TO THE FUTURE

## OTHER FEATURES OF HOPE

When our family goes on trips, we ask the inevitable questions as we pull out the driveway: "Are the doors locked?" Is the oven turned off? Iron unplugged?" One remaining question we cannot yet answer: "What have we forgotten?" Time will tell and always does.

As I come to this last chapter, I ask myself the same question: "What have I forgotten?" Time will tell, but I already know quite a few things. On this trip through the Bible I have covered what are commonly referred to as "the historical books." With few exceptions I have left the others behind. My choice was to cover the Old Testament's backbone, the part Christians often avoid because it smacks of names and dates and—let's say it—history.

If you've come this far with me, perhaps your notion of these books has changed. They are not a dusty record of facts and events—on par with some modern, dryly detailed account of the Crimean War. Biblical writers selected key events and carefully linked them so we might discover the divine lessons of Israel's history. The accounts of David and Goliath, Gideon with his lamps, and Samuel hearing the voice in the night are not incidental stories, but part of a larger mosaic—the whole of which carries a greater impact than the sum of its parts.

Oh, I admit to sneaking in a chapter on wisdom. Like chocolate, it was too tempting and enjoyable not to give you a taste. And though the prophets Haggai and Zechariah also are not "historical books," I did treat them since Ezra and Nehemiah alone give us too little of the outlook of the returning exiles.

But what have I forgotten? Plenty. I omitted most of the prophets. As you move on to study them, I believe you'll find their message harmonizes with the themes we have already seen for each period of God's working.

Space left no room for the books of:

- *Ruth*—about God's grace in accomplishing what was impossible according to the Law, and so providing a continuing family in Israel—the family of David.
- *Esther*—which shows, like Ezra and Nehemiah, that God was in control even while the Jews were outside the land and under foreign kings.
- *Song of Solomon*—a wisdom book which, to handle properly, would take more ability than I have. One of my students confessed his delight as a teenager in choosing verses from the Song of Solomon to quote during church meetings when the congregation was asked to share "their favorite verse." My favorite verse about Song of Solomon is Proverbs 5:18-19. All the rest is commentary.

So much for the intentional omissions. As my family always finds, there is only so much room in the trunk. But some omissions compel us to stop our vehicle and retrieve valuable cargo. We would not want to reach our destination without them.

## Themes for the Future

The first theme we cannot leave only partially treated is the prediction of a new covenant. Jeremiah, though announcing the catastrophe of captivity, nevertheless trumpeted a message of hope to those on their way out of the land. As we saw earlier, he pictures Rachel, the mother of Israel, weeping for her children as they leave and "are no more" (Jeremiah 31:15). But this nation that was no more was not forgotten by God. Jeremiah does not end his prophecy on this note of despair. In fact, he tells them to dry their tears because the exiles "will return from the land of the enemy" (31:16).

Weeping provides the background to the announcement of a new covenant (31:31-34). The old covenant which shaped Israel when she left Egypt is found inferior "because they broke my covenant, though I was a husband to them."

The failure of the old covenant is not in its laws, but in its inability to guarantee heartfelt obedience. The new covenant will remedy this failure.

> I will put my law in their minds
> and write it on their hearts.
> I will be their God,
> and they will be my people.
> No longer will a man teach his neighbor,
> or a man his brother, saying,
> "Know the LORD,"
> because they will all know me,
> from the least of them to the greatest,
> declares the LORD.
> For I will forgive their wickedness
> and will remember their sins no more.

Universal knowledge of Yahweh, forgiveness, and spiritual enablement are the hallmarks of the coming new covenant. The new covenant will guarantee the restoration of God's people. Because it will overcome the weak link of human frailty, achieve forgiveness, and produce a response of gratitude and obedience, there is a blessed future for Israel's descendants (31:35-37). But how will God accomplish this?

## Born by Water and Spirit

The prophet Ezekiel also prophesies of Israel's restoration and describes the same enablement that Jeremiah announced as part of the new covenant.

> I will sprinkle clean water on you, and you will be clean; I will cleanse you from all your impurities and from all your idols. I will give you a new heart and put a new spirit in you; I will remove from you your heart of stone and give you a heart of flesh. And I will put my Spirit in you and move you to follow my decrees and be careful to keep my laws. You will live in the land I gave your forefathers; you will be my people, and I will be your God. I will save you from all your uncleanness (Ezekiel 36:25-29).

No wonder Jesus told Nicodemus that "unless a man is born of water and the Spirit, he cannot enter the kingdom of God," and chided that teacher of Israel for not understanding these things (John 3:5-12). Without cleansing from God and the promised new heart and the work of God's Spirit within, no restoration can last. With these things, we are looking at none other than the arrival of the promised kingdom.

## The Pouring Out of the Spirit

The work of the Holy Spirit of God, promised in Ezekiel, is also the subject of Joel 2:28-32:

> And afterward,
> I will pour out my Spirit on all people.
> Your sons and daughters will prophesy,
> your old men will dream dreams,
> your young men will see visions.
> Even on my servants, both men and women,
> I will pour out my Spirit in those days.
> I will show wonders in the heavens
> and on the earth,
> blood and fire and billows of smoke.

The sun will be turned to darkness
and the moon to blood
before the coming of the great
and dreadful day of the LORD.
And everyone who calls
on the name of the LORD will be saved;
for on Mount Zion and in Jerusalem
there will be deliverance,
as the LORD has said,
among the survivors
whom the LORD calls.

This prophecy looks for Israel's universal experience of the Spirit of God. In the past the Spirit spoke through the prophets. In the future everyone will speak God's word and see visions from God. Communication with God will be direct.

**The Prophetic Combination**

When we combine these aspects of the future hope of Israel with those we saw in Zechariah and Haggai, we arrive at the following picture:

- Israel is looking for an ultimate restoration under the Davidic Messiah who will reign as King and Priest.
- Israel's restoration will be effective because God will initiate a new covenant to replace the old one (which failed because it did not supernaturally change men's hearts, as the new covenant will).
- This change will involve forgiveness, cleansing, and a new spirit produced by the work of God's Spirit.
- God's Spirit will be universally experienced and everyone will know God.
- The nations will oppose Israel, but Yahweh will deliver her by direct intervention. Many from the nations will be drawn to worship Yahweh at Jerusalem.

Such is the package of hope as we close the Old Testament. And in spite of disappointment at waiting years with no national restoration, it is still the hope of the faithful as we open the pages of the New Testament. Here we find priests and teachers able to name the place of Messiah's birth (Matthew 2:5-6) and to question John the Baptist about his place in the prophetic scheme (John 1:19-21). How many, like Simeon, were "waiting for the consolation of Israel" (Luke 2:25)? Apparently old Anna's devotion and expectation were such that she never left the temple precincts (Luke 2:36-38). Nor did she have difficulty finding those "who were looking forward to the redemption of Jerusalem" so she could tell them the news of Jesus' birth (Luke 2:38).

## NEW TESTAMENT UPDATE

The New Testament brings some surprises, however. In the Gospel records of Jesus' life there is no rise of this Son of David to an earthly throne, no overthrow of the Gentile rulers, and no intervention by Yahweh for the final deliverance of Jerusalem. What has happened? How does the New Testament relate the life of Jesus to these hopes and expectations?

### Two Advents

Predictions, when fulfilled, often happen in a way which—dare I say it?—are *unpredictable*. Or to put it another way, while futuristic prophecy often tells us *what* will occur, *how* it comes to pass may surprise us. I suspect that many bestselling books on prophecy will blush (were it possible) when prophecies "as clear as the headlines in your daily newspaper" actually come to pass. The details surrounding fulfilled prophecy are recognized when they happen, not before.

This does not mean prophecy is less than exact. Micah 5:2 predicted Messiah would be born in Bethlehem. And he was. But who would have predicted that a manger would be his first cradle and that his parents, in the kingly line of David, would be there only temporarily because of a Roman edict about a census?

One of these unpredictable items facing the Jewish believer during Jesus' lifetime was the Bible's silence concerning the fact that Messiah would come twice, not just once. The Old Testament told of both a suffering Messiah (Isaiah 53, Zechariah 13:7) *and* a victorious and reigning Messiah. The idea that Messiah would deliver them from Gentile rule dominated Jewish thinking in the New Testament period. That Messiah would come without restoring Israel to nationhood was unthinkable.

From a human perspective, the Israelites' problem was their lack of freedom and the absence of a restored Davidic monarchy. From the divine standpoint, however, the greatest problem was their need for forgiveness and for faith in God. For God, the prerequisite for restoration was the work of the new covenant with its ability to change hearts. That must come first. And that is what the First Advent is all about.

If Israel was granted a restored kingdom no different from great Gentile kingdoms, what would be gained? Even a restored kingdom as righteous as the past monarchy would not do.

Our knowing that two comings of Messiah are needed to fulfill all that the prophets have spoken helps us to understand that not everything was fulfilled during Christ's first advent. Much is still future.

This new knowledge about two comings also causes problems. Take God's sending of the Holy Spirit in Acts 2. Peter quotes Joel 2 to explain to his audience what was happening at Pentecost. Yet it is obvious that Pentecost does not fulfill all the features of Joel's prophecy. Where are the signs in the heavens, the sun turning to darkness and the moon to blood?[1] Even more, where is the gift of universal prophecy? Paul is quite clear that prophecy and knowledge are not universal in the church, even if gifts of the Spirit are (1 Corinthians 12:29). In fact, apart from receiving the Spirit himself, there is little similarity between Pentecost and Joel 2.

**Partial Fulfillment**

Experiencing part of a fulfillment, yet not to the full extent of the original prophecy, has gathered a variety of labels. Some call it *partial fulfillment*. Others use the term *double fulfillment*, suggesting that a prophecy can be fulfilled more than once. Still others see all such cases as *token fulfillments* that look forward to a full and final fulfillment. But the label is not so important. What is important is the *reason* we need these labels.

We have this problem because Messiah's two comings were unforeseen in the Old Testament. Therefore some predicted events and blessings that began at the first coming await ultimate and universal fulfillment until Christ's return, when he sets up his kingdom in full operation.

**Already, but Not Yet**

In fact, there is a whole list of predicted blessings which believers enjoy today.

- We have the promised Spirit of God (1 Corinthians 6:19, Romans 8:9).
- We are under the benefits of the new covenant, rather than the limitations of the Mosaic Covenant (Hebrews 8:6-13).
- We are new creatures in Christ Jesus, part of the new creation yet to be fully revealed (2 Corinthians 5:17).
- We are citizens of the promised Kingdom (Colossians 1:12-14).
- We have every spiritual blessing provided by Messiah, who now sits at the right hand of the Father in the place of authority and power (Ephesians 1:3, 1:18-23).

The Jews spoke of the present age and the age to come. Jesus, in his death and resurrection, provided forgiveness of sins and made available the power of the age to come (Ephesians 1:19-21). This means we are already in "the last days" spoken of by the prophets. We are in the time of fulfillment—the end times, if you please (Hebrews 1:2, 1 Peter 1:20, 1 Corinthians 10:11). We who believe already experience the age to come by being united to Messiah, by being under the new covenant, and by experiencing the power of the promised Spirit.

The age to come is here; yet it is not fully revealed. Already . . . but not yet. Some may enjoy it now, but all the earth will experience it at Christ's return. The time of fulfillment has begun. The Rule of Messiah has commenced. He has been given the position of authority and power (Ephesians 1:21-22). Yet he sits at the right hand of the Father, waiting for the time when all things are subject to him (Psalm 110:1, Hebrews 10:12-13). The kingdom has begun, but the kingdom has not yet been fully revealed.[2]

## Gentiles and the Church

Another difficulty: What is the period like between these two comings of Christ? This era is unseen by the prophets. This has been well illustrated by a diagram of two mountain peaks, one behind the other. These two peaks represent the two comings of Christ. From the distance of the Old Testament, they appear as one peak with no hint of a gap in between.

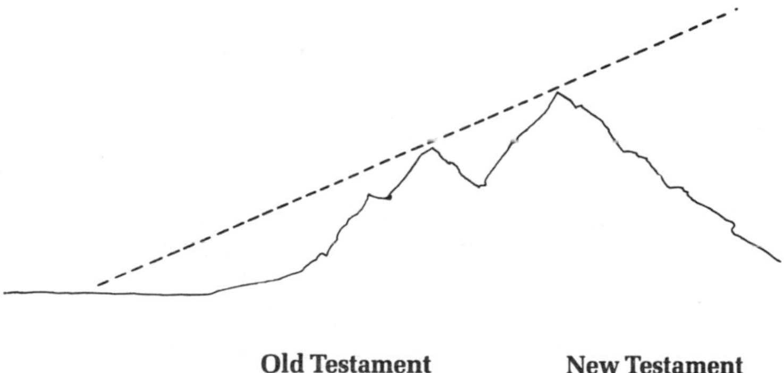

**Old Testament** **New Testament**

So what is the period in between the two comings like? The people of God in this period are called the church. The church is "in Christ." It has entered into the work of Messiah, for it has been forgiven of its sins through his sacrificial death on the cross, and operates as his representative on earth by the power of the Spirit.

But what about Gentiles? May they be considered part of the people of God? Or can only Israelites be full citizens under Israel's king?

**The Mystery Revealed**

Understandably, Jewish believers were reluctant to accept that Gentiles could be fully part of Christ without becoming part of Israel. But the fact that God gave to the Gentiles the gift of the Holy Spirit when they believed in Jesus as Messiah was convincing evidence that God had accepted them (Acts 10, 11:15-17, 15:1-3).

The "mystery," which had not been revealed in the Old Testament but has now been revealed through apostles and prophets, is that "one new man" has been formed in Christ. That new man is made up of Jew and Gentile—all who believe in Christ (Ephesians 2:11—3:6).

**The New Covenant**

The new covenant promised by Jeremiah is now made available to Jews and Gentiles through the blood of Christ (Luke 22:20, Hebrews 9:15). Paul is a minister of the new covenant, and all who trust in Christ participate in the new covenant's benefits (2 Corinthians 3:6-18). Kingdom life—eternal life—may now be had by those who have believed in Christ, whether Jew or Gentile.

But a question arises: How can Gentiles participate in a covenant promised specifically to the Jews? We Gentiles had no covenant, old or new. We were "foreigners to the covenants of the promise, without hope and without God in the world" (Ephesians 2:12). How do we get a new covenant?

Because the idea of *covenant* is like a *contract* today, perhaps an example from modern business will make clear what has happened:

The head of a manufacturing firm has two plants in different states. One is unionized, the other is not. Workers in the unionized plant, who are under a contract with management, go out on strike for additional pay and benefits.

After negotiation, a settlement is reached which gives workers in the unionized plant a ten-percent raise and better medical coverage. Union members refer to this settlement as the "New Contract."

To the workers in the other plant, nothing new is promised at all. But shortly after the union shop returns to work, the owner of the firm travels to his nonunionized plant, calls the workers together, and makes an announcement: "You may have heard that my other plant has negotiated a New Contract. I know you were not part of that arrangement. I have no obligation to you under either the Old Contract or the New Contract. But I am giving you the same New Contract I promised them."

That is what the New Testament says about the New Covenant. Gentiles who had no covenant promises are accepted when they believe in Christ and come under the New Covenant.

The New Testament has a name for this:

It's called *GRACE.*

> For the grace of God has appeared, bringing salvation to all men, instructing us to deny ungodliness and worldly desires and to live sensibly, righteously and godly in the present age, looking for the blessed hope and the appearing of the glory of our great God and Savior, Christ Jesus; who gave Himself for us, that He might redeem us from every lawless deed and purify for Himself a people for His own possession, zealous for good deeds. (Titus 2:11-14 NASB)

And this is the place to end our trip. It has brought us to Jesus, the Author and Finisher of our faith, (Hebrews 12:2)

> who for the joy set before him
> endured the cross, scorning its shame,
> and sat down at the right hand of the throne of God.

# FOR PERSONAL INTERACTION & DISCUSSION

SUGGESTED SCRIPTURE READINGS:

John 3:1-21
Acts 2
Ephesians 2

1. How has this trip through the Bible sharpened your focus on the future?
2. What aspects of the future has Jesus already made available to individuals who belong to his kingdom? What difference does this make?
3. Why did Jesus not set up a restored kingdom on earth at his first coming?
4. What is the mystery that was not known in the Old Testament? Why is this so important to Gentiles? How does it relate to God's promise to Abraham?
5. Why do Gentiles experience the benefits of the new covenant when it was promised to Israel?
6. Can any individual become a member of the coming Kingdom of Jesus? How?
7. Because of what you have now learned, how will your journey on the way to Jesus be different?

# NOTES & COMMENTS

**Abbreviations Used in These Notes**

| | |
|---|---|
| *ANET* | *Ancient Near Eastern Texts* (Princeton University Press, 1969), ed. James B. Pritchard |
| *BDB* | F. Brown, S.R. Driver, C.A. Briggs, *Hebrew and English Lexicon of the Old Testament* (Oxford University Press, 1959) |
| *BSac* | *Bibliotheca Sacra* |
| *CBQ* | *Catholic Biblical Quarterly* |
| *CTM* | *Concordia Theological Monthly* |
| *EQ* | *The Evangelical Quarterly* |
| *Int* | *Interpretation* |
| *JBL* | *Journal of Biblical Literature* |
| *JETS* | *Journal of the Evangelical Theological Society* |
| *R&E* | *Review and Expositor* |
| *RKH* | R. K. Harrison, *Introduction to the Old Testament*(Grand Rapids: Wm. B. Eerdmans, 1969) |
| *TDOT* | *Theological Dictionary of the Old Testament* (Grand Rapids: Wm. B. Eerdmans, 1978), ed. G. Johannes Botterweck and Helmer Ringgren |
| *TWOT* | *Theological Wordbook of the Old Testament* (Chicago: Moody Press, 1980), ed. R. Laird Harris *et al.* |
| *WTJ* | *Westminster Theological Journal* |

## NOTES ON CHAPTER ONE—

### The God of Creation (A Fresh Look at Genesis 1)

1. See W. F. Albright, *Archaeology and the Religion of Israel*, fifth edition (Baltimore: Johns Hopkins Press, 1968), p. 73.

2. U. Cassuto, *The Goddess Anath*, translated by Israel Abrahams (Jerusalem: Magnes Press, 1971), p. 65.

3. *Epic of Baal*, Tablet V AB, 2nd section, lines M, N, as translated in Cassuto, *The Goddess Anath*, p. 89.

4. *Ibid.*, Tablet V AB, 5th section, lines O, P, p. 99.

5. For examples of deceit and murder among gods see "A Babylonian Theogony" in *ANET*, pp. 517-518. For intrigue among the gods see *Enûma Elish*, Tablet I. For a more detailed coverage of pagan cosmology as the background of Genesis 1 see Gerhard F. Hasel, "The Significance of the Cosmology of Genesis 1 in Relation to Ancient Near Eastern Parallels," *Andrews University Seminary Studies*, X (1972), 19.

6. Most ancient and modern philosophies recognize the necessity of starting with some concept of God and his relationship to the world. Some recent philosophies, however, have attempted to start with a denial of any reality beyond the natural. These lead straight to nihilism, despair, or a denial of rationality. For a helpful analysis of world views see James W. Sire, *The Universe Next Door* (Downers Grove, Ill.: InterVarsity Press, 1976).

7. We have called *Enûma Elish* "the Babylonian creation story." This must be qualified with the reminder that the pagan "creation stories" were not attempts at historical cosmologies, but were intended primarily for magical, ritual recitation to influence natural events. Cf. Alexander Heidel, *The Babylonian Genesis* (Chicago: University of Chicago Press, 1951), pp. 10-11, 16-17; and Bruce K. Waltke, *Creation and Chaos* (Portland, Ore.: Western Conservative Baptist Seminary, 1974), p. 47, also published in *BSac*, 132 (1975), 327.

8. *Enûma Elish*, Tablet IV, lines 137-140, as translated in Heidel, *The Babylonian Genesis*, p. 42. To make the quotation easier to read, I have omitted the indicators for supplied and partially missing words.

9. Heidel, *The Babylonian Genesis*, p. 9. Other views of creation in the ancient Near East are summarized in Gerhard F. Hasel, "The Polemic Nature of the Genesis Cosmology," *EQ*, XLVI (1974), 87-88.

10. *Enûma Elish*, Tablet V, lines 50-60, translated in *ANET*, pp. 501-502. The translator's editorial marks have been omitted.

11. A variety of interpretations have been suggested for verses 1-3. For a discussion of these as well as a detailed discussion of the grammar involved see Bruce K. Waltke, *Creation and Chaos*, pp. 18-36; also published in *BSac*, 132 (1975), pp. 136-144, 216-228.

To summarize Waltke's main conclusions, which we follow in the text: The arrangement of Genesis 1:1-3 is parallel to that of 2:4-7. In 2:5 we have a description of prevailing conditions at the time of 2:4. 2:4 is a summary statement, similar to 1:1. 2:7 begins the details of the story, as does 1:3. This parallel pattern shows that 1:2 should be understood as providing the background conditions for the creation announced by the topic sentence of 1:1 ("In the beginning God created . . . ) and detailed in 1:3ff. ("And God said, . . ."). Waltke concludes that Genesis 1 does not tell us about the origination of the "waste and void" state of 1:2.

Von Rad agrees that 1:2 speaks of a "preprimeval period," but also insists that v. 2 also comes under the truth of v. 1. Cf. Gerhard von Rad, *Genesis*, revised edition (Philadelphia: Westminster Press, 1972), pp. 50-51.

12. Von Rad, p. 49, takes *Elohim* in a figurative sense—meaning "great" as in the expression, "mountains of God" for great mountains. This, combined with translating *Ruah* ("spirit") by its alternate meaning as "wind," produces the idea of a great wind as an additional element of the description of chaos in 1:2. This must be rejected, however. It would be difficult to expect the readers to take *Elohim* as figurative here when it is used in its normal sense for God in the rest of the account. Cf. U. Cassuto, *A Commentary on the Book of Genesis*, I (Jerusalem: Magnes Press, 1961), p. 24, who confirms the traditional translation, "Spirit of God."

13. Cassuto, *Genesis*, I, 13, also rejects the notion that the pattern of days in Genesis is *merely* a literary device. He observes that the normal pattern for pairs of days in Akkadian and Ugaritic literature is 1 with 2; then 3 with 4, and finally, 5 with 6. For a comparison of wisdom motifs with Genesis 1—3 see R. Dennis Cole, *Foundations of Wisdom Theology in Genesis One to Three*, unpublished Th.M. thesis, Western Conservative Baptist Seminary, Portland, Or., May 1, 1978.

14. F. Delitzsch, *New Commentary on Genesis*, p. 100, and von Rad, p. 59, agree that the image of God in man is not dominion itself. The dominion is the result of the image. Neither is "male and female" the image, but rather an indication of the scope of the image. Most Old Testament scholars relate the idea of "image" to the practice of kings in setting up their statues in lands over which they were claiming dominion. Man, then, is to be God's representative, proclaiming and implementing God's rule over earth. Cf. Hans Walter Wolff, *Anthropology of the Old Testament* (Philadelphia: Fortress Press, 1974), pp. 159-165. That man was given the creative capacities necessary to operate as God's regent, of course, follows.

15. This creation by the word of God (Psalm 33:9, 2 Peter 3:5) is distinctive in the literature of the ancient Near East. The closest parallel is the use of words in Egypt in a superstitious way to repeat a magical formula. The commanding of creation and the naming of the elements

of creation demonstrate God's sovereignty and distinguish him from the material world.

16. The use of the term *têhom* in Genesis 1:2 for the "deep" has been seen by some to be a link to the Babylonian creation story where Tiamat is the primordial saltwater ocean goddess. Hasel, "The Significance of the Cosmology of Genesis 1," p. 7, points out that though the words derive from a common Semitic root, there is no direct borrowing. In fact, "the description of the depersonalized, undifferentiated, unorganized, and the passive state of *têhom* in Genesis 1:2 is not due to any influence from non-Israelite mythology but is motivated through the Hebrew conception of the world. In stating the conditions in which this earth existed before God commanded the light should spring forth, the author of Genesis 1 rejected explicitly contemporary mythical notions." Cf. Hasel, "The Polemic Nature of the Genesis Cosmology," pp. 82-85.

17. Derik Kidner, *Genesis* (Downers Grove, Ill.: InterVarsity Press, 1967), p. 49. See Hasel, "The Polemic Nature of the Genesis Cosmology," pp. 85-87, for the discussion of myths regarding sea monsters. In Genesis 1:21 and Psalm 104:25-26, the large sea creatures are simply creations of God—nothing more. Waltke discusses this sea monster motif as found in the rest of the O.T. in *Creation and Chaos*, pp. 1-17, or *BSac*, 132 (1975), 32-36.

18. See note 17 above for the rejection by Genesis 1 of the mythological notion of the sea.

19. Von Rad, p. 55.

20. Kidner, p. 49.

21. Cole, p. 14. Cf. Hasel, "The Significance of the Cosmology of Genesis 1."

## NOTES ON CHAPTER TWO—

### Man and His Relationships (The Added Contribution of Genesis 2)

1. A. Heidel, *The Babylonian Genesis*, p. 46 (Tablet VI), 1., lines 5-8. Editorial marks of the translator have been dropped from this quote.

2. The apparent contradiction with Genesis 1—that vegetation came before man, but in 2:5-6 has not yet sprouted because man is not available to cultivate it—is due to the more limited reference in Genesis 2. The verse is not speaking of all vegetation, but about cultivated fields, as indicated from the switch from "earth" in Genesis 1 to "field in the earth" in 2:5. "Field" (*sadeh*) may refer to a particular cultivated field (as here and Genesis 37:7, 47:24) or a pastureland (Genesis 29:2) or open country (Genesis 25:29). See *BDB*, p. 961. The "plants of the field" refer to "wheat and barley and the other kinds of grain from which *bread* is

made" (U. Cassuto, *Genesis*, I, 102). See Genesis 3:18-19 for the same phrase. Cf. TWOT, pp. 700-701.

3. Nahum M. Sarna notes other ancient Near Eastern parallels to creation of man out of "clay." Yet he sees a distinct difference in the biblical account. "Man, alone, has the breath of life blown into his nostrils by God Himself. Only by virtue of this direct animation did man become a living being, drawing directly from God his life source." *Understanding Genesis* (New York: Schocken Books, 1966), pp. 14-15.

The AV translation "Man became a living soul" has misled many modern English readers to conclude that the distinctiveness of man involves having a "soul." The Hebrew word translated "soul" may simply refer to *life* of a creature. Animals are living souls too. The same expression is used for the creation of animals in 1:20, 1:21, and 1:24. It simply means then that man became an animate, living creature.

4. Von Rad, *Genesis*, p. 82.

5. Another apparent difficulty arises in comparing Genesis 2 with 1. It appears that 2:19 teaches a creation of animals and birds *after* man's creation. As Keil points out, this is due to Hebrew style: "The writer, who was about to describe the relation of man to the beasts, went back to their creation, in the simple method of the early Semitic historians, and placed this first instead of making it subordinate; so that our modern style of expressing the same thought would be simply this: 'God brought to Adam the beasts which He had formed.'" (C. F. Keil and F. Delitzsch, *The Pentateuch*, I [Grand Rapids: Wm. B. Eerdmans, 1971], p. 87). This literary practice of "starting over" with the sequence of events and bringing it up to the present time of the narrative is, of course, not our Western pattern. To place it in sequence the verb must be translated, "had formed" as NIV. See 2:7-8; when was man "formed"? NIV, NASB, and RSV translate "had formed" in 2:8.

6. For the significance of naming as an indicator of rule see Cassuto, *Genesis*, I, 130. As Cassuto notes, this emphasis on man's rule is clear from 2:19 when Adam's work is accepted as final. God's rule is also indicated by naming in Genesis 1:5, 1:8, 1:10, and 5:2. Parental rule is exercised by Eve in 4:25.

7. Claus Westermann, *Elements of Old Testament Theology*, trans. Douglas W. Stott (Atlanta: John Knox, 1982), p. 95, has clearly stated the relational viewpoint of man as taught in Genesis 2: "The creation of humanity includes the living space (the garden), the means of life (the fruit of the garden), the occupation or work (cultivate and preserve), and the community (man and woman) and, as a medium of the community, language. This complex understanding of the creation of human life has largely been overlooked in theology. . . . [Anthropology] is a matter—in the relationship to God as well—of people in all their relationships . . . : living space, nourishment, work, and the social realm."

8. We will discuss the personal name for God, *Yahweh*, in chapter 6.

9. Those who discount the apostle Paul's argument for submission based on man being created first argue that order has nothing to do with role, because last meant highest in Genesis 1. Cf. Paul K. Jewett, *Man as Male and Female* (Grand Rapids: Wm. B. Eerdmans, 1975), pp. 126-127; Letha Scanzoni and Nancy Hardesty, *All We're Meant to Be* (Waco, Texas: Word, 1974), pp. 27-28. Of course, the chronological order in any account does not have any set significance. In Genesis 1 the order was ascending with humanity as the climax—and order was not the only indicator of this. In Genesis 2 the distinctive context of gracious provisions for the newly created man beginning in 2:8 is often overlooked. Order is actually climactic here, too. As Adam affirmed in poetry, *last is best* in Genesis 2—the greatest gift was the woman.

10. Bruce K. Waltke, "The Relationship of the Sexes in the Bible," *Crux* 19 (Sept., 1983), pp. 10-16. Waltke points out that the word "helper," if used by itself, would imply superiority, if anything. Certainly this word cannot be used to imply inferiority. Even when taking this as a statement of her primary role as I have, she does not thereby become inferior in personhood. Nor does the role become a menial one.

11. Jewett, p. 124. As quoted, Jewett rightly rejects the role of a menial servant for the woman. However, I do not agree with the unproven assumption of Jewett's book—that equality of person cannot exist when there is differentiation of role. This assumption leads him to conclude that the truth of equality as found in the word *helper* must imply no male leadership in carrying out the joint mandate of rule. Cf. Hans Walter Wolff, *Anthropology and the Old Testament*, pp. 159-165, where differentiation of role is seen as part of the human mandate. Dominion requires the whole community of mankind. "They are to be able to generate children and thus to increase mankind. The increase of mankind and dominion over the earth and the beasts are directly linked together" (p. 162).

12. The play on the words *ish* for man and *ishah* for woman comes out well in the English translation "man" and "woman." That *ishah* may not be derived directly from *ish* is beside the point. Assuming Hebrew was not the original language of the garden, it follows that Adam derived her designation from his in whatever language was spoken. The closest parallel in Hebrew was *ish* and *ishah*. English is blessed with two sets of acceptable terms to convey the idea: man/woman and male/female.

13. The absurd deduction that God's "surgical operation" on Adam produced an *inherited* shortage of one rib per man is an obvious *non sequitur*, but has had an interesting history. Cf. Jewett, pp. 121-122. But why should Jewett use such a faulty deduction to support the notion that a literal reading of Genesis contradicts modern biology?

14. The strength of the statement that a man leave his father and mother to be joined to his wife, coupled with no mention of the wife leaving her parents, have led some to suggest that the earlier marital

practice was for the couple to live with the wife's family. In contrast with this is the patriarchal pattern of the rest of Genesis. It is more likely that the man's leaving is to stress his commitment to his wife over his parents with the patriarchal pattern as the background.

15. Paul's quotation of Genesis 2:24 in 1 Corinthians 6:16 is often read as if it equates the sex act with the one-flesh arrangement God ordained in Genesis 2. But if that is the case, why would Paul call it fornication? It is, therefore, not really the "one flesh" as intended by Genesis, but a distorted "one flesh." This is what makes it fornication and a perversion of God's original intention. It takes what God made for marriage and uses it in a way that sins against God's plan for mankind.

16. Cole, p. 133.

## NOTES ON CHAPTER THREE—

### The Mess We're In (The Reality of Sin in Genesis 3)

1. "The Journey of Wen-Amon to Phoenicia," *ANET*, pp. 25-29.

2. Cassuto, *Genesis,* I, 112, takes "knowledge of good and evil" as "objective awareness of all things, both good and bad." Von Rad takes it as omniscience (*Genesis,*, p. 81). But 3:22 certainly eliminates both of these. Man has not become omniscient. It is best to follow Geerhardus Vos, *Biblical Theology* (Wm. B. Eerdmans, 1948), pp. 39-43, who shows that the tree functions as a tree of probation intended to teach man moral discernment at the highest level—obedience to God. See also H. C. Leupold, *Exposition of Genesis* (Grand Rapids: Baker Book House, 1942), I, 120-121. "Good and evil," if developed positively, may well be equivalent to "wisdom" in the Old Testament (see chapter 12).

3. Both Cassuto, *Genesis,* I, 139-143, and Sarna, *Understanding Genesis,* p. 26, recognize that the text explicitly rejects a mythological interpretation by identifying the serpent as one of the beasts of the field. Both, however, ultimately see the existence of a serpent myth as the reason for the choice of a serpent as the tempter. Cassuto takes the serpent to be allegorical for the slyness of Eve's own mind as she seeks to discover the reason for the prohibition. But this makes the shift of blame in 3:13 meaningless and the curse upon the serpent (3:14-15) even more so. In spite of his own interpretation, Cassuto also notes that the Pentateuch avoids allegory. It would be more consistent to see the serpent-myth tradition as getting its start here in this real event as a distorted memory of man's fall.

4. Vos, pp. 43-44, rightly rejects any allegorical interpretation in which the events here are reduced to nonhistorical representations of everyman's temptation. Walter Kaiser, *Toward an Old Testament Theology,* p. 77-78, has suggested a grammatical solution to the problem of the serpent. He takes "serpent" as only a title for Satan—not a designation of an animal. According to Kaiser, 3:1 ("more crafty than any beast

of the field") compares Satan with the beasts of the field, but does not identify him as one of them.

5. Sarna, p. 26, summarizes the serpent imagery available. "This reptile figures prominently in all the world's mythologies and cults. In the Near East the serpent was a symbol of deity and fertility, and the images of serpent-goddesses have been found in the ruins of many Canaanite towns and temples."

6. Vos, pp. 44-45. Leupold, I, 141-142.

7. The three differences between Eve's response and the original form of the commands and description are distinguished by Bruce K. Waltke, "The Fall of Man," Bueermann-Champion Lectures, Western Conservative Baptist Theological Seminary, Portland, Ore., October, 1974, who sees them all as significant departures.

8. Waltke sees the difference in the grammatical form as indicating a shift from command ("You shall surely") to optional permission ("We may") and, therefore, a modification of emphasis on God's goodness. Leupold, I, 148, finds no difference in meaning due to the grammatical differences, but does see the omission of "all" (every) as significant. "She was beginning to lose sight of the goodness of God."

9. Waltke takes Eve's identification of the tree being in the middle of the garden as a direct geographical error caused by a faulty focus on the restriction. Leupold, I, 149, argues that both trees are in the middle and sees no problem with Eve's statement identifying the tree of knowledge as being in the middle. But Cassuto here agrees on a shift of focus: "Although there was in the *centre* of the garden also the tree of life, and possibly there were other trees as well, her interest is focused at the moment on the *forbidden tree,* and for her it is *the tree*—with the definite article—in the centre of the garden" (I, 145).

10. Cassuto disagrees that "You shall not surely die" is intended to be the opposite to the "you shall surely die" of 2:17. He argues that it is too distant from 2:17 and that "you" is plural here, but singular in 2:17 (I, 145). That change, of course, is necessary to include the woman. Otherwise, it is a direct contradiction.

11. R. Obadiah Sforno, quoted in Cassuto, I, 137.

12. As Cassuto notes, I, 155-156, to suggest that God's question, "Where are you?" (3:9), is an indication of some lack in God's omniscience is to fail to note the purpose of the question. He was not seeking information, but seeking them out. See Genesis 4:9 for a similar question followed by the already known answer.

13. Von Rad, p. 91.

14. This reversal of the divine order is indicated by the literary order of the account. The temptation moves from serpent to woman to man. The announcement of the curse moves from man to woman to ser-

pent and back to woman to man, a chiastic arrangement—the only purpose of which can be to indicate an order of responsibility.

15. My comments about rebellion against insignificant rules should not be taken as approval of such rules (cf. Colossians 3:21 and 2:20-23).

16. Regarding Jesus' temptation by Satan, Matthew seems to be most concerned with its parallel to Israel's temptations—a theme we will address in a later chapter. Luke, however, with the inserted genealogy which takes us back to Adam, seems to be making the comparison which we develop here—Jesus as the Man qualified to save.

## NOTES ON CHAPTER FOUR—

### The Effects of Sin (Loss of Order and Balance, Genesis 3—11)

In this chapter, due to space limitations, we have not been able to follow the divisions of the book given to us in the phrase, "These are the generations of" or "This is the history of." These divisions occur at 5:1, 6:9, 10:1, 11:10, and 11:27. (Cf. 2:4, 25:12, 25:19, 36:1, 36:9, 37:2). Except for the genealogy of Shem (11:10-26), a scene of deterioration and judgment climaxes each of these sections.

1. As Kidner, *Genesis*, p. 70 points out, the serpent's manner of locomotion would not be changed, just surrounding conditions. The wording may involve a pun and so indicate the judgment in words appropriate to the physical traits of the serpent.

2. For a detailed analysis of the parallels in wording and grammar of 3:16 as well as a consideration of other views, cf. Susan T. Foh, "What Is the Woman's Desire?" *WTJ*, 37 (1975), pp. 376-83. An alternate interpretation of 4:7 is found in *Matthew Henry's Commentary*, I (Old Tappan, N.J.: Fleming H. Revell, n.d.), 39. This view sees the rule as Cain's position as firstborn. Cf. John Calvin, *Commentaries on the First Book of Moses Called Genesis*, I (Grand Rapids, Baker Book House), 203-204. Abel's (positive) desire would recognize Cain's status, and Cain would rule over Abel. This positive idea of desire, if applied to 3:16, would have the Lord predict that the woman will be a willing subject, which does not fit with the need to command subjection (Ephesians 5:22, 1 Peter 3:1). The context of a curse in 3:16, which announces the effects of entering a fallen state with its struggles in relationships and goals, makes Foh's interpretation most compatible with both contexts.

3. This rationale was suggested to me by my colleague at Multnomah School of the Bible, Edward Goodrick. More recently, Ronald B. Allen, *The Majesty of Man* (Portland, Ore., Multnomah Press, 1984), pp. 145-149, has noted the same parallel. He, however, uses the parallel to suggest that 3:16 itself is predicting a fallen, harsh rule by the man. Though he accepts Foh's argument based on the parallel to 4:7 to define

"desire," he does not follow her in seeing the grammar of the last line as also parallel ("But you/he must . . .")—a statement stressing moral necessity. Allen's view is also weakened by the observation that the word "rule" does not imply invalid or harsh rule elsewhere in the O.T., even being used of God's rule. However, he is undoubtedly correct in his understanding that, since the Fall, man has distorted his pre-Fall leadership function.

4. Sarna, *Understanding Genesis*, pp. 29-30.

5. Modern translations have preferred to find sin "crouching" at Cain's door rather than the AV's "couching." This change may have come from commentaries which suggest that sin is like a wild animal ready to pounce on Cain. Yet a study of the other uses of this term in the O.T. suggest that the animal would be more likely resting after a meal than looking for one (Exodus 23:5, Genesis 49:9 and 49:14, Isaiah 11:6), cf. *BDB*, p. 918. "Lying" or "couching" pictures the responsibility which rests at Cain's door, if he does not do well.

6. The qualification of Noah as righteous is another contrast with the Babylonian flood stories, in which personal favoritism is the basis for the choice. Cf. Sarna, p. 51.

7. The description of Ham's sin includes, as a minimum, parental dishonor. Calvin says: "Ham, by reproachfully laughing at his father, betrays his own depraved and malignant disposition. . . . This Ham, therefore, must have been of a wicked, perverse, and crooked disposition, since he not only took pleasure in his father's shame, but wished to expose him to his brethren" (I, 302). Cassuto, *Genesis,* II, 152, defines it as "looking with unclean intent." It could involve more than mockery. The idiom used can involve more direct actions than "seeing" (Leviticus 20:17).

Allen P. Ross, "The Curse of Canaan," *BSac,* 137 (1980), pp. 223-40, examines these options and rejects any greater sin than seeing Noah's nakedness, yet he adds: "To the writer of this narrative this [viewing nakedness] was apparently serious enough to incur the oracle on Canaan (who might be openly guilty in their customs of what Ham had been suspected of doing)" (p. 230).

8. In addition to the article above, Ross has discussed the place of Canaan and the function of the table of nations in "The Table of Nations in Genesis 10," *BSac,* 137 (1980), pp. 340-353.

9. Sarna, pp. 70-74, has gathered evidence for the accuracy of the Babel account regarding ancient Mesopotamian building practices and terminology.

10. O. Palmer Robertson, "Tongues: Sign of Covenantal Curse and Blessing," *WTJ,* 33 (1975) pp. 43-53. provides an excellent study of the O.T. significance of tongues. His N.T. conclusions regarding 1 Corinthians 14:20-25, however, are less convincing.

## NOTES ON CHAPTER FIVE—

### A New Beginning (The Covenant with the Patriarchs)

1. When we point out that we are beginning again with one man, this is not to suggest an absolute break with the previous material. The introduction of Abraham was anticipated in the selection of earlier material. The genealogies are leading toward Abraham. The comments about Shem also anticipate God's choice of Abraham.

2. Some, using the ages given, criticize Abraham for an apparent delay in coming to Canaan. The text (12:4) gives no hint of censure. See Kidner's appropriate remarks (*Genesis,* pp. 113-114).

3. Sarna, *Understanding Genesis,* pp. 126-127, should be consulted for the significance of the ritual of Genesis 15. He says, "The covenant completely lacks . . . mutuality. It is a unilateral obligation assumed by God without any reciprocal responsibilities being imposed upon Abraham. The use of established legal forms of treaty-making to express such a situation is a dramatic way of conveying the immutable nature of the divine promise."

4. We should not miss the additional lesson which the story of Abraham's lack of faith in Egypt teaches. "If Yahweh did not go astray in his work of sacred history because of the failure and guilt of the recipient of promise, then his word was really to be believed" (von Rad, *Genesis,* p. 170). This again shows that the point of these narratives is the certainty of the promise.

5. Von Rad, p.180, finds an inconsistency in the account of Abraham's not accepting anything of the booty, yet tithing it. The inconsistency is possible only if the order of the account is reversed. Abraham tithes the booty as appropriate for the deliverance, then refuses the offer to take something for himself.

6. As here in Genesis 15, visions often follow actions of faith in the narrative. See 12:7 following the entrance into the land; 13:14 after allowing Lot his choice of land; and, most notably, after Abraham's willingness to sacrifice Isaac in 22:11. Additionally, Yahweh's speaking to Abraham introduces new steps: 12:1, 17:1, 18:1, 22:1.

7. The Nuzi Tablets, dated only slightly later than Abraham, illumine the nature of Eliezer as heir. The Nuzi texts include actual legal documents of such adoptions. One document reads: "As long as Nashwi is alive, Wullu [the adoptee] shall provide food and clothing; when Nashwi dies, Wullu shall become the heir. If Nashwi has a son of his own, he shall divide (the estate) equally with Wullu, but the son of Nashwi shall take the gods of Nashwi." *ANET,* p. 219.

8. Sarna, pp. 121-122, finds four connections of this renewed promise of land to Abraham in Genesis 15 with the previous context dealing

with the booty of the kings. One connection is the "possessions" that Abraham's descendants would have, corresponding to the possessions (14:21, same word) which Abraham refused from the king of Sodom.

9. Marrying a slave from the land of Lullu is specified as the way to guarantee an heir if the wife is barren, *ANET*, p. 220. If this is done, the original wife "may not send the offspring [of the slave-wife] away." Cf. Sarna, pp. 128-129. It is clear from the Rachel story that when the slave is the wife's, the children are to be counted as the wife's (Genesis 30:3—"that she may bear on my knees, that through her I too may have children" NASB). "The slave was born 'on the knees' of the wife, so that the child then came symbolically from the womb of the wife herself (cf. 30:3,9)!" (von Rad, p. 191). Talk about surrogate motherhood!

10. Sarah's statements in 16:5 are confusing since she, not Abraham, had suggested Hagar as a substitute. How could Abraham be responsible? Von Rad, pp. 191-92, points out that the maintenance of justice was the husband's responsibility. The allowance of the new "wife" to despise her mistress was an injustice. Sarah utters this legal formula calling for redress of the wrong. Abraham's verdict is to reassert Hagar's status as Sarah's personal servant and her right to do what she wished with her. Hagar flees after Sarah's rough treatment, but is sent back by God with directions to submit. A similar case appears in the Code of Hammurabi (#146) with the same verdict (*ANET*, p. 172).

11. The summary of 16:15—17:1 informs us of a thirteen-year time gap. Is this gap due to Abraham's desire to use Ishmael as a substitute? Is it significant that it is 13 years—long enough for Ishmael to grow out of childhood? The summary also appears to act as a hinge in the movement of the narrative. Following this summary and prior to the birth of Isaac, earlier threads are picked up. Another incident with Lot and Sodom, another encounter with a king involving Sarah, and the reaffirmation of the promise are renewed themes.

12. Note the language similarity in the blessing on Ishmael and the wording of the original blessing of Genesis 1:28.

13. Abraham's recognition by God in the Sodom account is impressive. It is heightened by the fact that Abraham realizes he is pressing his point as he arbitrates, and so is presuming upon God's patience (18:27-32). God's willingness to allow Abraham to press the issue highlights Abraham's position.

A second point is observed by von Rad (pp. 213-214). Abraham's objections are really questions of justice. He believes it unworthy of God that a significant minority should die with an admittedly perverse majority. Additionally, the account shows that he misjudged God's grace. He bargained all the way down to ten, but God exceeds his request and delivers the four who "qualify" anyway! This has its relevance to the Israelites. They are to understand that their invasion of Canaan was under a God who was not just eliminating the whole nation because the majority were perverse. No, God would have saved it even if only a slight minority were good.

On the sin of Sodom see Sarna, pp. 144-146. C. F. Keil argues that it is not Abraham's position, but the object lesson for his descendants that is the primary reason for God's consultation. *The Pentateuch* (Grand Rapids: Wm. B. Eerdmans, 1971), pp. 229-230.

14. As Kidner, *Genesis*, p. 117, points out, this second incident of Sarah being desired for a king's harem is not due to beauty as was the first at a younger period in her life, but probably represents a desire by Abimelech to enhance his own position by an alliance with Abraham who is now well-off.

15. In stating that Abraham was looking forward to a *city*, the writer of Hebrews demonstrates an understanding of the culture of the land of promise in Abraham's time. The city he was looking forward to was not heaven. Further discussion of the interpretation of Hebrews on this point is found in chapter 9.

16. The narrative of "Jacob out-of-the-Land" is enclosed by the two events at Bethel, one on the way out and the other on the way back in. For some literary observations see: Steve McKenzie, "You Have Prevailed," *Restoration Quarterly*, 23 (1980), pp. 225-231; also, Michael Fishbane, "Composition and Structure in the Jacob Cycle" (Genesis 25:29—35:22), *Journal of Jewish Studies*, 28, pp. 15-38.

17. Kaiser, *Toward an Old Testament Theology*, p. 153, includes a revealing comparison between the language of the Davidic Covenant and the Abrahamic. Our discussion of the Davidic Covenant comes in chapter 10.

18. Some maintain that the Abrahamic Covenant was conditional all along and could be canceled for disobedience. Cf. Dan Fuller, *Gospel and Law* (Grand Rapids: Wm. B. Eerdmans, 1980), pp. 121-145. Fuller fails to recognize the distinction between an unconditional covenant, in which enjoyment of the covenant at any point in time is conditioned by faithfulness, and a conditional covenant. Thus he turns the whole issue on its head and declares all the covenants conditional. It will still turn out the same, he assures us, because both Ezekiel 36 and Genesis 18 make "certain both the end that God would unite Israel in the land, and the means necessary for achieving this end, namely, that Israel be godly" (p. 143).

He finds one passage, Genesis 18:18-19, which, unlike other passages, seems to have a condition attached. He reads the passage's final (result) clause—"so that the LORD will bring about for Abraham what he has promised him" (NIV)—as a condition. Yet both verses are clearly a prediction and guarantee that God's covenant will surely come to pass for Abraham. One must simply ask of the verses: Do they indicate God has promised something to Abraham? Do they indicate God will bring it to pass? What else do we mean by unconditional? The last clause merely reaffirms the assured result. These things will occur, so that God will establish His covenant. On the other hand, to make the covenant conditional ignores all of the contextual indicators that the covenant is totally guaranteed on God's part. To introduce a condition as late as chapter 18 is to destroy the significance of the earlier narrative. Cf. Kaiser, pp. 91-94.

Fuller's treatment might imply that only dispensationalists see the Abrahamic Covenant as unconditional. Such is far from the case. Cf. Sarna, p. 127; John Bright, *A History of Israel,* third edition (Philadelphia: Westminster Press, 1959), pp. 102-103; Leupold, I, 489.

19. It is important to recognize that Paul uses the term "Israel" here for physical descendants of Abraham, whether in or out of the church. "All Israel shall be saved" (Romans 11:25-26) cannot, therefore, be referring to those not physically Israelites.

20. A wider array of scholars are recognizing that a future is predicted for Abraham's physical seed in Romans 11. Cf. Anthony A. Hoekema, *The Bible and the Future* (Grand Rapids: Wm. B. Eerdmans, 1979), pp. 144-147, though he takes Israel's salvation to be an ongoing process not distinct from the present remnant; and Gordon J. Wenham, *The Book of Leviticus* (Grand Rapids: Wm. B. Eerdmans, 1979), p. 333.

Hopefully in decline is the view that God has promised something to one group but is fulfilling it to another, and has renamed the second group so that they supposedly are the original group. It is a credit to God's grace that he gives covenant benefits to those with whom he had no promise (Gentiles), but it is an unworthy accusation that God has cast away those to whom the promise was given originally.

## NOTES ON CHAPTER SIX—

### A Redeemed People (Calling Out a People for God)

1. I have not attempted to identify individual Pharaohs in the account, following the pattern of the book itself. For discussion of the possible identifications and dating see the commentaries.

2. I have used the term "mini-ark" intentionally to bring to mind Noah's ark. Apparently the writer wants us to compare the two boats. As Cassuto notes, "The word *ark* . . . occurs in only two sections of the Bible: here and in the section of the Flood. This is certainly not a mere coincidence. By this verbal parallelism Scripture apparently intends to draw attention to the thematic analogy. In both instances one worthy of being saved and destined to bring salvation to others is to be rescued from death by drowning. In the earlier section the salvation of humanity is involved, here it is the salvation of the chosen people." *A Commentary on the Book of Exodus,* trans. by Israel Abrahams (Jerusalem: The Magnes Press, 1967), pp. 18-19. We should additionally note that the use of this term at this point in the narrative continues the emphasis on God's providence without explicitly stating it.

3. The fellow Hebrew's statement—"Who made you a prince or judge over us?"—is not the only statement of "providential irony" in

the passage. Moses also names his son Gershom (meaning "an alien there"), explaining that he has become an alien in a foreign land. Undoubtedly we are to raise the question: What land is not foreign to Moses and the Israelites? Which land would be considered home? Egypt or Canaan?

4. In light of the rest of the book, the purpose for the suffering of the Hebrews seems to be to allow the iniquity of the Egyptians to become full (cf. Genesis 15:16). God does not bring judgment—and with it relief for his people—at the first injustice. God's patience toward the ungodly often involves allowing his people to suffer. Paul seems to have this in mind in Romans 8:31-39 where he quotes Psalm 44:22, "For your sake we face death all day long; we are considered as sheep to be slaughtered."

5. The use of the term *come down* indicates God's intervention to bring justice on earth as we saw in its earlier usage in Genesis for Babel and Sodom. Here it is connected to deliverance which will take place in the context of judgment on the Egyptians (cf. Cassuto, p. 34).

6. The call of Moses becomes the pattern for the call to the office of prophet. Brevard S. Childs, *The Book of Exodus* (Philadelphia: Westminster Press, 1974), p. 56.

7. *Ibid.*, p. 119. Childs notes that by chapter 6 "the whole focus falls on God's revealing of himself in a majestic act of self-identification: I am Yahweh. . . . To know God's name is to know his purpose for all mankind from the beginning to the end."

8. Scholars argue about the derivation of names. Do they actually derive from the words used to explain them and the meaning given in the text? Or are they names chosen because of a similarity, but not a direct linguistic connection, to the significance attached? It does not matter. The name was given to imply a significance whether by direct derivation or by similar sound.

9. Because Hebrew is a consonantal language, only the consonants YHWH are provided. Later Jewish readers, who did not want to pronounce the name YHWH lest they use it in vain, substituted their word for "Lord" whenever they came to the name YHWH in the text. The spelling JeHoVaH was mistakenly produced by combining the consonants for YHWH (or JHVH) with the vowel sounds of Adonai, the Hebrew word for "Lord." Due to this practice, the correct pronunciation of YHWH is in doubt. Because the name is built on the verb meaning "I am," most scholars conclude that it should be spelled as Yahweh.

10. I have substituted "Yahweh" in the biblical quotations for "the LORD" in this quotation and in many others throughout the rest of the book so as to bring out the full emphasis on the Name. This substitution takes place in quotations from both the NIV and the NASB.

11. The Hebrew tense represented may be translated either "I will be" or "I am." The suggested translation "I cause to be" is impossible in 3:12, and therefore should be rejected for 3:14. Cf. TWOT, I, 211.

12. T. C. Vriezen as quoted in Childs, p. 69. Vriezen's article is not available to me. The LXX (Greek Septuagint) translates the Hebrew: "I am the One who is." Though we have taken the meaning of Yahweh to represent primarily his presence and faithfulness along with many other interpreters, it seems a bit hasty to dismiss the notions of eternality and independent existence as implications of "I AM" as well (cf. Revelation 1:8, John 8:58). Certainly the use of "I am He" for the exclusive existence of the true God against all other gods is common (Deuteronomy 32:39, Isaiah 48:12). Cf. *TDNT*, II, 343-354. Childs, pp. 82-83; and, TWOT, I, 210-212.

13. The grammar itself is not clear about who the Lord sought to kill, Moses or his son, nor even whose feet were touched in 4:25. Many theories have resulted (Cf. Childs, pp. 95-101). The view I have taken is that of both Jewish tradition and the history of Christian interpretation.

14. Many attempt to show that Pharaoh first hardened his own heart because they want to avoid a doctrine of predestination or the accusation that God is unjust. On the other hand, those who find predestination here often fail to see that this hardening does not precede the moral failure of Egypt in mistreating God's people. God has determined to judge Egypt; therefore he has hardened Pharaoh's heart.

Attempts to place God's hardening after Pharaoh's hardening of his own heart (Cf. Walter C. Kaiser, Jr., *Toward Old Testament Ethics* [Grand Rapids: Zondervan, 1981], 252-256) can be successful only by reducing God's announced determination to harden Pharaoh's heart to mere predictions. These passages rather seem to be statements of intention which form the background and explanation of Pharaoh's response (Exodus 4:21, 7:3). Also neglected are the verses which see Pharaoh's hardening of his own heart as the result of God's already announced intention to harden Pharaoh's heart (7:13,22; 8:15,19). God did not predict that Pharaoh would harden his own heart; rather, God indicated that he himself would harden Pharaoh's heart, and we are told that Pharaoh's hardening is the fulfillment of this. Exodus 4:21 and 7:3 are, therefore, not predictions about what would come at the sixth plague and later, but state Pharaoh's response and God's control of it from the very beginning.

This creates an ethical problem only if we do not see Pharaoh and Egypt as deserving this judgment before Exodus 9—if we picture Pharaoh as an innocent participant who deserves a chance to respond before God hardens him. But if we understand the picture provided by our book that Egypt's cup of iniquity is already full, that God is determined to bring a judgment against her, and that Pharaoh as head of Egypt must be hardened so as not to let the people go before

God has decimated Egypt—then we have no ethical difficulty with the Pharaoh's hardening.

15. The emphasis is mine and not that of the version quoted.

16. For these identifications of Egyptian gods see John J. Davis, *Moses and the Gods of Egypt* (Grand Rapids: Baker Book House, 1971), p. 100, pp. 86-129.

17. *Ibid.*, p. 100.

18. Cf. John R. Kohlenberger III, *Jonah and Nahum* (Chicago: Moody Press, 1984), pp. 113-114. Kohlenberger suggests a chiastic arrangement of this material with the protection in battle by Yahweh being recognized at the beginning and end (15:1-21 and 17:8-16) and the incidents of provision being in the center.

19. Childs, p. 13, puts it: "Direct theological statements concerning God's activity are used sparingly." Cf. pp. 17, 24-25 for Childs's helpful discussion of providence which I have largely followed here.

20. *Ibid.*, p. 115.

## NOTES ON CHAPTER SEVEN—

### A New Nation (One Nation under God)

The whole issue of the Mosaic Law and its relationship to the New Testament is one of today's most intensely discussed issues. The Reformed, Lutheran and dispensationalist traditions have all distinguished Law and Gospel in their own ways. Despite obvious gains in our understanding in this area, any final conclusions may be premature, and it was with great hesitancy that I wrote this chapter.

Growing interest in the study of Old Testament theology has brought the recognition that the Law and its originally intended function should not be equated with the legalistic use of the Law.

1. Charles C. Ryrie, *The Grace of God* (Chicago: Moody Press, 1963), p.34. As this citation shows, not all dispensationalists viewed the Law as a burden. Ronald M. Hals, *Grace and Faith in the Old Testament* (Minneapolis: Augsburg, 1980) is an excellent work from a Lutheran reassessing the place of grace under the Law. Cf. Kenneth L. Barker, "False Dichotomies between the Testaments," *JETS*, 25 (1982), pp. 3-16.

2. Apparently Egypt, with its divine king, was an exception to this statement that nations need laws and did not have a law code.

3. George E. Mendenhall, "Covenant Forms in Israelite Tradition," *The Biblical Archaeologist*, 17 (1954), pp. 50-76, was the first to discover this parallel. A good general introduction to the parallels and dating can be found in K.A. Kitchen, *The Bible in Its World* (Downers Grove, Ill.: InterVarsity Press, 1977), pp. 79-85. Shalom M. Paul, *Studies in the Book of the Covenant in the Light of Cuneiform*

*and Biblical Law* (Leiden: Brill, 1970), pp. 32-33, maintains that the decalogue is not the text of a covenant—that a more personal relationship is sustained between God and Israel than that of king to vassal. He does accept Deuteronomy as a good example of the treaty pattern.

4. We will take up the full format of Hittite treaties in Deuteronomy.

5. For "kingdom of priests" as a people who would act as priests for the world, see Paul, pp. 30 and 32, and the other studies cited there.

6. Allowing other compensation to the family of the murder victim rather than capital punishment is found in the Middle Assyrian Laws (hereafter, MAL), A10 and B2, also the Hittite Laws (hereafter, HL), #1-5, *ANET*, pp. 180-181, 185, 189. See Paul, pp. 61-62, 69, where he notes that requiring capital punishment for the death of a slave is "without precedent in all other ancient Near Eastern collections."

7. Passages in Exodus on capital punishment for human life are in chapter 21, verses 12, 14, 15, and 20. Verse 20 calls for proper vengeance for the slave, that is, the penalty of v. 12. Cf. Paul, pp. 69-70.

8. The equation of "equal justice for all" and "an eye for an eye" is that of W. F. Albright in *History, Archaeology, and Christian Humanism* (New York: McGraw-Hill, 1964) p. 74. Albright observes that the application of this model seen in Israel's laws (that is, the rich receiving the same punishments as the poor) has not yet been reached in modern society.

9. LH 116, 210, 230, in *ANET*, p. 170-176.

10. In the situations described in Exodus 21:28-31 and 22—24, no vicarious punishment was allowed in the case of sons and daughters. Though the Bible often recognizes that divine punishment comes on a family or a nation as a result of sin, its Law does not allow human judges to penalize other members of the family instead of the one committing the crime.

11. The application of "an eye for an eye" in a nonliteral fashion (freedom for the slave, rather than requiring loss of the master's eye or tooth) shows that the principle of equal justice is in view—not an exacting literalness demanding the same injury. In all other law systems the slave was treated as property, and damage to a slave was an economic loss to the master.

Of course, slavery's very existence in the Mosaic Law bothers us. A number of factors should be remembered, however: (1) Slavery as regulated by the Law was more humane than our own country's practice just over a century ago. (2) Specifically for that time and place, the Law's provisions were righteous. It limited fallen society and encouraged improvement. Divorce, for example, was permitted by the Law and regulated, though never viewed as the ideal. (3) The slave was given legal rights in Israel, the same legal rights as those of a hired man. (4) Temporary slavery to pay off debts was a fairer way of dealing with unpaid obligations than debtor prisons and perhaps contained more justice than declaring bankruptcy. (5) Runaway slaves were set free (Deuteronomy 23:15-16). Cf. Exodus 20:10, 12:44; Leviticus 25:35-55; Deuteronomy 16:11-14, 15:12-18.

For a helpful discussion of the relationship of the Law to polygamy, divorce, and slavery, cf. Christopher J. H. Wright, *An Eye for An Eye* (Downers Grove, Ill.: InterVarsity Press, 1983), pp. 174-182.

12. LH 12, *ANET*, p. 166.

13. Laws of Eshnunna 13, *ANET*, p. 162.

14. MAL 15, *ANET*, p. 181. There is only one case of bodily mutilation as a penalty in the Mosaic Law: Deuteronomy 25:11-12. Compare MAL A8 *ANET*, p. 181.

15. Note the distinction between apodictic (stated principles or prohibitions, but no penalties) and casuistic or case-laws usually in the form, "If a man does such-and-such, then he shall (make restitution, be put to death, etc.)."

16. The provision in a case of accidental death that the man not leave the city of refuge until the death of the high priest also supports the notion that blood must be shed for blood. For unsolved murders a special ritual also involving atonement with blood was necessary to keep that failure of justice from counting against the community (Deuteronomy 21:1-9).

17. G.J. Wenham, *The Book of Leviticus*, NICOT (Eerdmans, 1979), p. 223, points out that the uncleanness through sexual contact meant that no sex would take place in connection with the tabernacle as well as in holy wars. This insulates against Canaanite orgiastic practices as well as the evils of ravishing women in warfare (cf. Judges 5:30).

18. Walter Breuggemann, *The Land* (Philadelphia: Fortress Press, 1977); and C.J.H. Wright, *An Eye For An Eye*, have shown the importance of the land as a feature of Israel's ethics.

19. G.J. Wenham, *The Book of Leviticus*, and R.K. Harrison, *Leviticus* TOTC (Downers Grove, Ill.: InterVarsity Press, 1980), provide two excellent conservative commentaries on Leviticus. They take differing views on the laws of cleanness. Harrison prefers to see them as largely related to health. Wenham, following Douglas, sees more theological concerns involved. Cf. Gordon J. Wenham, "The Theology of Unclean Food," *EQ*, 53 (1981), pp. 6-15; and Jacob Milgrom, "The Biblical Diet Laws as an Ethical System," *Int*, 17 (1963), 288-301.

20. See *The Mishna*, Shabbat 7.2.

21. A great deal of current discussion concerns Paul's use of the term *Law*. Some believe Paul often uses it for "Jewish legalism" as

well as for the Mosaic Law. Cf. C.E.B. Cranfield, "St. Paul and the Law," *Scottish Journal of Theology* 17 (1964), p. 51; C.F.D. Moule, "Obligation in the Ethics of Paul," *Christian History and Interpretation: Studies Presented to John Knox*, eds. W.R. Farmer *et al.* (Cambridge, 1967), pp. 392-393; and Daniel P. Fuller, *Gospel and Law,* who cites the previous two, pp. 86-88.

Douglas J. Moo in a thorough study entitled "'Law,' 'Works of the Law,' and Legalism in Paul," *WTJ*, 45 (1983), 73-100, has argued that "law" *(nomos)* does not mean "legalism" in any passage of Paul and that the expression "works of the Law" is not equivalent to legalism either, as Fuller maintained. He sees the main distinction in Paul as between whether Paul is viewing the Law as a covenant in the progressive history of salvation or whether he is using it for the Mosaic body of commands. Moo may be right in questioning whether *nomos* is ever used technically to mean legalism. Both the Judaizers and Paul, of course, have reference to the Mosaic commands when they speak of Law. It is the different use of the Law, not the meaning of the word, that makes one context speak of the (Mosaic) Law as Paul's opponents understood it and another that makes it the (Mosaic) Law as really intended by God.

No matter who wins the linguistic argument, we shall still have to recognize with Calvin that when arguing against Judaizers "to refute their error [Paul] was sometimes compelled to take the bare law in a narrow sense." *Institutes*, 2.7.2; cf. 2.11.7, cited in Moo, p.85.

22. Here I agree with Moo, pp. 80-82, that some of these statements in Galatians are Paul's own view of the Law, not those of his opponents. The distinction drawn by Paul involves seeing the positive but temporary function of the Law as the Mosaic Covenant. Paul clearly does not see himself as operating under the Mosaic Covenant or Law (1 Corinthians 9:20-21).

I believe both distinctions are necessary. Paul sometimes speaks of Law as it is used by his opponents, and sometimes as a covenant God gave, but which believers are no longer under. Fuller's treatment, *Gospel and Law*, stresses so strongly the continuum between Law and Gospel that it is difficult to see why we are not refraining from pork or at least keeping the seventh day. We are left believing that the believer today is to do *all* that is commanded in Scripture (p. 110). Cf. Douglas J. Moo, Review of *Gospel and Law*, *Trinity Journal*, 3 (1982), 99-103.

23. C. J. H. Wright, pp. 148-173 and 187-196, seems to be advocating the use of the Law in a similar way. The tentativeness of some of his examples combined with his care to avoid oversimplistic, direct applications show that the use of the Law in this way will not be an easy hermeneutical exercise. But then, this is true for the application of any O.T. passage—for example, Joshua 1:1-9. The whole of O.T. Scripture needs to be read in light of the progress of revelation and redemptive history. Yet it is still Scripture.

24. The strong contrasts in Hebrews between the covenant that is passing away and the new covenant makes it difficult to accept W. C. Kaiser, Jr.'s thesis that the new covenant is simply the old covenant "renewed."

25. For a summary of views on Romans 10:4 see C.E.B. Cranfield, *A Critical and Exegetical Commentary on the Epistle to the Romans*, ICC (T. & T. Clark, 1979), pp. 515-520. See also the view of Felix Fluckiger, detailed by Fuller, pp. 69-81. I appreciate Robert D. Brinsmead's emphasis in "Jesus and the Law," *Verdict*, 4 (October 1981), pp. 5-30. The N.T. focus of ethics is on the work of Christ, just as the Old Testament Law centers its ethics in gratitude around the Exodus salvation. In my judgment, however, Brinsmead in his justified reaction against sabbatarianism as a holdover of the Mosaic Covenant has now neglected the use of the O.T. for instruction in righteousness and greatly underplayed Paul's use of the Law as Scripture.

## NOTES ON CHAPTER EIGHT—

### Living the Life
### (The Challenge of Deuteronomy)

Deuteronomy, taken at face value, contains addresses of Moses to the second generation of Israelites out of Egypt at the border of the land. Most nonconservative scholars, impressed by the reoccurrence of Deuteronomy's theology in the former prophets (Joshua—2 Kings), have suggested a later date, either shortly after the fall of Samaria or shortly before or after the exile of Judah. For a summary of these views see *RKH*, pp. 637-53.

It should be noted that most of these attempts to date Deuteronomy as the work of a later author involve a theory of a "pious fraud." Cf. Gerhard von Rad, *Deuteronomy: A Commentary* (Philadelphia: Westminster Press, 1966), p. 28. Though the theology of Deuteronomy extends its influence through the former prophets, it is, as Walter Kaiser points out (*Toward an Old Testament Theology*, p. 122), entirely another matter to assign it to an author at the end of this period. What is so difficult about recognizing this theology as having been the *base* for the "school" of thinking that followed and evaluated Israel's history? It is as if Adam Smith had to be invented after his economic school developed. Did Marxists invent Marx?

As Harrison points out, the work of Kline on Deuteronomy (see note 2 below) has provided significant historical support for the earlier dating of Deuteronomy.

1. Deuteronomy 8 is devoted to the danger of land. The possibilities of land as a temptation for Israel to focus on the gift rather than the covenant is spelled out by Walter Brueggemann, *The Land*, pp. 53-54.

2. Deuteronomy follows the pattern of the Hittite treaties of the fourteenth and thirteenth centuries B.C. This pattern is discussed by K. A. Kitchen in *The Bible in Its World,* pp. 79-85. Kitchen cautions that none of the biblical accounts (Exodus, Leviticus, Deuteronomy, Joshua 24) are the actual treaties themselves, but narratives about them. We should, therefore, expect some differences. The student should also consult Meredith G. Kline, *Treaty of the Great King* (Grand Rapids: Wm. B. Eerdmans, 1963), for his more extensive treatment of Deuteronomy. Compare also Kitchen's earlier work, *Ancient Orient and Old Testament* (Chicago: InterVarsity Press, 1966), pp. 90-102.

3. On the meaning of love in the Old Testament, see Larry L. Walker, "'Love' in the Old Testament: Some Lexical Observations," *Current Issues in Biblical and Patristic Interpretation,* ed. Gerald F. Hawthorne, pp. 277-88. Walker lists examples where love is found in contexts of treaties to indicate faithfulness and loyalty. Cf. W. Moran, "The Ancient Near Eastern Background of the Love of God in Deuteronomy," *CBQ,* 25 (1963), 77-87. L. E. Toombs has pointed out the third aspect of love in Deuteronomy—i.e. justice (10:19)—in "Love and Justice in Deuteronomy," *Int,* 19 (1965), pp. 399-411. J. A. Thompson's analysis of distinctive vocabulary of Deuteronomy has shown the dominance of covenant loyalty as a theme. Cf. *Deuteronomy* (Downers Grove, Ill.: InterVarsity Press, 1974), pp. 30-35.

4. The words *heart, soul,* and *strength*—especially the first two—often are misunderstood because the Hebrew words carry different connotations than our English counterparts.

Biblically, *heart* is not to be contrasted with mind. In fact, in the Old Testament it is often translated "mind." The heart represents the *true inner person*—his thinking, motives, plans, and feelings. Wolff observes: "In by far the greatest number of cases it is the intellectual, rational functions that are ascribed to the heart—i.e., precisely what we ascribe to the head and, more exactly, to the brain." (Hans Walter Wolff, *Anthropology of the Old Testament,* p. 46.)

The word *soul* also is subject to misunderstanding. Too often the Greek idea of "soul" is applied to the Old Testament as if it were referring to the immaterial part of man, as is the tendency of our English word. In the Old Testament the word has in view the physical life of the person, the person as an individual, or the particular passions and appetites of the person. It is, therefore, often translated "life" or "self." McBride sees these terms as concentric in Deut. 6:5 [TDOT, IX, pp. 617-37; cited in TWOT, I, p. 487]. For a comparison of O.T. and N.T. usage, see D. M. Lake, "Soul," *ZPEB,* V, 496-98.

The word translated "strength" looks at abundance or excess, so I have used the word *exuberance.*

5. Because Yahweh owns all the earth, he may disestablish the Canaanites when his justice demands it and give the land to Israel.

Neither action involves giving up his own claim to ultimate ownership of the whole earth. Marvin E. Tate, in an otherwise very helpful article on Deuteronomy's theology, has misread the book on this point. Following von Rad, he concludes: "It [the land] could not have been Israel's without Yahweh's taking it away from other people—for it did not originally belong to either Israel or Yahweh" (*R&E*, 61 [1964], 315). He neglects Deuteronomy 10:14. Kaiser, pp. 125-26, answers von Rad. John D. W. Watts, "The Deuteronomic Theology, *R&E*, 74 (1977), pp. 328, puts it succinctly: "The foundation of all that Deuteronomy teaches about the land is the understanding that it belongs to Yahweh. He made it. He cares for it by sending rain. And now he is in process of throwing the latest tenants out to make room for his chosen people."

6. The issue of Yahweh's wars and *ḥerem*, total destruction and dedication to Yahweh, will be discussed in the next chapter.

7. See Michael L. Goldberg, "The Story of Moral: Gift or Bribes in Deuteronomy?" *Int*, 38 (1984), pp. 15-25, for further aspects of uniqueness in the laws themselves.

8. Edward P. Blair, "An Appeal to Remembrance," *Int*, 15 (1961), pp. 41-47. This excellent article details the importance of memory to the dynamics of Deuteronomy in a way I could only partially reflect in this overview. Cf. Brueggemann, pp. 54-55.

9. Other references in Deuteronomy designating the land as an inheritance include 4:38, 12:10, 20:16, 21:23, 24:4, 25:19, and 26:1.

10. This is Walter Brueggemann's summary of the theology of land in "The Kerygma of the Deuteronomistic Historian," *Int*, 22 (1968), p. 395. Cf. Brueggemann, *The Land*, 53-59, on the danger of land to the memory of Yahweh's gift and covenant.

11. The use of "good" in covenants indicating covenant faithfulness also adds a covenantal flavor to the expression "good land." Cf. Brueggemann, "The Kerygma of the Deuteronomistic Historian," pp. 387-402.

12. Patrick D. Miller, Jr., "The Gift of God: The Deuteronomic Theology of the Land," *Int*, 23 (1969), pp. 459-60, shows the distinctive emphasis on land even in the more detailed stipulations of chapters 12—27: "A large number of the laws in the legal corpus of Deuteronomy are specifically associated with the land and Israel's existence on it: the year of release (15:1ff); judicial procedure (16:18-20); law of kingship (17:14ff); law against abominable practices (18:9ff); cities of refuge (19:1ff); not removing a landmark (19:14); expiation for an unknown murder (21:1ff); law against leaving a hanged man's body on a tree (21:22 ff); just weights and measures (25:13-16); divorce law (24:1-4). Introductory or motive clauses relative to land appear in all these laws. In some cases disobedience of the law brings

defilement or guilt upon the land itself (21:23; 24:4). In other cases long life and blessing are motivations for obedience."

13. See Goldberg, p. 22.

14. James (in 2:8-11) does quote the Law three times: Leviticus 19:18, and two commandments of the ten which could be from either Exodus 20 or Deuteronomy 5. It is clear that James is thinking of law in these chapters.

15. This parallel was suggested by L. E. Toombs, pp. 399-411.

16. Brueggemann notes W. D. Davies' belief that Psalm 37:11 is spiritualized in the N.T., but comments that this conclusion must be reached "only with a troubled conscience" (*The Land*, p. 183, n.36). His own treatment of land in the N.T. is filled with misgivings about divorcing the promise from land (pp. 167-183).

M.H. Woodstra, *The Book of Joshua* (Grand Rapids: Wm. B. Eerdmans, 1981), pp. 18, 35, seems to believe Matthew 5:5's use of Psalm 37:11 proves a widening of the land promise in the N.T. because of the change from "the land" to "the earth." He fails to note, however, that the LXX already had translated "land" as "earth" without apparently intending to announce something new. As Matthew's wording follows the LXX text here, too much should not be made of any supposed switch.

17. Verses which relate to Israel's deliverance include Romans 11:26-27, Acts 3:19-21, and Luke 1:32-33. Blessing on the whole world is anticipated in Luke 2:30-32 and Isaiah 42:1-6 and 49:6.

18. C.S. Lewis, *Mere Christianity* (New York: Macmillan, 1952), p. 104.

## NOTES ON CHAPTER NINE—

### Living by Faith (God's Rule in Joshua and Judges)

1. Among the debates about the history of Joshua, surely none stands out more than the account of "Joshua's Long Day." An extensive number of theories have been developed to explain it in scientific terms. Cf. the list by John J. Davis and John C. Whitcomb, *The History of Israel* (Grand Rapids: Baker Book House, 1969-71), pp. 66-70. No objection should be brought against this miracle because the text uses phenomenological language (the language of appearance rather than the language of scientific explanation). Such language is the normal language of observation, such as is used today for "sunrise" and "sunset."

Another problem associated with the southern campaign is the chronology of Joshua 10. In 10:15 he returns to the camp at Gilgal, but the next verses show him in hot pursuit of the fleeing kings. At the chapter's end, Joshua returns to Gilgal (10:43). This is likely another example of the Hebrew literary pattern of a summary account followed by a more detailed one (see Genesis 1 and 2). The return to Gilgal then is the same return in both verses. The events of 10:16-42 fit between verses 14 and 15.

2. I have distinguished the practice of *ḥerem* at Jericho from the rest of the towns by understanding that Jericho was the exception. M. H. Woodstra, *The Book of Joshua*, p. 113, sees various degrees of *ḥerem*. He understands this most rigorous application of *ḥerem* at Jericho to have been for purposes of example. There is a problem, however, with understanding the original intent of Deuteronomy 20 in terms of livestock and plunder. I discuss this further in note 11 below.

3. The activity of God in history is an important biblical theme, going under the German term *Heilsgeschichte*. See Graeme Goldsworthy, *Gospel and The Kingdom* (Exeter, Paternoster Press, 1981) for a use of it as the Bible's central theme. Any use of God's acts as a replacement for God's words, as others have done, is an unbiblical dichotomy. Both God's words and his acts in history function as revelation of himself and his program.

4. Trent Butler has summarized the Deuteronomic themes in Joshua under four headings: the land, leadership, law, and the Lord. He also suggests that the structure of Joshua is marked out by Deuteronomic emphases (*Word Biblical Commentary: Joshua* [Waco: Word, 1983], pp. xxiv-xxv). Gordon J. Wenham, "The Deuteronomic Theology of the Book of Joshua," *JBL*, 90 (1971), pp. 140-148, sees five themes which bind Deuteronomy and Joshua together: "The holy war of conquest, the distribution of the land, the unity of all Israel, Joshua as the successor of Moses, and the covenant" (p. 141).

5. NIV translates 4:9 so that there is only one memorial. NASB has two—one in the middle of the Jordan and the one at the camp, which God commanded for teaching purposes.

6. Terence E. Fretheim, *Deuteronomic History* (Nashville: Abingdon, 1983), p.80, adds to what we have said about the place of memory in Israel by pointing out that Israel's worship was designed to actualize past events so "the worshipers understand themselves to be involved in these events. . . . This gives the people historical depth so they may see that it has always been Yahweh, and no other god, who has enabled their history."

7. Carl Graesser, Jr., "The Message of the Deuteronomic Historian," *CTM*, 39 (1968), pp. 542-551, indicates that "more than 50 percent of the speech to Joshua (1:2-9) can be reproduced from verses in Deuteronomy." Cf. Deuteronomy 5:31, 11:24, 11:26, 31:23, 5:32, and 31:6. Cf. Butler and Wenham (note 4 above) as well as Walter C. Kaiser Jr., *Toward an Old Testament Theology*, pp. 122-23.

8. Regarding the need for covenant obedience, Fretheim, p. 78, quite rightly points out that Joshua 24 emphasizes "one clear point:

the future of the community in the land is finally determined by whether it worships Yahweh alone, or turns to the worship of other gods." Again, the problem with Israel is not that they were sloppy in following all the details of the Law, but that they failed in the most basic commitment.

9. Though we are treating the theology of Joshua, the fact that Joshua 24 assumes the covenant pattern we saw earlier in Deuteronomy should not be overlooked. Cf. K. A. Kitchen, *The Bible in Its World*, pp. 79-84.

10. Peter C. Craigie, *The Problem of War in the Old Testament* (Grand Rapids: Wm B. Eerdmans, 1978), p. 48-50, notes that the expression "holy war" is not a biblical one and objects to it with the statement: "While war was religious by association, it was no more a cultic and holy act than was sheep shearing." In the light of the priestly activities surrounding the initiation of war (cf. Peter C. Craigie, *The Book of Deuteronomy*, NICOT [Grand Rapids: Wm. B. Eerdmans, 1976], p. 271, n. 5), the comparison seems extreme. As Craigie notes, the biblical expression is equally forceful: "Wars of Yahweh."

11. *Ḥerem* was followed outside Israel, as the Moabite Stone of a later period (c., 830 B.C.) shows. Cf. *ANET*, p. 320.

The instructions of Deuteronomy 20:16-18 indicate that the Israelites are to destroy "all that breathes" when practicing *ḥerem*. Robert Polzin, *Moses and the Deuteronomist* (New York: Seabury, 1980), pp. 114-115, understands Deuteronomy 20 to include the destruction of animals and so sees a modification of the law in the case of Ai. He sees (pp. 122-123) the same fluctuation between a rigorous interpretation of the law during the southern campaign and at Hazor—where "all who breathed" (Joshua 10:40, 11:11) are destroyed—and the other northern cities where "all who breathed" is understood to require killing people but to allow cattle to be taken (11:14-15). Polzin is arguing a thesis that Joshua and Judges are giving new hermeneutical applications of Deuteronomic law.

It is true that "all that breathes" applied literally would include animals, yet the term is not always used as widely as that, and depending on the context may refer to human beings alone (Joshua 11:13-14, Psalm 150:6). Deuteronomy 20 at once defines the objects of destruction in the land by the national identifications and warns that to fail to destroy everyone that breathes would invite learning from them detestable ways. The writer clearly has people in mind at this point. Cf. Keil and Delitzsch, *The Pentateuch*, III, p. 403.

The fact that Deuteronomy's practice of *ḥerem* did not include animals (Deuteronomy 2:34-35, 3:6-7) weakens Polzin's thesis. The understanding of Joshua 11:14-15—that Israel was fulfilling the command to put to death "all that breathed" even when they were keeping livestock—need not be a new understanding of Deuteronomy 20, but one intended in Deuteronomy itself. That leaves Jericho as the only clear case where livestock were put to death. This is likely for other reasons, as indicated in note 2 above. Woodstra, as indicated, has simply taken the view that there were various levels of *ḥerem*. Later, under specific command of Samuel, Saul was to destroy Amalek, including the livestock (1 Samuel 15:2-3).

12. The explanation that *ḥerem* was God's use of sinful human agents and the fallen institutions of society to accomplish his purposes is a favorite explanation for those who do not wish to reject the God of Joshua outright. Cf. G. Ernest Wright and Reginald H. Fuller, "God's Gift of a Land," *Perspectives on Old Testament Literature*, edited by Woodrow Ohlsen (New York: Harcourt Brace Jovanovich, 1978), pp. 99-101. Fretheim in *Deuteronomic History*, pp. 69-75, after listing views which try to avoid the reality of the destruction, settles for a similar view, though with much more qualification.

13. All three destructions—the Flood, Sodom and Gomorrah, and the Canaanites—involved judgment which came upon the *whole community*: men, women, and children. We may add to this the immediate *family* of Achan. In each case the unity of the family and nation is accepted. All Israel came under the ban when Achan disobeyed. If they as a nation did not want to accept responsibility for that sin, then they must remove the guilty party from their society. A society is viewed as a unit. What it allows is its responsibility. A family suffers the effects of the sins of its members as well. There are other aspects to what has been called *corporate solidarity* or *corporate personality* in the Bible. See Kaiser, pp. 67-70. Cf. Sarna, *Understanding Genesis*, p. 124, on the guilt of the Amorites and God's absolute justice.

14. This inadvertent but negligent sin of allowing the Gibeonites to live does not seem to have received further punishment. They dare not further sin by violating an oath taken in Yahweh's name.

15. It is difficult to date Judges 1. Verse one begins "after the death of Joshua," yet some of the material (1:10-15) repeats material given in Joshua (15:14-19). Arthur E. Cundall, *Judges* (Downers Grove, Ill.: InterVarsity Press, 1968), p. 51, suggests that the phrase is a title to the whole book and that 1:1b—2:5 serve as an introduction to the time after the death of Joshua (that is, the period of the judges), by giving background material from the Book of Joshua. But Joshua 15:14-19 clearly occurs at a later time than the gathering to dispense the land.

16. The observation that the Lord may not have given total control of the land to Joshua's generation—even though they were obedient—but waited for at least two generations to be obedient is that of R. Polzin, p. 152.

17. I do not know who originally suggested this more alliterated outline of the cycle. The cycle itself is noted by nearly every writer.

The usual weakness with the presentation of the cycle in this alliterated form is in the first step: SIN. The cycle in Judges is not built around sin in general, but that most basic sin: the violation of the first commandment. It is also possible that the cry to God does not always mark a full repentance. In Judges 6 the response to their cry is the prophetic announcement of the problem: worship of the gods of the Amorites. God's speech in 10:11-14 and their response suggests that they may not always have put aside their idolatry before previous deliverances.

18. Robert C. Boling, *The Anchor Bible: Judges* (Garden City, N.Y.: Doubleday & Co., 1969), p. 210, 214, suggests that Jephthah was the most exemplary judge since Othniel. This is hard to justify. It is more likely that in Jephthah and especially Samson we reach a low point.

Of course, Jephthah's vow is a perennial problem. Did he commit child sacrifice, clearly unacceptable to the Law? Or did his daughter become devoted to the Lord's service? Or, was an animal sacrifice made to redeem her as was the case with every first-born male? See Keil and Delitzsch, *Commentaries on the Old Testament: Joshua, Judges, Ruth* (Grand Rapids: Wm. B. Eerdmans, n.d.), p. 388-392 , who conclude that the grammar supports actual sacrifice, but the historical situation of Israel's laws makes this unacceptable. Davis, *The History of Israel*, pp. 124-128, summarizes the views and concludes that this type of legal confusion, given Jephthah's background, is very possible and in line with the period of confusion of the judges. Cf. Cundall, pp. 147-149.

19. The observation at 10:7 of dual oppressors, the Ammonites and the Philistines, followed by the judgeships of Jephthah against the Ammonites and Samson against the Philistines suggest that these judgeships overlapped. Jephthah served in Gilead and Samson served in the west where the tribes of Dan and Judah lived next to the Philistines on the coastal plain. Cf. the chronology in Davis and Whitcomb, *The History of Israel*, p. 16.

20. Keil and Delitzsch, p. 101, are responsible for the insights concerning the significance of Samson and his importance for the theme of the book, although they have taken a more positive stance concerning his contributions as a judge than I have.

21. It is interesting that the phrase "everyone did that which was right in his own eyes" occurs in Deuteronomy for the practice of religious activities outside the land. Clearly in Judges we are talking about more than a lack of strictness in how and where to worship, but the extreme of false worship. It should be noted as well that the phrase "in those days there was no king in Israel" (17:6, 18:1, 19:1, 21:25) is given as an explanation to the reader as to how things could get this far out of line. Of course, a king who worshipped falsely could get things even farther out of line, but our readers lived during

the early monarchy where Saul and David both worked to correct the problem of false worship and pagan practices.

22. In spite of the emphasis on futility, there is in the actual numbers of Judges an emphasis on the grace and mercy of God. In a time of such consistent disobedience the periods of rest far exceed the periods of oppression. "The fourteen judges were an overplus of grace for the five lapses into idolatry" Charles C. Ryrie, *The Grace of God*, p. 35.

23. It is common to interpret this as a totally different kind of rest here than Joshua provided. But the writer does not say that. Neither does Psalm 95 which he is quoting. Rather, he argues that Joshua did not give them rest and this is proven by the fact that Psalm 95 says Israel does not yet have it.

24. 2 Samuel 7:8-11 still reads as open to fulfillment.

25. See Stanley D. Toussaint, "The Eschatology of the Warning Passages in the Book of Hebrews," *Grace Theological Journal* (Spr., 1982) , pp. 71-72, for reasons why the "rest" is not present spiritual rest.

26. See Walter C. Kaiser, Jr., "The Promise Theme and the Theology of Rest," *BSac,* 130 (1973), pp. 135-50, who finds 11:9 to state the promise of the land as Abraham's.

27. The uses of "heavenly" in Hebrews are 3:1, heavenly calling; 6:4, heavenly gift; 8:5, copy of the heavenly things (plural); 9:23, copies of things in the heavens (plural); 9:23, heavenly things themselves (plural); 11:16, heavenly country; and 12:22, heavenly Jerusalem. See *BAG* which also indicates the variety of uses and the notion of source, pp. 305-306.

28. Anthony A. Hoekema, *The Bible and the Future* (Grand Rapids: Wm. B. Eerdmans, 1979), has developed a form of amillennialism which sees the fulfillment of the Old Testament promises on the new earth rather than in "heaven." Thus, the fulfillment to Abraham does take place on earth (p. 278-279). Toussaint, "Eschatology," pp. 72-74, and Kaiser, "Promise Theme," pp. 142-146, see the use of Psalm 95 in the context of other enthronement psalms—all millennial—and conclude that the rest must be millennial.

29. Fleming James, "Some Thoughts on Joshua's Religion," *Perspectives on Old Testament Literature*, p. 98.

## NOTES ON CHAPTER TEN—

### Modification to Monarchy (A King from among Your Own Brothers)

1. When the Book of Samuel opens, the Israelites are largely subject to the Philistines. The Philistines had transplanted themselves from southwest Asia Minor, settling in Crete and along the

Mediterranean coast of Canaan. They formed five city-states: Ashdod, Ashkelon, Ekron, Gath, and Gaza. Though each city was under its own ruler, together they formed a united front (cf. 1 Samuel 5:11, 6:4). They integrated with the local Canaanite population and were especially skilled in warfare and the use of iron. Cf. F.F. Bruce, *Israel and the Nations* (Grand Rapids: Wm. B. Eerdmans Publ. Co., 1963), pp. 21-27. The Philistines, in fact, had kept the skill of iron-working to themselves, attempting to enforce a monopoly even in agricultural tools so as to control the ability to make weapons (1 Samuel 13:19-22). As a result Saul's army was drastically short of modern weaponry.

2. Gilbert K. Chesterton, *What's Wrong with the World* (N.Y.: Dodd, Mead & Co., 1922), p. 48.

3. The exact nature of Saul's first sin is debated. Some take it as a violation of the priesthood by offering a sacrifice himself. Cf. John Bright, *A History of Israel*, p. 192; and G. L. Carr, "'ōlâ," *TWOT*, II, p. 667. Others see it as a violation of Samuel's instruction to wait for him. It was at least that.

It seems to me that the words "offered a sacrifice" are too quickly understood to mean the priest's function. The offerer too "offers a sacrifice" even though a priest is there to carry out the duties of his office. Since we know a priest was present among Saul's men (1 Samuel 14:2-3, cf. 13:15), and Samuel himself was not a priest, but a Levite only (1 Chronicles 6:33-38), normal usage assumes the meaning to be that Saul offered the sacrifice to begin the battle by providing the sacrificial animal, killing and preparing it (the worshiper's responsibility, Leviticus 1), and having the priest put it on the altar. Since the same words are used for both David's and Solomon's offering of sacrifices to Yahweh (2 Samuel 24:24, 1 Kings 3:3-4), it is stretching the vocabulary too much to see intrusion into the priest's office for Saul.

Samuel's rebuke and a comparison with 1 Samuel 10:8 yields only the conclusion that Saul failed to wait for Samuel to come to initiate the campaign with the sacrifice. It is this command that he failed to keep. Cf. C. F. Keil and F. Delitzsch, *Biblical Commentary on The Books of Samuel* (Grand Rapids: Wm. B. Eerdmanns, n.d.), pp. 128-129.

4. The Israelite function of king may be contrasted with that of the other kings. For instance, in the prologue of the Code of Hammurabi King Hammurabi says he was commissioned by Marduk to guide the people and he offers his set of laws as his fulfillment of that function (*ANET*, p. 164-165). Later in biblical history we experience the "Laws of the Medes and Persians" which were to be unchanged once the monarch had decreed them.

5. Keil and Delitzsch, p. 129, also point out this distinction between the penalties announced for Saul's first and second sins of dis-

obedience. This solves any supposed problems of duplication, cf. *RKH*, p. 702.

6. There are several issues raised in the latter part of 1 Samuel worthy of discussion. Among these are David's honoring Saul's office so that he will not kill him. His conscience bothered him in even cutting off a corner of Saul's robe (24:4-5). Only Yahweh has the right to take Saul's life, either in battle or by natural death (26:8-11). To take Saul's life would have placed David in the same position as any other usurper of a throne. The tradition of assassination would not be introduced into Israel's history by David.

Another problem is David's becoming a mercenary under the Philistine king, Achish of Gath (1 Samuel 27). Was this right? David's thought and motive for his move (27:1)—a thought which even Saul in his saner moments knows is untrue (26:25, 24:20) shows that David's move was not based on faith in God's promise.

While under Achish, the account continues to inform us that David is carrying out his responsibilities as king. Rather than attacking Israel and her allies, David carries out raids against the enemies of Israel (1 Samuel 27:8-12). He completely eliminates these villages—not for any reasons of *ḥerem*, but to keep the report of his activities from Achish. Prior to this, David had delivered Keilah from the Philistines (1 Samuel 23), even though they were not committed to him.

7. Joab's killing of Abner is totally outside of the Law. Joab is taking vengeance on Abner for the death of his brother, Asahel (2 Samuel 2:18-23). But Joab had no right of revenge because Asahel's death was in warfare. Even if it were in peacetime, Abner would have been considered only defending himself under the circumstances. But, in addition to all this, Joab does his misdeed in the very gates of Hebron—one of the cities of refuge—at the very place where Abner's case should be heard. David knows Abner's death was unjustified homicide as indicated by the curse he calls on Joab (3:29-30). Joab should have been executed.

8. All attempts to shift some of the blame to Bathsheba tempting David go beyond the statements of the narrative and seem designed to lessen the character of the sin here. It is likely that Bathsheba assumed the right of the king to do what he wanted.

9. Nathan's rebuke of David includes the statement from the Lord: "I delivered you from the hand of Saul. I gave your master's house to you, and your master's wives into your arms." This has raised the question as to whether David took Saul's wives. I'm sure David could find his own wives (and did!) without the older women that belonged to Saul. The statement is more a reflection of a cultural practice that occurs a number of times in Samuel and Kings. To take a former king's wives was one way of indicating a claim to kingship. So, Ishbosheth in 2 Samuel 3:7 is upset when Abner takes one of

Saul's concubines. Also, in the fulfillment of the judgment of 12:11, Absalom will go in to David's concubines publicly to certify his claim to the throne (16:21-22). Additionally, in 1 Kings 2:13-25 Solomon rightly interprets his brother Adonijah's request for Abishag as another plot to take the throne. In 2 Samuel 11:8, therefore, we simply have another way of saying that David was given the throne rights which had belonged to Saul. There is no evidence that he actually took Saul's wives, though we may speculate that he might have made sure no one else did either!

10. Brevard S. Childs's observation that the appendix (2 Samuel 21—24) to the book has an important function in focusing on the book's important issues is a helpful one (*Introduction to the Old Testament as Scripture* [Philadelphia: Fortress Press, 1979], pp. 273-277). Each supplemental item, though too cumbersome to insert in the narrative, adds a needed perspective to a theme of the book.

The first story in the appendix helps explain David's innocence in the near demise of Saul's house, though he had promised earlier not to carry out the normal practice of eliminating the previous king's line (1 Samuel 24:21, 20:14-15). As we noted in the main discussion, the two psalms in the middle of the appendix bring us back to the major themes of Yahweh as the true Rock of Israel, the propriety of righteous rule, and the Davidic Covenant. Surrounding these are the exploits of David's loyal troops; especially noteworthy is the inclusion among the Thirty Mighty Men—and listed last so we cannot miss it—of Uriah the Hittite. The last incident (2 Samuel 24) provides the background to the site of the temple as the place where God's mercy was again shown.

11. Walter Brueggemann, *The Land*, pp. 71-89, stresses the danger of kingship for seeking self-security. Seeking to hold the land by alliances and military might rather than by attention to Torah and covenantal memory would ultimately lose the land.

12. The statement of David in 2 Samuel 12:13: "I have sinned against Yahweh" has its equivalent in Psalm 51:4: "Against you, you only, have I sinned and done what is evil in your sight." The contrast is not one between Uriah and Yahweh, but between Yahweh and other gods. David has sinned against Yahweh and against no other god. His faithlessness has been to Yahweh's covenant.

13. See Terence E. Fretheim, *Deuteronomic History*, pp. 108-121; and Walter C. Kaiser, Jr., *Toward an Old Testament Theology*, pp. 156-157, for more complete discussions of the unconditional nature of the Davidic Covenant. Kaiser also has a list of linguistic parallels which show the continuity of this covenant with previous ones (p. 153).

14. The last sentence in 2 Samuel 7:19 is difficult to translate. See discussions in Keil and Delitzsch, pp. 350-351; S. Goldman, *Samuel*, Soncino Books of the Bible (New York: Soncino Press, 1949),

p. 229; and Kaiser, pp. 154-155. Because of the parallel in 1 Chronicles 17:17 it seems best to stick with the context of amazed gratitude rather than a statement of new information.

15. The statement of Yahweh's love for Solomon is the only hint in Samuel of who the next king will be. The notion of God's loving often includes the idea of His choosing (cf. Deuteronomy 4:37, 7:7-8, Nehemiah 13:26, Psalms 78:68, Malachi 1:2). 1 Chronicles 22:9 indicates that God's choice of Solomon was told to David.

16. Kaiser, p. 157.

## NOTES ON CHAPTER ELEVEN—

### Nation Heading for Judgment (The Theology of Kings)

For years the chronology of the kings of Israel and Judah was a puzzle to scholars, many concluding that the writer was a poor historian. The work of E. R. Thiele, *The Mysterious Numbers of the Hebrew Kings*, rev. ed. (Grand Rapids: Zondervan, 1983) has changed all that. By discovering and following the practices of the time for counting king's reigns (differing calendars, differing ways of counting partial years, coreigns), Thiele found that the years for reigns given in Kings fit together perfectly with only one exception. A popular summary of Thiele is available under the title, *A Chronology of the Hebrew Kings* (Grand Rapids: Zondervan, 1977). Thiele's one unresolved case has been resolved using the same methods by K.A. Kitchen and T.C. Mitchell in the *New Bible Dictionary*, pp. 192-193.

1. Idolatry was not Solomon's only sin as king. He also sinned in multiplying horses and wives and accumulating wealth (Deuteronomy 17:14-17). It is clear also that a growing economic burden fell upon the people, which becomes an immediate cause of the break following Solomon's death (1 Kings 12:4-19).

2. Some have attempted to make David's sin with Bathsheba the turning point for Israel's history. As we have seen in Samuel, it was the turning point for David's own reign. The historian-theologian of Kings is aware of David's sin with Bathsheba (1 Kings 15:5), nevertheless he uses David as the model of obedience and traces the slide of the nation from the failure of Solomon in accommodating false worship.

3. Omri's fame is indicated by the Assyrian records which refer to Israel as the "House of Omri" (*ANET*, p. 280, 284, 285). Jehu, the destroyer of Omri's house, is even referred to as the son of Omri on the Black Obelisk of Shalmaneser III (*ANET*, p. 281).

4. Walter C. Kaiser, Jr., *Towards an Old Testament Theology*, pp. 130-133, and G.J. Wenham, "Deuteronomy and the Central Sanctuary," *Tyndale Bulletin*, 22, pp. 103-108, suggest that

Deuteronomy does not require a limitation of one central site for sacrifices. It is not clear how this view avoids putting the Book of Kings into conflict with Deuteronomy. The most straightforward understanding of Deuteronomy 12 is the same as the apparent position taken by the writer of Kings—sacrificial worship was to be limited to the central sanctuary, wherever it happened to be located. For the writer of Kings, its location is no longer in doubt.

5. It is apparent from the Book of Jeremiah that Josiah's reign, though turning official policy and formal practice back to true worship of Yahweh, did not change the heart of the people generally.

6. I believe this colorful expression which handily summarizes this longest and darkest reign in Judah was originated by Howard G. Hendricks.

7. For a literal translation of Elijah's mockery read the text in *The Living Bible* (Wheaton, Ill.: Tyndale House, 1971).

8. Leah Bronner, *The Stories of Elijah and Elisha*, (Leiden: E. J. Brill, 1968), esp. pp. 50-122. Bronner also suggests that Elijah's ascension may have been an answer to Baal as the "Rider of the Clouds" (pp. 123-127), and that the two prophets' parting the Jordan River may be an answer to Baal's power over the waters (pp. 127-138). This last miracle, however, has other possible motivation than as an answer to Baal worship. It copies the Exodus and entrance into the land. It, therefore, validates the two prophets as the spokesmen of Yahweh, who brought Israel out of Egypt and into Canaan—i.e. the God to whom the nation owes its very existence.

9. Elijah is often portrayed as discouraged and irrational in facing Jezebel's threat after Mt. Carmel. He wants to die, yet he flees for his life! Ronald B. Allen, "Elijah, the Broken Prophet," JETS, 22 (1979), pp. 193-202, has provided a better explanation. Elijah thought his ministry had failed and that Israel would never turn from her rejection of prophets. He did, therefore, want to die, but not at Jezebel's hands. That would be an opportunity for Baal to claim victory over Yahweh. Therefore, he escapes to Judah and wants God to take his life there.

10. Carl Graesser, Jr., "The Message of the Deuteronomic Historian," *CTM*, 39 (1968), pp. 542-551, has identified the themes of repentance and hope and also the central focus of Kings on worship practices.

11. I. Howard Marshall, *Luke: Historian and Theologian* (Grand Rapids: Zondervan, 1970), pp. 126, 147, and *Commentary on Luke*, NICOT (Grand Rapids: Wm. B. Eerdmans, 1978), pp. 178, 188-89, 276, 283, 286, 388, 412, has recognized the occurrence of the Elijah comparison in many of these passages. Cf. Charles P. Baylis, *The Elijah-Elisha Motif in Luke 7-10*, unpublished Th.M. theses, Dallas Theological Seminary, Dallas, Tex., April 1985.

## NOTES ON CHAPTER TWELVE—

### Prudent Living (Wisdom for Life)

1. Benjamin Franklin, *Poor Richard's Alamanack*, January, 1736, ed. by Benjamin E. Smith (New York: The Century Co., 1899), p. 79.

2. B.K. Waltke, "The Book of Proverbs and Old Testament Theology," *BSac*, 136 (October, 1979), pp. 302-317. Waltke, in fact, finds ten lines of agreement between the outlook of Proverbs and that of Deuteronomy and the prophets. Moshe Weinfeld, "Wisdom Substrata in Deuteronomy and Deuteronomic Literature," *Deuteronomy and the Deuteronomic School* (Oxford: Clarendon Press, 1972), 244-274, listed extensive parallels between the instruction of Deuteronomy and Proverbs. A partial list is cited by Walter C. Kaiser, *Toward an Old Testament Theology*, p. 167.

3. J. Kenneth Kuntz, "The Canonical Wisdom Psalms of Ancient Israel—Their Rhetorical, Thematic, and Formal Dimensions," *Rhetorical Criticism: Essays in Honor of James Muilenburg* (Pittsburgh: The Pickwick Press, 1974), pp. 211-215. Kuntz lists four thematic elements present in wisdom psalms. These include: (1) The Fear of Yahweh and veneration of the Torah; (2) The contrasting life styles of the righteous and the wicked; (3) The reality and inevitability of retribution; and (4) Miscellaneous counsels pertaining to everyday life.

4. See Kaiser, pp. 168-170.

5. Gerhard von Rad, *Wisdom in Israel* (Nashville: Abingdon 1972), p. 26, makes the startling suggestion that memorized proverbs were "of greater importance for the decisions of daily life and thus for orientation in the thick of everyday activity than, for example, the ten commandments which were pronounced over the cultic assembly only rarely on great festivals."

6. Derek Kidner, *Proverbs* (Downers Grove, Ill.: InterVarsity Press, 1977), p. 13.

7. The debate over taking "Son" as an indication of parental instruction or as a term used by a teacher continues.

8. For discussion of the concept of a created order and its relationship to the Egyptian concept of *Ma'at* see Bruce K. Waltke, "The Book of Proverbs and Ancient Wisdom Literature," *BSac*, 136 (July, 1979), 232-234; and von Rad, p. 72.

Roland E. Murphy, "Wisdom—Thesis and Hypothesis," *Israelite Wisdom: Theological and Literary Essays in Honor of Samuel Terrien*, eds. J.G. Gammie, W.A. Brueggemann, W.L. Humphreys, J.M. Ward (New York: Union Theological Seminary, 1978), pp. 35-36, objects to the notion of a created "order" because of the Israelite view that the Lord is the primary cause of everything. If, indeed, an order was proposed as independent of Yahweh's direct involvement—a kind of deistic watchmaker's universe, then we could agree with Murphy. We do not think, however, that the notion of a regular order and Yahweh's direct involvement should be seen as alternatives. There is order, but it is directly ordered and upheld by Yahweh.

9. The translation of Proverbs 8:22 is difficult. In this personification, is wisdom "possessed," "created," or "begotten" before the creation of the world? See Kidner, pp. 78-81, who summarizes recent discussion and concludes that wisdom is here a personification as in the following 9:1-18 and "possessed" is the best translation to indicate that wisdom "comes forth from Him [God]."

10. See C. Hassell Bullock, *An Introduction to the Old Testament Poetic Books* (Chicago: Moody Press, 1979), pp. 58-62, for a summary of recent scholarship on the doctrine of a future life in wisdom literature. Cf. Waltke, "The Book of Proverbs and Old Testament Theology, pp. 314-315.

11. For a more complete overview of Ecclesiastes see J. Stafford Wright, "The Interpretation of Ecclesiastes," *Classical Evangelical Essays*, ed. Walter C. Kaiser, Jr., (Grand Rapids: Baker Book House, 1972), pp. 133-150, originally published in *EQ*, 18 (1946), 18-34. For a more painstaking literary analysis which arrives at much the same conclusion see Addison G. Wright, "The Riddle of the Sphinx: The Structure of the Book of Qoheleth," *CBQ*, 30 (1968), 313-334; reprinted in *Studies in Ancient Israelite Wisdom*, edited by James L. Crenshaw (New York: KTAV Publishing House, 1976), pp. 245-266.

12. The connection between wisdom and royal wisdom is developed by Norman W. Porteous in "Royal Wisdom," *Wisdom in Israel and in the Ancient Near East*, ed. by M. Noth and D. Winton Thomas, Supplements to Vetus Testamentum, Vol. III (Leiden: E. J. Brill, 1969), 247-261.

13. Ibid., pp. 258-261. Porteous concludes that Matthew 11 identifies the royal Messiah as the wisdom of God. *Sirach* 6:24-31 also identifies wisdom as a yoke that gives rest. Cf. James M. Ward, "The Servant's Knowledge in Isaiah 40-55," *Israelite Wisdom: Theological and Literary Essays in Honor of Samuel Terrien*, (New York: Union Theological Seminary, 1978), pp. 121-136.

## NOTES ON INTRODUCTION TO PART FOUR—

### Restoration and Hope
### and
### CHAPTER THIRTEEN—

### A Peg in the Holy Place
### (Concerns of Ezra and Nehemiah)

1. John Bright, *A History of Israel*, pp. 345-346. Biblical references which indicate the organization and community life of the

exiles in Babylon include Ezekiel 3:15, 8:1, 14:1, 33:30ff; Jeremiah 29:5ff; Ezra 2:59, 8:17.

2. Ezra 1:8 and 5:14 indicate that the return took place under "Sheshbazzar the prince of Judah." Much debate has taken place about the relationship of Sheshbazzar to Zerubbabel (Ezra 3:2, 5:2). It is interesting to note that only official documents use the name "Sheshbazzar." The narrative gives all the credit for actual activity to Zerubbabel. This observation supports the view that they are one and the same—"Sheshbazzar" being the official Persian name for Zerubbabel. This same tacit identification is present in Josephus as well (*Antiquities*, XI, 11-13).

On the other hand, W. F. Albright identified Sheshbazzar as the same as the Shenazzar of 1 Chronicles 3:18, seeing both as corruptions of a Babylonian name like Sin-ab-user [*JBL*, 40 (1921), pp. 108-110]. Cf. Bright, pp. 361-364, for the implications of the latter view. F. F. Bruce, *Israel and the Nations*, pp. 100-101, sees them as joint leaders with Sheshbazzar returning to Persia as soon as the altar is reestablished.

3. Ezra 4:6-23 follows a common Hebrew literary pattern in choosing to follow out the topic of opposition beyond the time of the surrounding events of the narrative. Thus, the biblical writer goes beyond the opposition to building during the rule of Cyrus and Darius and includes in these verses opposition under Artaxerxes. This opposition was against the building of the walls (4:16). The narrative returns to the time of Darius in verse 24.

4. Much ink has been expended on the dating of Ezra's return. Bright, pp. 391-402, provides a good summary of the current views. We have followed the traditional view based on Ezra 7:7. We believe that Gleason Archer, *A Survey of Old Testament Introduction*, pp. 396-398, has adequately answered Bright's hesitations about the traditional view which has Ezra preceeding Nehemiah. CF. F. Charles Fensham, *The Books of Ezra and Nehemiah* (Grand Rapids: Wm. B. Eerdmans Publishing Co., 1982), pp. 6-9.

5. The insidious influence of Tobiah was helped no doubt by the apparent fact that he was Jewish. His name ("Yahweh is good") attests at least a nominal adherence to Yahweh, as do the names of his sons. It is also possible that Sanballat claimed to be a Yahweh worshiper. Cf. Derek Kidner, *Ezra and Nehemiah* (Downers Grove, Ill.: InterVarsity Press, 1979), p. 101; and *RKH*, pp. 1141-42.

6. The unfortunate English use of the word *heart* to refer primarily to nonrational feelings has caused many readers to believe this verse vindicates "God speaking to them" and telling them what to do through their feelings.

7. It is popular among scholars to find the beginnings of Phariseeism and legalism here. This period is then viewed as one which has reversed the original purpose of the Law. Cf. Paul J. and

Elizabeth Achtemeier, *The Old Testament Roots of Our Faith* (Philadelphia: Fortress Press, 1962), pp. 75-78. We, however, see here no contradiction with the earlier view of the Law. Certainly in Deuteronomy the Law was a gracious gift. But if there was to be blessing, it would have to be followed. The later legalism, which saw the Law as a way of earning righteousness, was a development which perverted this needed emphasis on a return to the Law.

8. Childs also rejects a clear "Second Exodus" theme in Ezra-Nehemiah, though he does find it typologically in Chronicles. Brevard S. Childs, *Introduction to the Old Testament as Scripture*, p. 634.

9. Fensham, pp. 129-130.

10. William J. and Gloria Gaither, "The King is Coming," *Let's Just Praise the Lord* (Alexandria, Ind: Alexandria House, 1974), 59.

## NOTES ON CHAPTER FOURTEEN—

### The Second Temple (Hope in Haggai and Zechariah)

1. This observation that the Jews did not return "by might and power," but by permission of Cyrus is that of Yehezkel Kaufmann, *The Religion of Israel*, IV (New York: KTAV Publishing House, 1977), p. 286.

2. Joyce Baldwin, *Haggai, Zechariah, Malachi*, Tyndale Old Testament Commentaries (Downers Grove, Ill.: InterVarsity Press, 1972), p. 33.

3. Kaufmann, p. 261, argues that the discussion of ritual uncleanness here is not intended as a parallel to the moral sins or injustice of the people, but that the incomplete temple made everything ritually unclean because it was impossible to carry out the prescribed rites acceptably with just an altar.

4. Kaufmann, p. 254, observes that Haggai contains 2 sets of two prophecies each. The first set is prior to the laying of the foundation (1:1-2:9), the second on the day it was laid (2:10-23). The first prophecy of each set deals with the present temple situation, the second is messianic. The first messianic prophecy (2:6-9) deals with the temple, the second messianic prophecy (2:21-23), the house of David.

5. The condition of moral repentance before Yahweh would return to His Temple reminds us of Judges 10:6-16 when God was so weary of their repeated failure that He would not deliver them until after they had demonstrated their willingness to serve Him exclusively. Also similar is our earlier observation that God did not give final rest to Joshua's generation, apparently requiring that more than one generation be faithful. A look at Ezra, Nehemiah, and Malachi suggests that the returned exiles never fulfilled this requirement.

6. The visions are grouped by twos, except for the first and the last which as a pair bracket the whole section. Joyce Baldwin, pp. 80, 85, 93, has suggested a chiastic arrangement for these paired visions. In addition to these suggestions, however, it should be noted that the second and third visions are also closely connected to the first in that 2:6-13 contains exhortations depending upon the united message of the first three visions, not just the third.

7. David L. Peterson, "Zechariah's Visions: A Theological Perspective," *Vetus Testamentum* 34 (1984), p. 201, calls attention to the city of Pasargadae, an unwalled ritual capital built by Cyrus during the period 545-530 B.C. This city was without walls and had fire altars on its perimeter. Yahweh's protection surely addressed the issue of the security normally handled by walls, which Jerusalem did not have. But, Kaufmann is correct when he cautions that the vision does not argue that no walls should be constructed. "The measurer goes to measure this great Jerusalem of the future whose extent no man now knows. This greater Jerusalem will have no walls; the Lord will be its shield. The messianic vision does not indicate any stance with respect to the building of the real wall" (p. 277).

8. John D. W. Watts, "Zechariah," *The Broadman Bible Commentary*, Vol. 7 (Nashville: Broadman Press, 1972), p. 327, has noted that "the ephah basket would be much too small for a full-sized person. The vision either has a very small woman or a woman-like figure, that is, an idol" (p. 328). This conforms very nicely to setting it up on its base in Babylon.

9. The oddity of having the high priest wear the crown and be called the branch has occasioned much discussion. For the view followed in the text see Merrill F. Unger, *Unger's Bible Commentary: Zechariah* (Grand Rapids: Zondervan, 1963), pp. 110-118; and Joyce Baldwin, pp. 133-35. An alternate interpretation finds both Joshua and Zerubbabel present. A crown is placed on the head of Joshua. To avoid problems of implied revolt, no crown is placed on Zerubbabel's head, but the predictions which follow are addressed alternately to Joshua and Zerubbabel as the two leaders. Zerubbabel represents the Branch of David's line who will build the Temple and sit on his throne (6:13a). The subject shifts now to Joshua: "And he will be a priest on his throne" (13b); then to the conclusion: "And there will be harmony between the two [king and priest]." The shift of reference within one verse without clearly identifying the person in view is taken as necessary by the political situation. Cf. Kaufmann, pp. 294-296; Watts, pp. 329-330.

10. The main fast was that of the fifth month which marked the destruction of the Temple (2 Kings 25:8). The tenth month was the month that Nebuchadnezzar began the siege of Jerusalem (2 Kings 25:1,2). The fourth month saw the army break through the city wall (2 Kings 25:3-4; Jeremiah 39:2) and the seventh month memorialized

the murder of Gedeliah, the Governor (2 Kings 25:25). Cf. Unger, p. 122.

11. Baldwin, pp. 77-81, here follows the work of P. Lamarche, *Zacharie IX-XIV, Structure Littéraire et Messianisme* (Paris: Gabalda, 1961), translating his headings into English. Lamarche has suggested that four essential themes are repeated in chiastic arrangement in Zechariah 9-14. These are: (1)judgment and salvation of neighboring peoples; (2) the king shepherd and false shepherds; (3) Israel's war and victory; and (4) judgment on idols. Whatever the merits of the details of Lamarche's literary analysis, the observation that there is repetition of several major themes is very helpful as is the suggestion that each time a theme is renewed, a new perspective is added. Also helpful is Baldwin's observation that the writer "in the manner characteristic of apocalyptic, is using past events to typify a supremely important future event. Just as successive armies swept through Syria and Palestine and claimed a right to each territory, so finally the Lord will see every proud city capitulate to Him" (p. 158).

A threat to Lamarche's chiastic arrangement comes from Paul Hanson, *The Dawn of Apocalyptic* (Philadelphia: Fortress Press, 1975), pp. 315-316, who sees Zechariah 9 as following the format of an ancient warrior hymn. See also Elmer A. Martens, *God's Design: A Focus on Old Testament Theology* (Grand Rapids: Baker Book House, 1981), pp. 203-205.

12. For a full discussion of the word *associate*, cf. E. W. Hengstenberg, *Christology of the Old Testament*, Vol. IV (Grand Rapids: Kregel Publications, 1956 [1872-78]), pp. 96-98. Some avoid the conclusion that Messiah is equal to God by taking the verse to be a judgment of the false shepherd. Cf. Eli Cashdan, "Zechariah," *The Twelve Prophets*, Soncino Books of the Bible, ed., A. Cohen (London: Soncino Press, 1948), p. 325.

13. We have not covered the other post-exilic book: Chronicles. Though it would have been more consistent with our format to do Chronicles and to neglect Haggai and Zechariah, we would have missed something of the Messianic element of the hope of the returnees.

Chronicles fits without difficulty into our understanding of post-exilic hopes. This history of Israel, written especially for the returning community, stresses the hope of the Davidic dynasty and the temple. These two related pillars are clearly seen as relevant to the reestablishment of Israel. Cf. James D. Newsome, Jr. "Toward A New Understanding of the Chronicler and His Purposes, *JBL*, 94 (1975), 201-117.

14. Franz Delitzsch, *Biblical Commentary on the Psalms*, III (Grand Rapids: Wm. B. Eerdmans), pp. 223-224, identifies this psalm as "without any doubt a post-exilic song." He decides in favor of the dedication of the second temple as the psalm's setting. J.J. Perowne,

*The Book of Psalms*, II, p. 338-339, also sees it as post-exilic, but identifies it with the celebration in Nehemiah 8. More recent interpreters are greatly divided on its setting (cf. Leslie C. Allen, *Word Biblical Commentary: Psalms 101-150*, (Vol. 21), Waco, Texas: Word, 1983), pp. 122-124.

The more recent recognition of the king as a main speaker in songs of praise for victory, especially those which are singular or shift from singular to plural (king to nation), accounts for some identification with pre-exilic worship. Its present place in the Psalms identifies it as being used in the post-exilic community, however. Perhaps an earlier psalm of victory was adapted and applied to the situation at the time of the second temple (see note 13). It would not be out of place in the mouth of the Davidic heir, Zerubbabel.

15. J. J. Stewart Perowne, *The Book of Psalms*, II, p. 343. So also A. Cohen, *The Psalms*, Soncino Books of the Bible (New York: The Soncino Press, 1945), p. 392. A similar view is taken by Delitzsch, pp. 229, though he identifies the rejecters as chiefs and members of Israel itself.

16. Ronald E. Clements, *Old Testament Theology: A Fresh Approach*, (Atlanta: John Knox Press, 1978), p. 151, believes that hope for the future restoration during the post-exilic period caused them to include royal psalms. Psalms originally speaking of a specific victory in the past for the Davidic king would, read through the eyes of God's promise of restoration, be sung as prophetic about what Yahweh would do in the future.

## NOTES ON CHAPTER FIFTEEN—

### On the Way to the Future (Other Features of Hope)

1. F. F. Bruce, *The Book of Acts* (Grand Rapids: Wm. B. Eerdmans Publ. Co., 1954), pp. 68-69. Bruce suggests the natural signs may have had some significance to those who had seen the unnatural darkness at the crucifixion nearly two months earlier. He recognizes as well, however, that this is at best a beginning of fulfillment (cf. Revelation 6:12).

2. *Ibid.*, p. 35. Cf. George E. Ladd, *A Theology of the New Testament* (Grand Rapids: Wm. B. Eerdmans Publ. Co., 1974), pp. 550-552.

# SCRIPTURE INDEX

### 1 JOHN



### REVELATION

# SUBJECT INDEX